Psychotherapist
REVEALED

Marci
Thanks for coming
on the side. Much
love on our journey

Love,
Roe

Psychotherapist
REVEALED

Therapists Speak About Self-Disclosure in Psychotherapy

ANDREA BLOOMGARDEN
ROSEMARY B. MENNUTI
Editors

Routledge
Taylor & Francis Group
New York   London

Routledge
Taylor & Francis Group
270 Madison Avenue
New York, NY 10016

Routledge
Taylor & Francis Group
27 Church Road
Hove, East Sussex BN3 2FA

© 2009 by Taylor & Francis Group
Routledge is an imprint of Taylor & Francis Group, an Informa business

Printed in the United States of America on acid-free paper
10 9 8 7 6 5 4 3 2 1

International Standard Book Number: 978-0-415-96383-1 (Hardback)

Library of Congress Cataloging-in-Publication Data

Psychotherapist revealed : therapists speak about self-disclosure in
    psychotherapy / edited by Andrea Bloomgarden, Rosemary B. Mennuti.
        p. cm.
    Includes bibliographical references and index.
    ISBN 978-0-415-96383-1 (hardback : alk. paper)
    1. Psychotherapy--Practice. 2. Psychotherapists--Professional ethics. I.
Bloomgarden, Andrea. II. Mennuti, Rosemary B., 1947-

RC465.5.P79 2009
616.89'14068--dc22   2008046110

Visit the Taylor & Francis Web site at
http://www.taylorandfrancis.com

and the Routledge Web site at
http://www.routledgementalhealth.com

Dedication

I dedicate this book to my parents, Joan and Charles,
and to all my clients, past and present. •
To my clients: Thank you for letting me know
who you are and what you've needed from me.
You have educated me, enriched my life,
and honored me. All that was missing in
classroom and text, I learned from you.

AB

To know me is to know my mom and dad, my brothers,
and my sister. I dedicate this book to all of you. Thank you
for the strong foundation, the gentle holding, and the
freedom to fly. Mom, your spirit remains with me always
and serves as my guide, fills my heart, and is my inspiration.
Your unconditional love grounds me each and every day.

RBM

Acknowledgments

Roe Mennuti and I have been colleagues and friends for over ten years, and we had previously worked together on therapist self-disclosure, collaborating on various writing projects, and copresenting on occasion. Two years ago, tucked away in a corner booth of a dimly lit Italian bistro, we decided to take our interest to the next level, plotting our book outline on a napkin we could barely see. Together, we conceptualized what would make for an interesting and useful book about therapist self-disclosure. Rather than close discussion with the final word on how to self-disclose correctly, it should open discussion. Rather than answer questions definitively and authoritatively, it should raise them. While we intended to leave readers with a clearer idea about what constitutes helpful, therapeutic, and wise self-disclosure than they had before reading our book, reaching this new awareness would come from open dialogue, ongoing exploration, and the collective wisdom of many. With such a broad range of factors to consider, there never will be, nor should there be, an exact formula applicable for every situation. What therapist self-disclosure needed most was to become a subject that could be openly discussed, researched, examined, and talked about without shame and inhibition, and accomplishing this would be something new and valuable for the psychotherapeutic community.

We wanted a book that would touch the reader with a personal element: a book on self-disclosure that was itself appropriately self-disclosing. Which authors would dare to participate and tell their stories? What publisher would trust our idea enough to pursue our project?

We found the answer to these questions, leaving us many people to thank. To our acquisitions editor, George Zimmar, and Routledge Publishers, who read our proposal, we are enormously grateful—you believed in it and in us, and together, we moved forward. Equally, we thank our contributing authors. You understood our purpose, shared our vision, and trusted us enough to join. Thank you for your hard work, collaboration, and willingness to be known. Later, when the book moved into the editing and production phases, we have Fred Coppersmith, Marta Moldvai, Kenya Pierre, and Tara Nieuwesteeg to thank—you were right there for us every step of the way.

On a personal note, the support of friends, family, and colleagues has been priceless. You have thoughtfully listened and shared your own ideas and supported ours, and we thank you all for your enthusiasm and interest. There are so many of you who have played this part over the years when we explored self-disclosure in previous research and writing; it would take up pages to personally thank everyone who has been helpful in informing our thought over the last ten years. So many of you—friends, family, colleagues, and clients—have shared your self-disclosure stories with us, providing us with a strong foundation for understanding the breadth of this topic. We thank you for your openness—you have all played a part in the creation of this book.

We would like to thank those of you who have been involved most closely during the past few years as we worked on this book, listening, encouraging, and firmly believing in our idea: Joan and Charles Bloomgarden, Jean and Alex Cobb, Ellen Ostroff, Marci Ostroff, Paula Sherman, Bill Sherman, Paul Miller, Leslie Parkes Shralow, Jeff Shralow, Terry Hall, Fran Gerstein, Davida Kelly, Barb Peterson, many pals and colleagues in Jake's Club, Amanda King, Vicki Dansky, Tim Campbell, Monica L'Tainen, Holly Kricher, Yuma Tomes, Lina Lukens, Linda Filetti, Stephanie Mattei, Harin Feibish, B. Hibbs, Suzanne Brennan, Alice Trisdorfer, Alex Wenz, Joni Stern, Elise Billock Tropea, Emily Chernicoff, Eva Feindler, and Ray Christner.

Some of you read parts of our manuscript: Fran Gerstein, Judy Rabinor, Linda Filetti, Ellen Ostroff, and Marci Ostroff—we thank you for letting us test our ideas on you, and for your useful feedback.

Thank you to those who have mentored us over the years, teaching us about therapy relationships and all relationships: Barb Peterson, Vic Malatesta, Carol Gantman, Robin Hornstein, Sybil Meyer, Georgia Sloane, Annie Steinberg, Eva Feindler, and the Jean Baker Miller Training Institute.

We would like to thank the Renfrew Center, our old stomping ground, for supporting us in doing research on therapist self-disclosure and for giving us a forum for our workshops on self-disclosure. Thank you to Judi Goldstein for giving us a platform in the Renfrew Conference—through that experience we met so many people and it provided a foundation and context for our work on therapeutic relationships.

Lastly, we thank our clients. You have allowed us to be with you in your most vulnerable moments. Without even knowing it, each of you has taught us something important, inspired us, and facilitated our growth. Mutuality occurs in all relationships; you have each had a part in making us better therapists, better listeners, and wiser people.

Contents

About the Editors

Andrea Bloomgarden, PhD, received her doctoral degree from the University of Pennsylvania in 1991 and became interested in exploring effective therapeutic relationships in the mid-1990s while she was director of outpatient services at the Renfrew Center. There, she became engaged in research, writing, and presenting at the national and local levels on a variety of topics, with particular focus on understanding therapist self-disclosure in the context of successful psychotherapy relationships. She has published articles and chapters on various aspects of psychotherapy including therapist self-disclosure, eating disorders, countertransference, EMDR, dialectical behavior therapy, adolescents, and relational-cultural theory. She has a diverse practice in Philadelphia, Pennsylvania, and is cofounder of the Center for Acceptance and Change. For more information, visit her Web site at http://www.centerforacceptanceandchange.com.

Rosemary B. Mennuti, EdD, NCSP, is professor and director of school psychology programs in the Department of Psychology at the Philadelphia College of Osteopathic Medicine. She comes to academia after a long career in public school education where she worked with children and families as a school psychologist. In addition, she served as an outpatient therapist at the Renfrew Center, conducting individual and group therapy for clients with eating disorders, and has a small private practice in New Jersey. She has authored several books (*Cognitive-behavioral interventions in educational settings; School-based mental health: A practitioner's guide to comparative practices*), was coeditor of the *School Practice in Action* series, has written various articles and book chapters, and has conducted professional training workshops locally, regionally, and nationally.

About the Authors

Meredith Barber, PsyD, maintains a private practice in Penn Valley, Pennsylvania. She is a past president of the Philadelphia Area Group Psychotherapy Society and an adjunct faculty member at Widener University, where she has taught Introduction to Group Psychotherapy.

Dana L. Comstock, PhD, is a professor of counseling and chair of the Department of Counseling and Human Services at St. Mary's University in San Antonio, Texas. She is the editor of the first RCT-based human development text, *Diversity and development: Critical contexts that shape our lives and relationships* (2005), and is featured in the first RCT casebook *How connections heal: Stories from relational-cultural therapy.*

Eva L. Feindler, PhD, is a professor of psychology and the program director of the Long Island University doctoral program in clinical psychology. She has authored several books (including *Adolescent anger control: Cognitive-behavioral techniques; Adolescent behavior therapy handbook; Assessment of family violence*) and numerous articles on parent and child anger and has conducted professional training workshops across the United States and internationally.

Linda Filetti, PhD, is a licensed clinical psychologist and cofounder of the Center for Acceptance and Change in Bala Cynwyd, Pennsylvania. She has been intensively trained in dialectical behavior therapy (DBT) and provides comprehensive DBT therapy to adolescent and adult women. Specializing in treating BPD, eating disorders, and self-harm, she maintains private practices in Bala Cynwyd and Chadds Ford, Pennsylvania.

Fran Gerstein, MSW, LCSW, has worked as a psychotherapist in private practice for over 20 years. In addition to working with teens and adults struggling with general issues like anxiety and depression, she specializes in the treatment of eating disorders and adolescent/parent separation problems. She treats individuals, couples, and families and currently works out of her home office in Wynnewood, Pennsylvania.

Dan Gottlieb, PhD, is a renowned family therapist, the radio show host of NPR's *Voices in the Family,* and a nationally known speaker. He is the author of four books, including *Letters to Sam,* written for his grandson, and *Learning from the heart.* He recently retired his celebrated weekly column, "On Healing," published in the *Philadelphia Inquirer* from 1993 until July of 2008.

Deany Laliotis, LCSW-C, is a psychotherapist and senior trainer for EMDR Institute, Inc. Deany presents on EMDR nationally and internationally, and is best known for her work with treating attachment issues and teaching EMDR as an integrative psychotherapy approach.

Victor J. Malatesta, PhD, is a licensed psychologist who maintains a practice in clinical psychology and neuropsychology in West Chester and Wynnewood, Pennsylvania. He is a clinical associate professor of psychology in the Department of Psychiatry at the University of Pennsylvania School of Medicine, a member of the professional staff of Pennsylvania Hospital, and editor of *Mental health issues of older women: A comprehensive review for health care professionals.*

Karen J. Maroda, PhD, ABPP, is a psychologist/psychoanalyst in private practice in Milwaukee, Wisconsin, as well as assistant clinical professor of psychiatry at Medical College of Wisconsin. She is the author of *The power of countertransference* and *Seduction, surrender, and transformation,* both from The Analytic Press, and the forthcoming *Interactive psychodynamic techniques* from Guilford Press.

Stephanie Mattei, PsyD, is a licensed clinical psychologist and cofounder of the Center for Acceptance and Change in Bala Cynwyd, Pennsylvania. She has been intensively trained in dialectical behavior therapy and is an adjunct faculty member in the psychology department at La Salle University. She specializes in treating women with eating disorders, borderline personality disorder, self-harm behaviors, and relationship distress.

Catherine McCoubrey, EdS, ADTR, LPC, is a recent graduate of the Educational Specialist Program, Philadelphia College of Osteopathic Medicine, and a school psychologist with the Upper Darby School District. She is also a dance/movement therapist on the faculty of the

Hahnemann Creative Arts in Therapy Program of Drexel University, Philadelphia, Pennsylvania.

Shaun McNiff, PhD, is a university professor at Lesley University in Cambridge, Massachusetts, an international leader within the arts and therapy field, and the author of many books that include *Art heals; Trust the process; Art as medicine; Creating with others; Art-based research; Depth psychology of art;* and *The arts and psychotherapy.*

Alyson Nerenberg, PsyD, a licensed psychologist who specializes in relationship counseling, codependency, and addictions, spent 5 years as the director of a residential addiction treatment program and is a board member for the International Institute of Trauma and Addictions Professionals. She has supervised many therapists, has lectured nationally on various topics, and has been featured in the media on TV stations including MSNBC, ABC, Fox, and CN8, and in many newspapers.

Jennifer J. Padrone, PsyD, is a clinical psychologist in independent practice on Long Island, New York. She provides supervision to doctoral candidates in clinical psychology at Long Island University, C. W. Post Campus. Her professional interests include serious and persistent mental illness, the interplay between language and psychosis, and family system functioning in eating disorders.

Jason Patton, LPC Intern, is a contract therapist at Waterloo Counseling Center, a community counseling clinic serving the needs of the GLBTQI population in Austin, Texas. He is currently obtaining his doctorate in counselor education and supervision at St. Mary's University in San Antonio, Texas. He is active in advocacy and training for issues pertaining to gender and sexual diversity at the national level.

Natasha Prenn, LMSW, is on the faculty of the AEDP (Accelerated Experiential Dynamic Psychotherapy) Institute. She is currently writing and presenting on the vocabulary of right-brain language in experiential treatments, on the effective use of self-disclosure, and on how to teach AEDP. She is in private practice in New York City.

Judith Ruskay Rabinor, PhD, is the director of the American Eating Disorders Center of Long Island, is the author of *A starving madness: Tales of hunger, hope and healing in psychotherapy,* and has written extensively on eating and body image disorders. She teaches, trains therapists, consults nationwide, and has private practices in both Manhattan and Long Island.

Elizabeth Sparks, PhD, is the associate dean of graduate studies in the Lynch School of Education at Boston College, a faculty member at the Jean Baker Miller Training Institute, and has a private psychotherapy practice. Her research areas are feminist psychotherapy, multicultural issues in practice and training, and culturally sensitive interventions for youth who are living in at-risk situations.

David C. Treadway, PhD, is a nationally known therapist and author who has been giving workshops and training around the country for the past 30 years. His next book is *Home before dark: A family's first year with cancer,* Union Square Press, 2009, which he is writing with his wife and two sons. He is the author of over 30 articles and is a 2002 Psychotherapy Networker award winner.

Elise Billock Tropea, MCAT, ADTR, a graduate of Hahnemann University's Creative Arts in Therapy program and faculty member since 1974, has supervised and mentored students internationally for the past 30 years. She has presented over 300 workshops and seminars to educators in the United States and in Taiwan on the power of nonverbal communication and assessment in understanding learning styles.

Ofer Zur, PhD, is a psychologist, an author, a presenter, and a forensic consultant from Sonoma, California. He is a prolific writer, and his latest book is *Boundaries in psychotherapy* (APA Books, 2007). He is the director of the Zur Institute (http://www.zurinstitute.com), which offers dozens of free articles and 100 innovative online courses for CE credits.

section one

Foundations

chapter one

Therapist self-disclosure
Beyond the taboo

Andrea Bloomgarden and Rosemary B. Mennuti

Behind closed doors

Behind closed doors, in workshops, at conferences, and in supervision meetings, therapists are talking. What are they talking about? Therapists who live in small communities are talking about what happens when they go to the same church as their clients or when they run into them in an AA meeting, at a parent-teacher conference, on the tennis courts, at the funeral of their own spouse, or, unexpectedly, at a wedding. Therapists are talking about how to navigate the newer forms of media: How does it affect their therapy relationships if they have an online blog or a Facebook page? What about e-mailing with clients? Is it acceptable to go to a client's special event? What happens when therapists write personal memoirs? Behind closed doors, therapists do talk. They tell each other which personal questions they've answered or what feelings they've shared with clients. They are hungry to learn from each other, to become better at knowing what to do in these situations.

Therapist self-disclosure is a controversial subject, but in private, in small groups where therapists feel safe, it is passionately discussed and often debated. Why the taboo? Isn't it natural that therapists are in some ways known to their clients? We will get into the reason for the taboo shortly, but first, let's just establish that this is still not a subject that therapists talk freely about. Therapeutic choices about how best to handle all of these sorts of self-disclosure and boundary dilemmas are among the most difficult and challenging set of decisions a therapist can make. Therapist self-disclosure, when wisely used as a therapeutic tool, has potential to promote positive change and to assist in the development of a good therapeutic alliance. Clearly, though, doing it well requires good clinical judgment and attunement to clients' needs.

Why this book?

The 21st century is a culture where self-revelation is an everyday and normal event, on the Internet, in all of the media, and on YouTube. Compulsory disclosure of personal details fills the World Wide Web, the television, the print media, and blogs. Many clients nowadays do some background research in choosing a therapist by simply "googling" us. Insurance companies may post our education and treatment specialties. If we've published anything or participate in any hobby, this information is often found online. It is becoming the norm for therapists to have Web sites. Thus, therapist "neutrality," in the old sense, is a thing of the past, like it or not. It is time too for therapists to "come out of the closet," so to speak, and talk more openly about this aspect of their work.

To create this book, we invited experienced therapists from different theoretical orientations, treating a varied clientele, asking them to discuss their views on self-disclosure and boundary crossings using real examples from their practice. Through their stories, they were asked to reveal what they believe, considering the implications for the client, the treatment setting, and their own feelings about being more known to their clients. Thus, the reader has the opportunity to benefit from the collective wisdom of the group. You will read about examples of self-disclosure that therapists thought were helpful, harmful, or something in between—mistakes that were made and later recognized, choices they thought had positive or negative effects based on some combination of feedback from clients, or how the disclosure (or nondisclosure) affected the course of therapy. In some cases the therapists tell you what they would do differently in the future.

In this book you will not find a chapter making either a blanket indictment or endorsement of all therapist self-disclosure. We don't believe that arguing for or against self-disclosure constitutes useful dialogue. Although many of our authors describe what they believe to be useful self-disclosure, they are not making a case for carte blanche self-disclosure. Rather, their examples are meant to elucidate for the reader good judgment in self-disclosure and boundary-crossing decision making. Our authors shared their stories, striving to reveal the complex and layered thought process behind their choices, to provide models, frameworks, or examples to stimulate the readers' thinking about their own clinical work.

In addition, you will get to know real therapists, talking about what they really did, sharing their real concerns and doubts and revealing their own humanity as they struggled with these sorts of decisions and faced issues for which there is no manual. Ideally, we have all read every theory pertaining to our field and know just how to apply it to each situation, but in the real world of therapy, we sometimes fly by the seat of our pants, make mistakes, and get feedback. At our best, we learn from our mistakes and recognize our idiosyncrasies, becoming better therapists and people in the course of this work.

A genuine bond between client and therapist

The subject of therapist self-disclosure is extraordinarily rich because regardless of clinical orientation, successful therapy depends on a good therapeutic relationship or "alliance." Part of the therapeutic alliance is the bond a person has with his or her therapist. How is that bond created? Some aspects of the therapist's real thoughts, feelings, values, and identity necessarily comes through in the creation of an authentic relationship between therapist and client. How do therapists choose to reveal something, or work with something that has already been revealed, in a way that is therapeutic? Under what circumstances are therapist self-disclosures of a particular kind helpful, harmful, inviting, distancing, effective, or ineffective? In what ways do nonverbal disclosures create connection or disconnection? Can a genuine bond between two people be created with a person who is completely unknown to the other? When is self-disclosure negative—distancing, distasteful, downright harmful, or the beginning of a slide into the realm of the unethical?

The self-disclosure taboo has stifled productive discussion, making therapists reluctant to talk openly about their self-disclosure practices and keeping it out of standard coursework in training programs. Being secretive has not served the psychotherapy community. Bravely, contributors to this volume decided to break their silence, paving the way for open dialogue about this important area of our work.

Overcoming self-disclosure's bad reputation

Why are therapists afraid of speaking openly? First, therapist self-disclosure has been unfairly stigmatized as being inextricably linked with extreme unprofessional behavior, and second, from a strict Freudian view, prohibited as bad practice. Let us briefly overview these two contributors to the self-disclosure taboo.

Sliding down a "slippery slope"

Regarding its untoward associations, as Zur explains in his comprehensive work *Boundaries in Psychotherapy* (2007a), an often repeated argument referred to as the "slippery slope" has treated therapist self-disclosure as the inevitable beginning of a slide into that most unethical and egregious boundary violation, having sex with a client. Although research about the small percentage of therapists who had sex with clients found that among other things, they self-disclosed to their clients, research also shows that almost all therapists who do not and never would have sex with their clients also self-disclose (Zur, 2007a). Thus, self-disclosing does not uniquely correlate with only one group, nor do correlations prove cause: To conclude that self-disclosure causes sexual relations with clients is erroneous. "To assert that boundary crossings [such as self-disclosure] are likely to lead to harm and sex because they statistically precede them is like saying that doctors' visits cause death because most people see a doctor before they die" (Zur, 2000). This logic though, has been largely responsible for much closed-mindedness about all therapist self-disclosure.

Additionally, in the extremely litigious culture in which we practice, therapists are given "risk-management" advice by lawyers often including blanket statements like "avoid doing anything that could appear unethical to a judge—thus, never cross a boundary, never self-disclose," even though having good judgment about these situations is the most clinically appropriate way of practicing. These extreme sorts of "risk-management" recommendations have serious drawbacks: they encourage therapists to practice in a way that both undermines their good clinical judgment and goes against the standard of care, and paradoxically, such "risk management" may actually *increase* the number of ethics complaints (Zur, 2007b; Williams, 2003).

The dread of being seen as unethical or getting into a lawsuit certainly shuts down open dialogue. Therapists are inhibited from talking honestly and comfortably about their boundary crossing and self-disclosure practices when they fear that their words and actions will be misconstrued as unethical.

Obedience to Freud

The view that self-disclosure is inherently bad practice originates with Freud. We would venture to guess that his famous metaphors about the ideal therapeutic stance have been taught to practically everyone who has been educated as a provider of mental health treatment, regardless of the particular orientation of the training program. Although many other orientations (e.g., feminist, cognitive-behavioral, humanistic) do not adhere to Freudian tenets, his words have still had a lasting impact on our thinking about therapeutic relationships nonetheless. Freud told us "like a mirror, reflect nothing but what is shown," (Freud, 1912/1963, p. 124) or "like a surgeon, [we should be] focused and devoid of all human sympathy" (Freud, p. 121).

In setting out guidelines for psychoanalysis, Freud may have assumed that most of us would exercise good clinical judgment, recognizing the flexibility in his statements. As Geller (2003) points out, in his letter to Ferenczi, Freud wrote,

> I thought it most important to stress what one should not do, to point out the temptations that run counter to analysis. Almost everything one should do in a positive sense I left to tact. What I achieved thereby was that the obedient submitted to those admonitions as if they were taboos and did not notice their elasticity. (Grubricht-Simitis, 1986, p. 270, in Geller, 2003)

Similarly, Freud's related concept of "therapeutic neutrality," meaning that therapists should be objective, has also been interpreted rigidly, implying that in order to be objective we have to be completely nondisclosing and distant. We have falsely pitted "neutral" therapists against self-disclosing, overemotional ones. Thankfully, after long debates about these topics in the literature, we have begun to break free of rigid interpretations of Freud's works, and many analysts have moved beyond extreme positions (e.g., Aron, 1996; Maroda, 1999, 2004; Orange, Atwood & Stolorow, 1997; Renik, 1995; Wachtel, 2008). There is now recognition that therapist self-disclosure is inherently a part of the therapy relationship, and the discussion should move from polarizing debates to thoughtful discussion about how the therapist's selfhood or subjectivity is appropriately integrated into a therapy relationship. Gediman (2006) asks that we stop having unnecessary debate over caricatures and stereotypes that falsely pit neutrality against self-disclosure:

> These false dichotomies and polarizations of objective versus subjective, like neutrality versus self-disclosure … serve only to foster pseudoarguments that do not advance our mutual interests. I believe that we can promote and facilitate productive dialogue between different schools once we recognize self-disclosure as a useful form of interactive intervention subject to a set of guiding principles that contribute to the patient's benefit and the analytic process. (p. 244)

Self-disclosure: A balanced view

Self-disclosure has been presented in a more balanced, nuanced way, acknowledging its value when done with clinical wisdom and skill by many psychological theorists (e.g., Aron, 1996; Baldwin, 2000;

Brown, 1994; Farber, 2006; Jourard, 1964; Kramer, 2000; Linehan, 1993; Maroda, 1999, 2004; Miller & Stiver, 1997; Norcross, 2002; Rogers, 1989; Shapiro, 1995; Stricker & Fisher, 1990; Walker & Rosen, 2004; Wachtel, 2008; Yalom, 2002; Zur, 2007a). There are even useful guidelines and suggestions for clinically appropriate, research-based, ethically sound therapist self-disclosure practices in the service of good therapy (e.g., Hill & Knox, 2002; Peterson, 2002; Zur, 2007a). As self-disclosure sheds its purely negative associations, it has arrived as a valid and ripe topic for conversation, research, and development of good practice. We believe that we are moving into a new era, where the collective focus will be that of thoughtful examination, clinical research, and the development of better clinical training to create a new generation of therapists who are educated about how to self-disclose appropriately and therapeutically.

What counts as therapist self-disclosure?

Therapist self-disclosure is a very broad term that has been defined differently by many authors and researchers. In a narrow definition, it refers only to the intentional disclosing of verbal information for the sake of having a therapeutic effect, often referred to in the literature as "intentional" self-disclosure. Stricker & Fisher (1990) defined it broadly as "the process by which the self is revealed" (p. 277). In this book, we use a broad definition: We define it to mean *anything that is revealed about a therapist verbally, nonverbally, on purpose, by accident, wittingly, or unwittingly, inclusive of information discovered about them from another source*. By this definition, everyone self-discloses to some extent, even if unintentionally.

The entire constellation of information revealed by any source impacts the therapeutic relationship, albeit in ways that are sometimes not easy to gauge. Therapy conducted in home offices, for example, yields a great deal about the therapist. Clients can infer the therapist's socioeconomic and marital status, as they are likely at some point to see a spouse, pets, children, and so on. Information about a therapist may be known via therapists' publications and presentations and from the World Wide Web. Therapists, too, may be seen at common locations—churches, supermarkets, the gym, yoga class, and so on. Therapists' physical presentation may be very self-disclosing, for example, and in the case of a therapist with either a disability or illness, the client is largely impacted by this information disclosed by the therapist just by seeing the physicality of the therapist. Nonverbal expressions are self-disclosing: we show what we think and feel with facial expressions and nonverbal utterances. Creative therapies like art therapy or dance/movement therapy raise a unique set of nonverbal disclosure issues.

"Boundary crossings" count as self-disclosure too. Reciprocally, self-disclosure is a considered by many a boundary crossing. What is a boundary crossing? A boundary crossing is any deviation from the narrowly defined traditional Freudian therapeutic frame: therapist self-disclosure, receiving an e-mail from a client, having a phone session with a client, doing therapy in any space other than your office, or running into a client accidentally in one's community are all deviations from the frame, thus they count as boundary crossings. Such boundary crossings may be inadvertently self-disclosing, such as in the example written about by Fish (2002) where she discusses the effects on a therapy relationship when a client saw her yelling at her children in the supermarket. With the advent of more behaviorally oriented therapies that utilized different settings for therapeutic effect in a well-planned and empirically supported framework (e.g., in vivo exposure therapy), the term *boundary crossing* came into being to refer to contact outside of an office that is purposeful and clinically appropriate within a particular treatment paradigm utilized for therapeutic effects (e.g., having a meal with an eating-disordered client or going to a feared place with a phobic client). This different term was needed to distinguish a legitimate, benign, or therapeutic boundary *crossing* from a boundary *violation* (Gutheil & Gabbard, 1998; Zur, 2007a). A boundary violation is a power-abusing, destructive, unethical act that is definitely not therapeutic, such as having any kind of sexual activity with a client. The term *boundary crossing* refers also to any inadvertent outside contact such as having a chance encounter with a client in a shared community, to intentional outside contact that has been carefully considered and deemed therapeutic or clinically appropriate. In sum, every therapist crosses boundaries sometimes, even if only by chance or in making clinically appropriate self-disclosures, and so the term *boundary crossing* will be used in this book, when relevant. "Boundary violations," by contrast, are destructive acts of power abuse and are not the subject of this book.

Therapist self-disclosure: Helpful or harmful?

When is it too much?

There is a possibility of destructive therapist self-disclosure: Abusive, excessive, or unattuned therapist self-disclosure does happen, and its effect can be quite damaging. Excessive and unattuned self-disclosure not done truly for the client's benefit will be, at minimum, unhelpful and possibly a harmful and truly destructive encounter.

Although we argued earlier that the slippery slope does not apply to most therapists and should not be used as a global argument against all self-disclosure, we agree that there is a subset of therapists, for which poor judgment and loose boundaries would beget increasingly more of that, hence the "slippery slope" phenomenon. For example, in a case that was published by Anonymous (2000), he rationalized that he was "helping" his client by revealing his sexual feelings to her, hiring her to work for him (since she did not have a job), and ultimately engaging in a sexual relationship with her. Anonymous committed a serious boundary violation, as we see it, not *because* he self-disclosed, but because he was not self-aware about his true motives, and not conducting therapy in the service of his client's well-being. The inappropriate disclosure of his sexual feelings was a byproduct of his underlying problem. He made his choices surreptitiously for his own need to be powerful, a savior, and ultimately to ameliorate his own loneliness. Thus, it was not self-disclosure that was the *cause* of his wrong actions. His inappropriate disclosure and choice to act on the feelings was the symptom of something that was deeper, a confluence of factors that contributed to his bad decision. Anonymous was a therapist who was not emotionally healthy enough to be doing this work, was not supported by a community where he could readily receive feedback (and not wise enough to seek it out), and who was not educated clearly enough about how to navigate his feelings when doing this complicated and intimate work.

Less egregious self-disclosures by therapists can be destructive on a smaller scale. Therapists who are too chit-chatty—who reveal, for example, willy-nilly about their children, their families, their own trials and tribulations—at the very least waste valuable minutes being paid for by their clients; in that, they violate their clients' trust because they are not able to stay focused on their clients' well-being. They are not listening or self-disclosing in the service of their clients' need for self-disclosure, and thus not doing their job very well. Clients do not always feel empowered to end their sessions with such a therapist and thus waste valuable time and resources, getting much less out of therapy than they could or should. This approach is neither judicious nor thoughtful with regard to their client's well-being and thus destructive as well as counter-therapeutic.

The negative effects of this loose-lipped over-sharing are many. In these situations, clients' treatment goals are unintentionally overshadowed and clients can be made uncomfortable with too much information. Ultimately, an unassertive client in this situation may stay way too long in an unproductive, counter-therapeutic relationship. Clients who are educated and savvy about what therapy should feel like will most likely know better, recognize the therapist's errors, and move on quickly. Unfortunately, not all clients are aware of what to expect and thus will not know that they are being ripped off and missing out on the valuable experience that therapy can be. In fact, some may leave therapy, scratching their heads in confusion about how therapy is supposed to help, ultimately concluding that therapy is a fruitless endeavor, provided and endorsed by purveyors of quackery. Based on this sort of experience, their minds may be closed to psychotherapy forever, and they will miss out on the chance to have the truly transformative and valuable experience that therapy can provide.

When is it "too little"?

On the other end of the continuum is the opposite extreme: a therapist who is too distant, adhering to Freudian metaphors as law, and attempting to be so uninvolved in the relationship that they are extreme in the other direction. Disconnected, distant, and detached are the feelings the clients may have and the client will miss out on the richness of a connected, attuned relationship that could facilitate positive change. There can be destructive effects too of this stance, which in the past were overshadowed by the taboo of "too much." For example, when a client is feeling so isolated, judged, abandoned and alone, having a therapy relationship that has this same quality could serve to reinforce the existential state of disconnection and perhaps convince the client that connection with another human being is not possible. Depression and isolation could worsen; hope for better relationships could be damaged or destroyed. Feeling that even one's therapist, who knows one most intimately, cannot reach out and metaphorically touch (emotionally connect) might make a client feel completely alienated and hopeless.

When is it therapeutic?

Thus, there is a bell curve continuum of therapist relatedness, and it is at the extreme end of "too much" or "too little" where the clients are most likely to be harmed. It is in murky middle where decisions about therapist self-disclosure are thoughtful, careful, but not always clearly understood: how much therapist self-disclosure is too much or too little for a given client, on a given day, in a given moment? How should clients' needs for therapist disclosure be balanced with therapists' needs for privacy? It is in this difficult and ambiguous space where therapists strive to make the best choices and the ideal amount of self-disclosure for a given client, in a given situation, may be found. When that balance is reached, it can also be among the most powerfully positive instigators of healing. This book provides many examples of therapists striving to find that ideal middle ground.

When the self-disclosure is used well, clients feel a comfortable bond or sense of connection with their therapist. Attuned and with sensitivity to clients' needs, therapists have to actively use their judgment to find the right fit for each client. There is no "one-size fits all"—every therapeutic relationship is so unique that therapists have to stay alert, constantly monitoring this aspect of the therapy. The very same disclosure that may be powerfully healing for one client will be unpleasantly experienced as "too much information" by another. Clients need vastly different amounts of connection, realness, and disclosure from their therapists, depending on so many variables that it is not possible to get it right every time. But when the therapist finds that balance, there is a good chemistry between client and therapist, and the client benefits enormously. The techniques of therapy are most effective in the context of a positive working alliance, which may serve to motivate clients in the hard work of healing and growing.

How to use this book

The book is organized into six sections. We begin Section 1 by providing a foundation of therapist self-disclosure in psychotherapy, in Chapter 1. In Chapter 2, a psychoanalyst well-known for her writing about countertransference and self-disclosure combines research, theory, and clinical examples to assert her case for judicious self-disclosure. In Chapter 3, an expert in boundaries and therapist self-disclosure provides a framework that includes a discussion of the standard of care, ethical considerations, and a review of relevant self-disclosure terminology. The next four sections all highlight clinical examples written by therapists, who in many cases are also expert in their fields.

In Section 2, therapists with clinical specialty areas and approaches share their considerations of self-disclosure choices via treatment from clinical orientations including psychodynamic, humanistic, dialectical behavior therapy (DBT), accelerated experiential-dynamic psychotherapy (AEDP), cognitive behavior therapy (CBT), and in vivo behavior therapy, using clinical examples that include adolescent and adult clients, eating disorders, depression, borderline personality disorder, anxiety, and addictions.

In Section 3, the therapist's selfhood is considered, with examples that refer to therapists' own ethnicity, race, and gender/sexual orientations as they enter the therapeutic alliance and raise self-disclosure issues. Two of these are written from a relational-cultural theory (RCT) perspective, and one is from an object-relations informed eye movement and desensitization reprocessing (EMDR) approach discussing the treatment of trauma and attachment problems.

Section 4 considers self-disclosure in different treatment modalities combining theories associated with these practices with clinical examples including schizophrenia, autism, eating disorders, and depression. Family therapy, group therapy, art therapy, and dance/movement therapy are discussed in this section.

Section 5 explores therapists' personal life challenges, including pregnancy, accidental injury, and illness, and highlights self-disclosure decisions within these personal realms. Section 6, the final one, highlights original research on self-disclosure in clinical supervision and concluding comments drawn from the entirety of this book.

The sections and/or chapters may be read in any order; the stories are independent, with the therapists writing in their own styles, their own voices. The writing style was not made uniform so that the uniqueness of each therapist—the special combination of training background, personality, culture/ethnicity, therapeutic identity, personal style, and clinical population specialized in—serves to show how that therapist works.

This book is a hybrid. Although it is academic enough to be used in training, it is also for the seasoned clinician. Some chapters are more academic in style, some more personal, and some are a combination of the two. And to break new ground, we encouraged all of our authors to write about this in an appropriately self-disclosing way. Therapists were encouraged to share relevant bits of information about themselves, to whatever extent they felt comfortable, to share the context of their identities as individuals and as therapists, thus to self-disclose a bit to you. Our authors shared not only their cases but also the journey of their evolution in their own consideration of human relatedness. In writing the chapters in this personal way, each author has now chosen to be a "psychotherapist revealed" to you.

References

Anonymous. (2000, March). Boundaries in therapy: The limits of care. *The Pennsylvania Psychologist, 1,* 3.

Aron, L. (1996). *A meeting of minds: Mutuality in psychoanalysis.* Hillsdale, NJ: The Analytic Press.

Baldwin, M. (Ed.). (2000). *The use of self in therapy* (2nd ed.). New York: The Haworth Press.

Brown, L. (1994). *Subversive dialogues.* New York: Basic Books.

Farber, B. (2006). *Self-disclosure in psychotherapy.* New York: The Guilford Press.

Fish, L. S. (2002, March/April). Nightmare in the aisle: A therapist caught in the act of being herself. *Psychotherapy Networker,* 36–37.

Freud, S. (1963). Recommendations for physicians on the psychoanalytic method of treatment. In S. Freud, *Therapy & technique.* New York: Collier. (Original work published 1912)

Gediman, H. (2006). Facilitating analysis with implicit and explicit self-disclosures. *Psychoanalytic Dialogues, 16*(3), 241–262.

Geller, J. D. (2003). Self-disclosure in psychoanalytic-existential therapy. *JCLP/In Session, 59*(5), 541–554.

Goldstein, E. (1994). Self-disclosure in treatment: What therapists do and don't talk about. *Clinical Social Work Journal, 22,* 417–433.

Grubrich-Simitis, I. (1986). Six letters of Sigmund Freud and Sandor Ferenczi on the interrelationship of psychoanalytic theory and technique. *International Review of Psychoanalysis, 13,* 259–277.

Gutheil, T. G., & Gabbard, G. O. (1998). Misuses and misunderstandings of boundary theory in clinical and regulatory settings. *The American Journal of Psychiatry, 155*(3), 409–414.

Hill, C. E., & Knox, S. (2002). Self-disclosure. In J. C. Norcross (Ed.), *Psychotherapy relationships that work* (pp. 255–266). New York: Oxford University Press.

Jourard, S. (1964). *The transparent self.* Princeton, NJ: D. Van Nostrand Company.

Kramer, C. H. (2000). Revealing our selves. In M. Baldwin (Ed.), *The use of self in therapy* (2nd ed., pp. 61–96). New York: The Haworth Press.

Linehan, M. (1993). *Cognitive-behavioral treatment of borderline personality disorder.* New York: The Guilford Press.

Maroda, K. J. (1999). *Seduction, surrender, and transformation.* Hillsdale, NJ: The Analytic Press.

Maroda, K. J. (1999, March). Creating an intersubjective context for self-disclosure. *Smith College Studies in Social Work, 69*(2), 474–489.

Maroda, K. J. (2004). *The power of countertransference* (2nd ed.). Hillsdale, NJ: The Analytic Press.

Miller, J. B., & Stiver, I. P. (1997). *The healing connection.* Boston: Beacon Press.

Miller, J. B., Jordan, J. V., Stiver, I. P., Walker, M., Surrey, J. L., & Eldridge, N. (2004). Therapists' authenticity. In J. V. Jordan, M. Walker, & L. Hartling (Eds.), *The complexity of connection* (pp. 64–89). New York: The Guilford Press.

Norcross, J. C. (2002). Empirically supported therapy relationships. In J. C. Norcross (Ed.), *Psychotherapy relationships that work* (pp. 3–16). New York: Oxford University Press.

Orange, D. M., Atwood, G. E., & Stolorow, R. D. (1997). *Working intersubjectively: Contextualism in psychoanalytic practice.* Hillsdale, NJ: The Analytic Press.

Peterson, Z. D. (2002). More than a mirror: The ethics of therapist self-disclosure. *Psychotherapy: Theory, Research, Practice and Training, 39,* 21–31.

Renik, O. (1995). The ideal of the anonymous analyst and the problem of self-disclosure. *Psychoanalytic Quarterly, 64,* 466–495.

Rogers, C. (1989). The therapeutic relationship. In H. Kirschenbaum & V. L. Henderson (Eds.), *The Carl Rogers reader.* Boston: Houghton Mifflin.

Shapiro, F. (1995). *Eye-movement desensitization and reprocessing.* New York: The Guilford Press.

Stricker, G., & Fisher, M. (Eds.). (1990). *Self-disclosure in the therapeutic relationship.* New York: Plenum Press.

Wachtel, P. L. (2008). *Relational theory and the practice of psychotherapy.* New York: The Guilford Press.

Walker, M. (2004). How relationships heal. In M. Walker & W. Rosen (Eds.), *How connections heal* (pp. 3–21). New York: Guilford Press.

Williams, M. H. (2003). The curse of risk management. *The Independent Practitioner, 23*(4), 202–205.

Yalom, I. D. (2002). *The gift of therapy: An open letter to a new generation of therapists and their patients*. New York: HarperCollins.

Zur, O. (2000). In celebration of dual relationships: How prohibition of non-sexual dual relationships increases the chances of exploitation and harm. *The Independent Practitioner, 2*(3), 97–100.

Zur, O. (2007a). *Boundaries in psychotherapy*. Washington, DC: American Psychological Association.

Zur, O. (2007b, July/August). The ethical eye: Don't let "risk management" undermine your professional approach. *Psychotherapy Networker*, 48–56.

chapter two

Less is more

An argument for the judicious use of self-disclosure

Karen J. Maroda

Historical overview

Self-disclosure has been rapidly shedding its reputation as the technique of last resort for the inexperienced or insufficiently trained therapist. Although analytic clinicians have historically been less inclined to self-disclose (Simon, 1988; Myers & Hayes, 2006), there were several analysts in the 1930s to 1950s who strongly advocated for self-disclosure, especially to confirm the client's reality and when the analyst had contributed to an empathic break or impasse (Little, 1951; Ferenczi, 1932/1988; Tauber, 1954). As Rachman (1993) said in discussing the work of Ferenczi, "by the analyst's self-disclosing his own contribution to the emotional experience, he becomes the parent who is willing to take responsibility for contributing to any, even unintentional, emotional difficulty" (p. 93). These pioneering attempts to endorse self-disclosure when it was needed to acknowledge the reality of the emotional scenario taking place between analyst and client were buried by the mainstream analysts in favor of ongoing "neutrality."

Self-disclosure resurfaced in the analytic world in the late 1980s and early 1990s, primarily with the work of analysts like Renik (1995), Ehrenberg (1982, 1992), Jacobs (1999), and Maroda (1991, 1999). Although self-disclosure has been acknowledged as ubiquitous and possessing therapeutic potential, it remains controversial. The problem with self-disclosure has been, and remains, whether the disclosure is done for the therapist's benefit, the client's, or both. When we disclose, what is our reasoning and our motivation? When is it helpful and when is it not? To whom should we disclose and to whom should we not?

Simon's (1988) now-classic study of therapist self-disclosure was one of the first efforts to compare therapists who were most likely to disclose versus those who were not. Twenty years ago, when this study was done, self-disclosure was not widely accepted and Simon's results probably did little to encourage any changes. The high disclosers in her study did not possess the characteristics most therapists aspired to. Simon says they were inclined to answer any question their clients asked; they initiated hugs and other minor physical contact; they were more likely to have social relationships with former clients; and they had fewer hours of personal therapy than low disclosers. Simon's study was limited to interviews with only eight therapists (chosen from the tails of a sample of 27 on the basis of frequency of disclosure), and her results have to be considered within those limitations. She also reported that her subjects found self-disclosure to be generally helpful. But for analysts, in particular, the lack of information regarding self-disclosure and the fear of becoming one of Simon's "high-disclosers" inhibit them from engaging in this behavior.

Yet at the same time we are seeing a movement among those who do disclose to hold almost nothing back. Disclosure of erotic countertransference (Davies, 1994; Rosiello, 2000; Mann, 1997), which I am almost always opposed to, has been touted frequently enough in recent years that it is rapidly insinuating itself within the acceptable parameters of therapist self-disclosure (in spite of the fact that most therapists still view it as ethically questionable; Goodyear & Shumate, 1996; Fisher, 2004; Pope, Sonne & Holroyd, 1993).

Those like myself who feel that disclosing sexual attraction to a client contains unique boundary and safety issues may shy away from all disclosure rather than embrace a technique that suggests all of the emotional responses of the therapist are grist for the mill. And without some meaningful conceptualization of the therapeutic action(s) of self-disclosure, we are bound to have as many failures as successes. As Levenson (1996) said,

> I have had some striking successes, but also some disasters. Self-disclosure often seems to be a reparative effort by the analyst after some acting-in on his or her part. It is a device to be used sparingly, and only with patients with whom one has a solid therapeutic outcome. (p. 247)

I doubt that there is any therapist who hasn't at one time or another blurted out something to a client that he later regretted having said. We are all too aware that Levenson's observation regarding our motivations for talking about ourselves may well be grounded in our guilt or other disturbance of our professional and personal equilibrium. Therapist defensive maneuvers are not therapeutic, including defensive self-disclosure.

The use of self-disclosure

The literature on self-disclosure provides some basic information that I want to briefly outline before going further with this discussion. The risk with any edited volume is that the reader will be subjected to repetitive literature reviews. So I will keep this as brief as possible. First, in spite of the controversy, self-disclosure appears to be therapeutic, at least some of the time (Hanson, 2005; Hill, 1989, 2001; Knox et al., 1997; Myers & Hayes, 2006; Simon, 1988). Second, the reasons given for this usually include modeling, providing needed reassurance, increasing openness in the relationship, confirming the client's perceptions and reality, and ending an impasse. Third, Myers & Hayes have also noted that not all clients are seeking self-disclosure and that they appear to benefit only if it occurs within the context of a strong, positive therapeutic relationship.

Most of us who write about self-disclosure seem to agree that it should be done with some consistency, not to be confused with high frequency. The therapist who gratuitously volunteers personal information and physical contact persists as a negative role model. I am reminded of a story I heard from a young woman who went to see a therapist, and by the second session this doctoral-level psychologist was filling silences by blabbing on about how she and her husband were going to China to adopt a baby. Self-disclosure as a response to therapist anxiety about what to say next is clearly not what we are talking about when we discuss therapeutic self-disclosure.

When and how is self-disclosure therapeutic?

The next logical question is, What *are* we talking about when we talk about therapeutic self-disclosure? The discussion in the analytic world regarding self-disclosure has shifted from "should we do it?" to "when and how is it therapeutic?" Analytic clinicians naturally wish to understand the therapeutic action of self-disclosure. We want to know not just that it works, but when, how, and why. Absolute answers to these questions are not possible, of course, but certainly we have, and will continue to have, valuable clinical reports regarding what seems to work and what doesn't. Over time as we gather this information, we can provide new therapists with some reasonable guidelines regarding self-disclosure, as well as other techniques (Maroda, in press).

No one who writes about self-disclosure recommends just saying whatever comes to mind. Even Renik (1999, 2006), who calls for us to be spontaneous, also says that ideally we would have some technical guidelines, as does Meissner (2002). The obvious benefit to understanding why therapist self-disclosure works is that we can formulate our self-disclosures in accordance with established therapeutic efficacy.

For example, early on (1991) I advocated for the use of self-disclosure from an attachment and relational perspective, promoting the therapist's expression of affect over providing personal information. And I continue to assert that providing the client with needed emotional feedback and a general awareness of how the therapist sees and experiences him is far more therapeutic than tales of the therapist's life. I also emphasized that self-disclosure should be done in response to the client's direct or indirect requests for an affective response.

Later (Maroda, 1999) I built on the work of Stern (1985) and Krystal (1988), proposing that the therapist's expression of emotion toward the client served to complete the cycle of affective communication that was insufficiently developed in childhood. In expressing emotion at the appropriate times, the therapist provides an emotional reeducation and remediates a developmental void.

I point out that it is not uncommon for the therapist's affect to be a feeling, like anger, that has been split off by the client. When the therapist constructively expresses his client's disavowed emotion, she is not only modeling awareness, and the naming and appropriate expression of emotion, she is also removing the taboo on that particular emotion. The client's fear that her anger will destroy her or her therapist is contradicted by the therapist's ability not only to silently contain but also to express that anger.

I said that whenever the client asks the therapist what she is feeling toward her, and does so in a heartfelt way, the therapist should probably answer. In the aforementioned case, when the client's affect is disavowed and stimulated unconsciously and repetitively in the therapist, that serves as a signal to the therapist to find a constructive way to express what she is feeling.

Lastly, I have advocated for the therapist to use self-disclosure to break any impasse that occurs. From Jourard (1959) to Truax and Carkhuff (1965) to Renik (1995), we have seen evidence that self-disclosure begets self-disclosure. And the literature on affect (Panskepp, 1994) tells us that change only occurs when there is a free flow of emotion in the brain. Our intra-session goal is the stimulation of emotion, with the hope of creating new experience. Emotional engagement, and to some degree, mutual disclosure of emotion, is the currency of therapeutic action.

Therefore, the primary reason to selectively and judiciously disclose emotion to a client is to complete the cycle of affective communication, model mature affective management, and in terms of brain function, provide the catalyst for change. I will elaborate on the other benefits of self-disclosure shortly, but I want to emphasize that the developmental and neural impact of felt emotion provides us with the most important answer to our initial question: How and why is self-disclosure therapeutic?

The other ways in which it can be therapeutic, to my mind, are not as essential and do not stimulate the same deep level of experience and potentiality for change that affective communication does. Providing personal information, including stories from the therapist's life, can be therapeutic, but I personally think this particular type of disclosure is overrated. Therapists or analysts who talk about their lives may, indeed, see a positive response from their clients. But, again, the question is: Why? What was it about the disclosure of personal information that was therapeutic?

There is no specific research on this subtopic, but from my clinical experience, I believe that clients are helped by a disclosure of personal information when that disclosure either resonates with the client's emotional experience, or makes the therapist emotionally vulnerable in that moment. It may also be therapeutic, if used infrequently, because of its novel stimulus value and the likelihood that the client will feel "special" due to the rarity of the event.

This takes us back to the notion of emotion as currency. It seems highly unlikely to me that personal information that does not "move" the client in some real way will be therapeutic. Other disclosures may be gratifying and therefore be rated positively in client self-report, but to my mind, this is not what we are trying to achieve. I agree with Meissner that it is not knowledge of the analyst per se that is nontherapeutic (he points out that the client may discover information about the analyst through a variety of venues) but rather actions on the part of the analyst to move away from a professional liaison in favor of a more personal one. If my client discovers my home address and drives by my house, this is qualitatively different than me providing the address and suggesting that he drive by and give his opinion on my new landscaping.

I am not saying that disclosure of personal information should not be done—only that the therapist take a moment to see if this is a substitute for a more relevant, but perhaps more threatening, disclosure of affect. If, in fact, the disclosure actually serves as a metaphor for the client's life or the relationship between the client and therapist, then it has a good chance of being therapeutic. The neuroscience literature says that few things light up areas across the brain like metaphor (Pally, 2000). And lighting up the brain is what we want to accomplish. So the question is, does the disclosure accomplish this or merely create greater familiarity between therapist and client?

I saw several clients who came to me after their therapist retired, and literally all of them recounted stories of him mentioning his favorite movies, Broadway shows, and sports teams. He would periodically regale them with stories on these subjects, which they found quirky but endearing. None of them seemed to be harmed by his disclosures, but they said they didn't really understand what purpose they served. And they were occasionally irritated by his self-indulgence. Before I tell a story to a client, I ask myself, Why I am doing it? Is it to amuse myself? Am I lonely from seeing clients all day and want to talk about myself? Is there something I need in that moment from that client? Is the session boring and therefore ungratifying? If so, perhaps I should dig into the client's experience a bit more rather than settling for self-reference. This is not to say that I never indulge myself in this way. I do. But I consider it a lapse, not something to strive for.

Self-disclosure in practice

This brings me to the subject of how I actually work with my own clients, all of whom are functional to highly functional, fairly intelligent people whom I see in my outpatient analytic practice. These are not all people seeking psychoanalysis. Some came for crisis intervention and stayed. Others are short-term, often coming to deal with the ending of a marriage or other relationship. Depression is their unifying symptom.

I think it will be most helpful for me to give examples of both therapeutic and nontherapeutic self-disclosure (as opposed to inevitable self-revelation that emanates from style of dress, office décor, the client seeing you drive up in your car, running into you accidentally outside the office, etc.). When I use the term *self-disclosure* I am talking about the therapist's verbal expression of some thought or feeling, preferably done consciously rather than something blurted out impulsively and unintentionally.

I wrote about a very difficult client in *Seduction, Surrender, and Transformation* (Maroda, 1999) whom I continue to write about because the therapy did not end well. I called this client Susan and will continue with this pseudonym. Susan and I had a very ambivalent relationship, yet she frequently insisted that I reveal my thoughts and feelings towards her. Excited by my therapeutic successes with self-disclosure, I proceeded to reveal more than I should have to Susan, especially in the area of my negative responses to her.

Susan was very seductive with me and assumed I would find her attractive, which I did not. In fact, she soon picked up on the fact that her overwrought attempts to gain my favor and persuade me to accommodate her annoyed me considerably. She felt my unstated but obvious negative reaction to her at these times was overdetermined. (And, yes, she did read the analytic literature, but was not a therapist herself.) Finally, after she had broached this topic many times, I decided to answer her honestly. She asked me to admit that I sometimes had a strong negative reaction to her. I admitted that I did. Then she said that she must remind me of someone from my past that I did not like, because I seemed to over-react to her.

I was very reluctant to respond to this inquiry, given that it required me to deviate from my own guidelines regarding very personal informa-tion. In the end, I decided to answer Susan's question and tell her that at times she reminded me of an aunt whom I disliked intensely. I quickly added that I did not feel this way all of the time, only part of the time. But it was too late. The damage had been done. Susan was both triumphant and distraught. She knew she was right. But the truth only fed into her exaggerated sadomasochism. Thompson (1964) warned us some time ago about this very scenario. She said,

> It is very important not to begin the truth telling on
> the part of the analyst too early. One must not offer
> oneself as a sacrifice to the patient's sadism. Also it
> is necessary, first, that the patient feels sufficiently
> secure and has some confidence in his own powers
> before he is called on to face the defects in the one
> on whom he leans. (p. 72)

Unfortunately, I had not read this particular passage of Thompson's prior to treating Susan. Too early into her treatment I fed her sadism through my significant error. Although the treatment proceeded with measurable successes, it ultimately ended in stalemate, and I believe this disclosure was the first of many errors I made due to my inability to manage my negative feelings toward Susan and hers toward me. In ret-rospect, I answered her question when I knew better because I felt guilty about the truth of her statement. On a conscious level, I thought she was entitled to having her reality confirmed, even if it was a negative real-ity. Unconsciously, I was probably seizing the opportunity to aggress against her.

I have not been faced with any similar situations since ending with Susan some 10 years ago but, in retrospect, my gut was telling me not to answer. I knew the information I was giving Susan was not what I normally disclosed, was too personal, and too negative to be helpful. And I was not at all comfortable with the disclosure at the time I was giving it which, again, went against my own guidelines (Maroda, 1991) for disclosing.

As stated earlier in this chapter, self-disclosure can be extremely ther-apeutic and I want to illustrate that as well. My most successful intense self-disclosure was also my first. I was treating a client with borderline personality disorder who constantly criticized me and said I was not helping her. If only I loved her and re-parented her, everything would be all right. But I constantly withheld this from her and made her miserable instead. If only I could love her the way she loved me, she would be saved. When this scenario kept repeating itself over and over again, with no interpretations or empathic statements making any lasting impression, I decided to try something else.

In *The Power of Countertransference* (1991, 2004) I illustrated in greater detail how I eventually told her that at that moment I felt frustrated and angry and that this encounter was more about hate than love. I definitely did not *feel* loved. Unlike the previous example of Susan, this disclosure of negative affect with Nancy was unbelievably therapeutic. She calmed down after asking me if I was going to "dump" her because I was right in what I said. Once I assured her that I was not, she said, "Why did it take you so long to say this?" She said she was afraid if I knew how much she hated me sometimes, I would reject and abandon her. She also reiterated that she does love me, too, and really wishes she could have a relationship with me outside of therapy. After that encounter, that impasse was never repeated and Nancy began to work productively with her rage.

These two cases shared many similarities, but also were quite different from each other. In the case of Susan, she was very aggressive and critical of me, and made many demands that were unreasonable regarding scheduling, fee reductions, and phone calls. From the beginning she was unable to accept the basic terms, especially the asymmetry, of the relationship. Her requests for personal information from me were just another attempt to equalize the relationship, but not in a positive way. She felt she was in a one-down position simply by being the client and frequently sought to turn the tables on me and prove that I was not better than she was.

Nancy, on the other hand, sincerely wanted therapy, needed a reduced fee because of her financial circumstances, but was grateful for it and always paid on time. She rarely called me and never asked for any special treatment. She was very difficult to work with in the sessions themselves, being frequently emotionally out of control. But she thrived in the safe environment I provided for her. Part of that safety was not talking about myself and limiting any disclosures to direct responses to her in the moment. She valued this feedback and used it productively. I believe that she was healthier and more motivated than Susan was, but we were also a better match.

Even though I didn't always like Nancy, I respected her earnest attempts to change her life for the better. With Susan I did not feel this and saw her as wanting to get better only if she could do it on her terms. Everything was a power struggle. We did not have the alliance I had with

Nancy and in one case I was giving mostly personal information with negative implications for Susan, while in the successful disclosure with Nancy I was expressing strong feeling in the moment.

Regarding my motivations, as I noted earlier, I was motivated to disclose a defensive response to Susan's criticisms and by the anger I felt in response to those criticisms. With Nancy I was able to consciously express my frustration and anger constructively, in part because she gave me the room to do so. Although these two clients shared a great deal in common, including an intense, regressive attachment to me, and a corresponding need to win my love and acceptance, they were also very different. Perhaps this is why some question the feasibility of guidelines for self-disclosure. These two clients had similar early experiences, shared the same general diagnosis, and were equally ambivalently attached to me. Self-disclosure guidelines based on categorization of client psychodynamics are clearly not workable. Individual differences in clients and client-therapist dynamics have to be included in any general technical advice. As Schwaber (1996) said, "One patient tells me I talk too much; another that I don't talk enough. I feel my degree of activity with each of them is about equivalent" (p. 6). Although she was not discussing self-disclosure per se, her comments are relevant nonetheless. Any therapist activity, including self-disclosure, has to be tailored to the individual needs of the client.

Returning briefly to my two case examples, the reader may have already noted a seemingly small but very important difference between these two self-disclosure incidents. In the case of Susan, I was responding to a demand for negative *information*. She was not asking for affective feedback, and she was not vulnerable herself. She was engaging in analyzing the analyst as a way of equalizing the power differential in the relationship. And I was pacifying her out of my guilt for being caught thinking ill of her.

With Nancy, however, we were both quite emotional and vulnerable. Even though she was unaware in the moment of her disavowed hatred of me, she was making herself very vulnerable when she begged me to love her. And I felt quite vulnerable, and scared, when I took the risk of telling her *how I was feeling toward her in the moment*. We were working together, affectively, to create a new emotional experience, and we had the strong alliance that allowed us to work through this painful exchange.

Also, I had given this disclosure a great deal of thought before implementing it. Before disclosing intense anger I had consulted with colleagues, tried everything else to break this impasse, and examined my feelings and motivations for even considering saying something like this (which I have never said to any other client since, by the way). It was anything but a "shoot from the hip" event, yet it was emotionally honest and immediate in that moment. I showed real emotion, but I was not out of control. I had thought through her possible reactions and prepared myself for dealing with them, especially her predictable fears of rejection and abandonment. And I did not do what Nancy was pushing me to do, which was declare love for her and reassure her. I did the opposite. I gave not what she was demanding, but what she needed. Had I done the same with Susan, which I did later (e.g., telling her that I didn't see any value in probing for negative comments and feelings), the result would have been more therapeutic.

What can current research tell us?

The research on self-disclosure has been limited and general, chiefly because it is not ethical to have clinicians try out different forms of self-disclosures in actual treatments. Most studies are done through showing videos or otherwise providing subjects with therapist disclosures and then noting their responses. Hanson's (2005) study involved interviewing actual therapy clients about their current experiences. Her conclusions were that self-disclosure was definitely helpful, but was highly dependent on a strong alliance between therapist and client, and on the skill and comfort levels of the therapist. Priest (2005), in a discussion of Hanson's work, said its weakness lay in the dependence of self-report by clients still in therapy. He doubts that they were in a position to objectively assess the impact of their therapists' behaviors.

I found two of the conclusions of a study done by Knox et al. (1997) to be particularly interesting and to resonate with my own experience. The first was,

> Although there were not enough data for us to investigate this fact more fully, different types of clients seemed to react differently to therapist self-disclosure. Some of these clients were voracious in their desire for therapist self-disclosure, wishing their therapists had disclosed more often or even arranging to meet with another client of the same therapist to share information about the therapist. (p. 282)

I think the topic of individual differences in receptivity to and therapeutic benefit of self-disclosure has not received enough attention and is something I address in my next book (Maroda, in press), but surely the "voracious" seekers of therapist personal information are not engaged in a healthy therapeutic process. They are those, like Susan, who seek knowledge of all sorts about their therapists out of a need to feel powerful and/or to feed a symbiotic merger. From my experience, most clients seek limited therapist self-disclosure, and many do not seek any at all. Knox et al.'s second conclusion discusses the fear some clients feel:

> Other clients, however, were less desirous of disclosures, worrying at times that the disclosures blurred the boundaries of the relationship or distinctly stating that self-disclosures were inappropriate because they removed the focus from the client and were unprofessional in their revelations about the therapist. (p. 282)

Clearly they were responding to receiving personal information about the therapist, which I expressed concern about earlier. But it also speaks to individual differences and against any notion that clients as a whole benefit from a predetermined level of therapist self-disclosure. These investigators did conclude that self-disclosure was therapeutic under the right circumstances, which included revealing only historical personal information, not information about the therapist's current problems. Goldstein (1994) rightly notes that the consequences of self-disclosure are both immediate and long-term. Something that the client works hard to accept and accommodate in the moment may linger and have longer-term negative effects.

And as many researchers have pointed out, relying on the client's self-report of benefit or harm is not a reliable barometer of therapeutic outcome. Clients of well-meaning and usually helpful therapists work hard to overlook their faults and self-indulgences. I have seen my own clients do this, yet at the same time their obvious discomfort when I disclosed something they were not seeking, not to mention the pervasive "tell" of looking at their watches, informed me that what I was saying was an intrusion.

Final comments

Although much remains to be done, it appears that the judicious use of self-disclosure can be quite therapeutic. It needs to be done in response to the client's direct or indirect request for a response. I believe it is the most effective when it involves giving an emotional reaction to the client in the moment. Watching the client's response carefully as you speak can potentially cut short an overly long or nontherapeutic disclosure. And there are two types of therapist self-disclosure that appear to be rarely, if ever, therapeutic: the disclosure of immediate personal problems, and the disclosure of erotic countertransference.

As with many topics in psychotherapy, more clinical reports and research need to be done. And clinicians need to be honest with themselves about what motivates their disclosures and whether or not the results are really therapeutic or simply not disastrous. It is not easy to study ourselves during our moments of vulnerability and occasional self-indulgence. But it is the best interests of our clients to do so.

References

Davies, J. (1994). Love in the afternoon. *Psychoanalytic Dialogues, 4,* 153–170.

Ehrenberg, D. (1982). Psychoanalytic engagement—The transaction as primary data. *Contemporary Psychoanalysis, 18,* 535–555.

Ehrenberg, D. (1992). *The intimate edge.* New York: Norton.

Ferenczi, S. (1988). *The clinical diary of Sandor Ferenczi* (J. Dupont, Ed.; M. Balint & N. Z. Jackson, Trans.). Cambridge, MA: Harvard University Press. (Original work published 1932)

Fisher, C. (2004). Ethical issues in therapy: Therapist self-disclosure of sexual feelings. *Ethics & Behavior, 14*(2): 105–121.

Goldstein, E. (1994). Self-disclosure in treatment: What therapists do and don't talk about. *Clinical Social Work Journal, 22*(4): 417–433.

Goodyear, R., & Shumate, J. (1996). Perceived effects of therapist self-disclosure of attraction to clients. *Professional Psychology: Research and Practice, 27*(6): 613–616.

Hanson, J. (2005). Should your lips be zipped? How therapist self-disclosure and non-disclosure affects clients. *Counselling and Psychotherapy Research, 5*(2): 96–104.

Hill, C., & Knox, S. (2001). Self-disclosure. *Psychotherapy, 38*(6): 413–417.

Hill, C., Mahalik, J., & Thompson, B. (1989). Therapist self-disclosure. *Psychotherapy, 26*(3): 290–295.

Jacobs, T. (1999). On the question of self-disclosure by the analyst: Error or advance in technique? *Psychoanalytic Quarterly, 68,* 159–183.

Jourard, S. (1971). *Self-disclosure: An experimental analysis of the transparent self.* New York: Wiley.

Knox, S., Hess, S., Petersen, D., & Hill, C. (1997). A qualitative analysis of client perceptions of the effects of helpful therapist self-disclosure in long-term therapy. *Journal of Counseling Psychology, 44*(33): 274–283.

Krystal, H. (1988). *Integration and self-healing: Affect, trauma, alexithymia.* Hillsdale, NJ: The Analytic Press.

Levenson, E. (1996). Aspects of self-revelation and self-disclosure. *Contemporary Psychoanalysis, 32,* 237–248.

Little, M. (1951). Countertransference and the patient's response to it. *International Journal of Psycho-Analysis, 32,* 32–40.

Mann, D. (1997). *Psychotherapy: An erotic relationship. Transference and countertransference passions.* London: Routledge.

Maroda, K. (1991). *The power of countertransference.* Chichester, UK: Wiley & Sons.

Maroda, K. (1999). *Seduction, surrender, and transformation.* Hillsdale, NJ: The Analytic Press.

Maroda, K. (2004). *The power of countertransference* (2nd ed.). Hillsdale, NJ: The Analytic Press.

Maroda, K. (in press). *Interactive psychodynamic techniques.* New York: Guilford.

Meissner, W. W. (2002). The problem of self-disclosure in psychoanalysis. *Journal of the American Psychoanalytic Association, 50,* 827–867.

Myers, D., & Hayes, J. (2006). Effects of therapist general self-disclosure and countertransference disclosure on ratings of the therapist and session. *Psychotherapy: Research, Practice, Training, 43*(2): 173–185.

Pally, R. (2000). *The mind-brain relationship.* London: Karnac.

Panksepp, J. (1994). Subjectivity may have evolved in the brain as a simple value-coding process that promotes the learning of new behaviors. In P. Ekman & R. Davidson (Eds.), *The nature of emotion: Fundamental questions* (pp. 313–315). New York: Oxford University Press.

Pope, K. S., Sonne, J. L., & Holroyd, J. (1993). *Sexual feelings in psychotherapy.* Washington, DC: American Psychological Association.

Priest, T. (2005). Comments on Hanson "Should your lips be zipped? How therapist self-disclosure and non-disclosure affects clients." *Counselling & Psychotherapy Research, 5,* 306.

Rachman, A. (1993). Ferenczi and Sexuality. In Aron, L. & Harris, A. (Eds.), *The Legacy of Sandor Ferenczi* (pp. 81–100). Hillsdale, NJ: The Analytic Press.

Renik, O. (1995). The ideal of the anonymous analyst and the problem of self-disclosure. *Psychoanalytic Quarterly, 64,* 466–495.

Rosiello, F. (2000). On lust and loathing: Erotic transference/countertransference between a female analyst and female patients. *Journal of Gay & Lesbian Psychotherapy, 4*(2): 5–26.

Schwaber, E. (1996). Toward a definition of the term and concept of interaction: Its reflection in analytic listening. *Psychoanalytic Inquiry, 16,* 5–24.

Simon, J. (1988). Criteria for therapist self-disclosure. *American Journal of Psychotherapy, 42*(3): 404–415.

Stern, D. (1985). *The interpersonal world of the infant.* New York: Basic Books.

Tauber, E. (1954). Exploring the therapeutic use of countertransference data. *Psychiatry, 17*(4): 331–336.

Thompson, C. (1964). Ferenczi's relaxation method. In M. Green (Ed.), *Interpersonal psychoanalysis: Papers of Clara M. Thompson* (pp. 67–82). New York: Basic Books.

Truax, C., & Carkhuff, R. (1965). Client and therapist transparency in the psychotherapeutic encounter. *Journal of Counseling Psychology, 12*(1), 3–9.

chapter three

Therapist self-disclosure
Standard of care, ethical considerations, and therapeutic context

Ofer Zur

Introduction

Self-disclosure in psychotherapy and counseling is defined as the revelation of personal rather than professional information by a therapist to a client. Generally, when therapist disclosure goes beyond the standard, most basic professional disclosure of name, credentials, office address, fees, emergency contacts, cancellation policies, and so on, it is considered self-disclosure (Farber, 2006; Stricker & Fisher, 1990; Zur, 2007). Psychotherapists often narrowly view self-disclosure as information of a personal nature that they intentionally and verbally reveal to their clients. They do not realize that self-disclosure encompasses vastly more than intentional verbal disclosure. In the most general terms, therapist self-disclosure can be intentional, unintentional, or accidental; verbal or nonverbal; or avoidable or unavoidable. Although the therapist initiates some disclosures, the client or a third party initiates others. All of the above types of disclosures can be gathered under the umbrella of "therapist self-disclosure," as they all disclose nonprofessional information to the client about the "self" of the therapist, regardless of how the information came to the attention of the client. Some personal information about the therapist may be available to the client without the therapist's knowledge or approval. In this Internet era the disclosure of information about therapists and the availability of such information to clients have become rather broad, extensive, and complex. As this chapter argues, Internet technologies have redefined the concept, meaning, and application of self-disclosure in psychotherapy.

This chapter reviews and defines the various kinds of self-disclosure, discusses the application of the standard of care in psychotherapy and counseling to self-disclosure, articulates the ethics of self-disclosure, and details how the meaning of self-disclosure can be understood only within the context of therapy. Finally, the chapter provides general clinical and ethical guidelines for psychotherapist self-disclosure and more specific guidelines in regard to online disclosures.

Types of self-disclosure

There are several different types of self-disclosure. Most generally, disclosures can be deliberate or nondeliberate. They can also be divided into avoidable, accidental, and unavoidable. As detailed below, they can be appropriate, benign, or inappropriate and can be differentiated between those disclosures by those that are therapist initiated and those that are initiated by clients. Following are brief descriptions of these different types of disclosures.

Deliberate self-disclosure

The deliberate form of self-disclosure is probably the one that therapists most readily identify as self-disclosure. This type refers to the intentional and deliberate disclosure by the therapist of personal information.

Verbal deliberate self-disclosure

Verbal disclosures are most common when therapists share with their clients personal information about marital status, parenthood, age, religious or spiritual orientation, personal history, sexual orientation, vacation destination, and so on.

Nonverbal deliberate self-disclosure

Besides the deliberate verbal expression of personal information, such information could be expressed by other deliberate actions, for example, intentionally placing a certain family photo or artifacts in the office or an empathic gesture that reveals personal information (Barnett, 1998; Farber, 2006); wearing certain attire, religious symbols, or jewelry. Similarly, deliberate nonverbal expressions of moral outrage or disappointment are part of this type of self-disclosure (Zur, 2007).

Deliberate online (Internet) self-disclosure

In recent years, deliberate online self-disclosure has become more popular, as increasing numbers of psychotherapists are posting a professional Web page. This is where they choose to reveal not only professional information but also personal information regarding former careers, marital status, hobbies, recreational activities, and so on. As the Internet culture continues to expand and dominate large parts of our modern lives, there is increasing pressure for therapists to be more transparent (i.e., personal), especially on their Web sites (Zur, 2008).

Within deliberate forms of self-disclosure there are two types of disclosures, self-revealing and self-involving (Knox, Hess, Petersen, & Hill, 1997). (a) *Self-revealing* includes the disclosure of information by therapists about themselves rather than about their opinions, thoughts, or feelings regarding situations or clients; (b) *Self-involving* has to do with therapists' personal reactions to situations, events, and clients that deliberately reveal information about the therapist. These include expressions of admiration, indignation, delight, or anger to clients' actions or reactions and to other occurrences that take place during sessions.

Nondeliberate and unavoidable self-disclosure

In contrast to the first type, this second type of disclosure is not deliberate and is often unavoidable. There are several subtypes within this form of self-disclosure, described below.

Unavoidable "everyday life" self-disclosure
This form of self-disclosure includes a wide range of unavoidable natural or routine disclosures that are part of everyday life, about which therapists have no choice whether to disclose or not. These include a therapist's gender, age, and distinctive physical attributes, such as pregnancy, obesity, some forms of disability, and so on (Farber, 2006; Stricker & Fisher, 1990).

Everyday, common self-disclosure
Therapists reveal themselves in many ways, including their manner of dress; hairstyle; use of makeup, jewelry, perfume, or aftershave; facial hair; wedding rings; or the wearing of a cross, Star of David, or any other symbol (Barnett, 1998; Zur, 2007). Obviously, these revelations can be deliberate acts of self-disclosure but can also be more benign everyday expressions of personal taste or cultural identity.

Nondeliberate nonverbal
Nonverbal cues or body language, such as a raised eyebrow or a frown, are also sources of self-disclosure that are neither always deliberate nor always under the therapist's full control. A therapist's spontaneous, habitual, or instinctive expressions of surprise, fear, joy, appreciation, or disgust are, more often than not, nondeliberate self-disclosures.

Unavoidable announcement
A therapist announcing an upcoming vacation or other times to be away from the office also constitutes unavoidable self-disclosure.

Settings that induce unavoidable or "forced" self-disclosure

There are a number of settings that inherently involve a wide range of unavoidable, nondeliberate self-disclosures or what has been called "forced transparency." These include home office settings, small communities, home visits, or other out-of-office interventions. When the therapy office is located at the therapist's home, it always involves extensive self-disclosures, such as economic status, information about the family and pets, sometimes information about hobbies, habits, and much more (Nordmarken & Zur, 2005; Zur, 2007).

In small or rural communities, remote military bases or intimate and interconnected spiritual, ethnic, underprivileged, disabled, or college communities, therapists must all contend with extensive self-disclosure and significant transparency of their personal lives simply because many aspects are often displayed in clear view of their clients by virtue of the setting. In many of these small community situations a therapist's marital status, family details, religion or political affiliation, sexual orientation, and other personal information may be readily available to clients (Farber, 2006; Schank & Skovholt, 2006; Zur, 2006, 2007). It is important to understand that small communities are not limited to rural or physically isolated communities and can also be composed of church, school, sexual orientation, or ethnic minority communities within large metropolitan areas.

In addition, therapists who conduct home visits, adventure therapy, anorexic lunches, or in vivo desensitization are often in situations where many aspects of their personal and private lives are inevitably being revealed (Zur, 2007). These personal aspects may include the type of car the therapist drives and how well-kept it is, eating and drinking habits, and comfort level in different social and other situations.

Accidental self-disclosure

This form of self-disclosure occurs when there are spontaneous verbal or nonverbal reactions, incidental or unplanned encounters outside the office, or other unplanned occurrences that happen to reveal therapists' personal information to their clients (Knox, Hess, Petersen, & Hill, 1997; Stricker & Fisher, 1990; Zur, 2007). This may include a therapist's unplanned strong, emotional, negative response to a client's surprise announcement of a decision to get married, quit a job, or quit therapy. Or it might be when a client unexpectedly witnesses the therapist's interaction with his or her family or friends in a public place, or a client seeing a surprised therapist naked in a local gym locker room.

Common investigative searches initiated by clients

This type of disclosure has received very little attention in the professional literature. Therapists, in this case, may wittingly or unwittingly reveal information about themselves to clients who are seeking information about them (Zur, 2008). There are a couple of general ways that clients can seek information about their therapists:

Gathering information in the community

Some curious clients may ask people in the community or other clients questions about the therapist. They may read about the therapist in the local paper or come and attend a church or other community gathering to learn more about the therapist. More determined clients may obtain the therapist's home address and drive by their home.

Stalking

Zealous, obsessed, or vindictive clients have been reported to stalk their therapists. Stalking is obviously illegal. In response to a stalking client, some therapists have sought restraining orders (Galeazzi, Elkins, & Curci, 2005). Clients who violate their restraining orders can face imprisonment and other penalties.

Online searches by clients about their therapists

Conducting online searches for the specific purpose of gathering information about the therapist has become very common and even expected in the modern digital era. Clients in the 21st century are accustomed to viewing themselves as "consumers" and feel entitled to a wide range of information about their caregivers so they can make informed decisions regarding their own care (Zur, 2007, 2008). The use of Internet search engines, such as Google or Yahoo! can reveal a great deal of professional and personal information. There are a number of ways that clients may go about finding information about their therapists online.

Reviewing the professional Web sites and online resumes of therapists

Many therapists have professional Web sites that often provide information about their education, training, professional experiences, fees, theoretical orientations, philosophy of treatment, resumes, and so on. Others include photos of the therapists, articles by the therapists, or links to articles on different clinical topics.

Conducting a simple Internet search

A simple Internet search is likely to unearth information that was posted by the therapist or by others with or without the therapist's knowledge. This information may include a home address, unlisted phone numbers and a personal e-mail address, information about family members, sexual orientation, volunteer activities, political affiliation, lawsuits, or a licensing board's sanctions or complaints. With the click of a mouse, clients can find their therapists' writings on a variety of Web sites and personal blogs. Such a search can reveal former clients' complaints, grievances, charges, accusations, and criticisms.

Joining social networks

Clients may choose to go a step further and join social networks, such as Tribe.net, Facebook, or MySpace, or join professional Listservs under a pseudonym and find very personal and private information about their therapists. Once clients join the social networks, they can befriend their therapists online and gain access to all sorts of personal information, including relationship status, sexual preferences, religious views, hobbies, and much more.

Paying for specialized online background checks

Clients can pay online companies to conduct legal or illegal searches about therapists. Using this approach, clients can become privy to a wealth of information, which may include financial and tax information, credit reports, debts, and bankruptcies; criminal records and lawsuits; divorce records and allegations of domestic violence or molestation; and cell phone records.

Reading therapists' postings on professional Listservs and in chat rooms

It is simple to join professional Listservs and chat rooms, on which therapists are active, especially the open sites. Clients who join such Listservs using a false identity may be privy to information about the other clients of therapists, ethical or unethical conduct by their therapist, and perhaps even the details of their own treatment.

Why clients gather information

Clients' search for information about their therapists may vary from normal curiosity to criminal stalking (Zur, 2008). Following are four different categories under which behavior of clients may fall.

Level 1: Curiosity

Clients who are appropriately curious about their therapist may conduct a simple Internet search or check their therapist's professional Web site. This search may yield information regarding the professional life of the therapist and personal information that a therapist elects to include on his or her own professional Web page.

Level 2: Due diligence

Clients who are seriously looking for information about their therapists may apply due diligence by conducting one or more thorough Internet searches about their therapists. This may include searching the licensing boards' Web sites to see if a potential therapist has had any complaints filed against him or her. In our modern era of consumer rights and consumer power, it is legitimate and common for clients to want to learn a significant amount about the people in whom they will place their trust.

Level 3: Intrusiveness

Clients may push the envelope and intrusively search for information about their therapists. They may search for a home address, marital status, or information about family members or sexual orientation. This may also include disguising one's identity and joining social networks, Listservs, and so on, in order to find out more. They may also pay for an online service which legally gathers information that is not readily available online. As noted above, this may include divorce or other court records that are considered public records. They may also locate a camera online, know as a "web cam," that films or televises 24/7 a certain public place or popular vacation destination where the therapist may visit.

Level 4: Illegal or cyber stalking

There are those clients who will hire certain unscrupulous online services to illegally gather information about the therapist. This is a much cheaper and more readily available digital version of hiring a "traditional" private detective and can be anonymous. Such private information may include credit reports, banking information, cell phone records, and tax and divorce records.

Categories of self-disclosure

Therapist self-disclosure also falls into three categories: appropriate, benign, and inappropriate self-disclosure.

Clinically appropriate self-disclosure

Appropriate self-disclosure is ethical and clinically driven, is done with the client's welfare in mind, and, like any other clinical intervention, is determined by the context of therapy.

Benign self-disclosure

This covers a wide range of deliberate and nondeliberate or avoidable and unavoidable self-disclosures. These are often part of everyday disclosures, which are part of normal human relationships, and are often determined by the setting in which therapy takes place.

Inappropriate or counter-clinical self-disclosure

This form of self-disclosure benefits the therapist rather than the client, burdens the client with unnecessary information about the therapist, or creates a role reversal where a client, inappropriately, takes care of the therapist (Knox et al., 1997; Stricker & Fisher, 1990; Zur, 2007). One of the most cited examples is when therapists inappropriately, unethically, and potentially illegally discuss their own sexual feelings or fantasies. Other examples are when therapists inappropriately and unethically discuss their own mental, relational, or financial hardships with their clients without any clinical rationale.

Standard of care and self-disclosure

The standard of care is one of the most important constructs in medicine and mental health. It guides practitioners in their practices, provides a minimum professional standard, and is an essential element in malpractice suits and hearings of state licensing boards. *Standard of care* is a legal term and is often defined as the degree of care that a reasonably prudent person would exercise in the same or similar circumstances. It describes the qualities and conditions that prevail, or should prevail, in a particular (mental health) service. While the standard of care is obviously an extremely important construct, it nevertheless remains very elusive and continuously is the subject of much debate and controversy. Surprisingly, there is not one national, professional, or universally accepted standard of care that can be found in any agreed-upon text. Oddly enough, the standard of care is primarily determined in courts by juries and judges and by licensing board hearings, which often rely on the testimony of expert witnesses who often disagree. In these hearings attorneys on both sides routinely present conflicting expert testimonies about the standard of care (Gutheil, 1998). The standard is determined by state and federal law and is based on professional and community standards, and as such, professionals are held to the same standard as others of the same profession or discipline, with comparable qualifications in similar localities (Bersoff, 1999; Caudill, 2004; Doverspike, 1999; Woody, 1988).

Elements

The standard of care is derived from the following, briefly described, six elements. The relevancy of each element to self-disclosure is discussed.

Statutes

Each state has many statutes, such as Child Abuse, Domestic Violence Reporting, and other laws. Not following these statutes puts therapists below the standard of care. When it comes to self-disclosure, to my knowledge, there is no specific statute that specifically mentions it.

Licensing board regulations

In most states there are extensive regulations governing many aspects of mental health practices. These often include rules for continuing education, supervision, record retention, having sex with former clients, and so on. None of these board regulations, to my knowledge, attend directly or specifically to the issue of self-disclosure.

Ethical codes of professional associations

The codes of ethics of professional associations are another important component of the standard of care. However, they are also controversial in regard to the standard of care. The ethical principles of the American Psychological Association (2002), National Association of Social Workers (1999), and American Counseling Association (2005) apply to all licensed psychologists, social workers, and counselors, respectively, regardless of whether they are members of the organizations or not, unless there is a state law or board regulation stating otherwise. The application of most codes of ethics and licensing board regulations or using them to clarify the standard of care can be a complex and challenging task. The codes are generally not specific about which behaviors are prohibited, and some parts of the codes are clearly aspirational rather than enforceable (Bersoff, 1999). The codes of ethics of all the major professional associations do not directly address the issue of self-disclosure. The general mandate for therapists to focus on their clients' welfare and not to exploit or harm their clients is relevant to almost all aspects of clinical practice, including self-disclosure. APA's Code of Ethics of 2002 introduced much needed clarity when it stated that therapeutic interventions, including self-disclosure, should be judged by the " ... prevailing professional judgment of psychologists engaged in similar activities in similar circumstances" (p. 162) rather than by certain theoretical orientations or arbitrary rules.

Case law

Case law is one of the cornerstones of the standard of care. Although I am not aware of a specific case law in regard to self-disclosure, case laws that may be relevant to self-disclosure are those that directly link certain disclosures by therapists (e.g., a scar or tattoo on the breast, sexual fantasy) as preconditions to therapist-client sexual exploitation.

Consensus of the professionals

In a field that is comprised of hundreds of therapeutic orientations and as many different settings and cultures, consensus among profession-als beyond "do not harm" is hard to come by and, as a result, is a rather vague aspect of the standard of care. Consensus among professionals can be derived from diverse professional publications, presentations at professional conferences, national surveys, and professional associations' guidelines (Younggren & Gottlieb, 2004; Zur, 2007). Research and national surveys have consistently established that self-disclosure is one of the most universally accepted behaviors among psychotherapists and counselors. In one of the largest of such surveys Pope, Tabachnick, and Keith-Spiegel (1987) reported that at least 90% of the therapist-respondents indicated that they engaged in self-disclosure behavior at least on rare occasions and concluded, "Thus, it appears that the more extreme versions of the therapist as 'blank screen' are exceedingly rare among psychologists" (p. 998). A survey (by the same researchers) reporting on therapists who are themselves in therapy yielded similar results, with many reporting that their therapists expressed feelings of care, disappointment, or anger. Other researchers (Borys & Pope, 1989; DeJulio & Berkman, 2003) found out that about half of the therapists reported that they disclosed details of current personal stresses to a client. Research on therapists who treated lesbian and gay male clients revealed that 63% of them were prescreened for gay-affirmative attitudes (Liddle, 1997). Rosie's (1974) finding that more experienced therapists are more likely to self-disclose is consistent with Williams's (1997) observation that older therapists are more comfortable with appropriate boundary crossing in psychotherapy.

Consensus in the community

Most scholars agree that some aspects of the standard of care are highly embedded in the community, local culture, and settings where the practice takes place. Different settings and communities, which abide by different cultural customs and values, have different standards (Lazarus & Zur, 2002). Conducting therapy on an Indian reservation is likely to be very dif-ferent from psychoanalytic sessions in New York City. Providing therapy on an aircraft carrier is also likely to be very different from therapy in a psychiatric unit in a hospital. This community element of the standard of care is probably the most relevant to self-disclosure, as numerous publications have repeatedly reported that significant self-disclosure is unavoidable in small communities, such as college campuses, rural communities (Barnett, 1998; Schank & Skovholt, 2006; Zur, 2006), and military bases (Johnson, Ralph, & Johnson, 2005); is expected in communities such as LGBT (Isay, 1996) and ethnic communities (Sue & Sue, 2003); and is extensive and unavoidable in home office and other settings (Nordmarken & Zur, 2005; Zur, 2007).

Misconceptions about the standard of care and its application to self-disclosure

The standard of care has often been viewed in several inaccurate ways, which led to misunderstanding in regard to the relationships between the standard of care and self-disclosure. Following is a nonexhaustive list of what the standard of care is not and the relevancy of each of these misconceptions to therapeutic self-disclosure.

The standard of care is not a standard of perfection

An innocent, infrequent, mistaken disclosure does not constitute substandard care. The standard is based on the average practitioner and on reasonable or "good enough" actions. Caudill (2004) describes it as a C student's standard. Simply making a common or ordinary mistake or common error in judgment does not automatically put a therapist's actions below the standard of care (Simon, 2001). Along these lines, an infrequent or occasional revelation of non–clinically significant or benign personal information to a client does not necessarily put the therapist's entire treatment below the standard of care.

The standard is not a black-and-white standard

Self-disclosure is neither a black-and-white concept nor an on/off practice. Compliance or noncompliance with the standard of care has gradations or shades of deviation from the standard. Gross negligence or extreme departure from minimum standard of care is different from simple departure from the standard of care, which is different from simple mistakes or errors in judgment. A consistent pattern of disclosing personal information to clients that is irrelevant to the treatment, is burdensome to the clients, and creates role reversal is below the standard of care. However, an occasional or infrequent mention of a mild personal difficulty or concern that may not be helpful or clinically advisable does not necessarily put the therapist's actions below the standard of care, unless it could have been reasonably predicted that such information could be harmful to the client.

The standard is not guided by risk management principles:
Clinical application of self-disclosure versus
defensive medicine guidelines

One of the most significant errors by experts, attorneys, courts, and licensing boards has been confusing the standard of care with risk management principles (Lazarus & Zur, 2002; Williams, 1997). Whereas the standard, as articulated above, is based on legal-professional-communal principles, risk management is geared to reduce the risk of malpractice accusations for therapists (Gutheil & Gabbard, 1993; Williams, 1997; Zur, 2007). While the standard of care focuses on what is good for the patient, risk management guidelines mostly provide preemptive protection of therapists and reduced financial liability for insurance companies. When it comes to self-disclosure, the typical principles of risk management to not disclose anything more than your name, credentials, and fees can easily translate into very cold, distant, and ineffective therapy.

The standard does not follow a particular therapeutic modality

The standard of care is theoretically blind and philosophically neutral. Attorneys and experts have often presented the psychoanalytic guidelines as the basis for the standard of care (Gutheil, 1998; Williams, 1997). When it comes to self-disclosure, as discussed below, it is important to realize that unlike psychoanalytic psychotherapy that advocates neutrality, "abstinence," and minimal self-disclosure for clinical reasons (Simon, 1994), most clinical orientations view self-disclosure as an effective clinical tool (i.e., Farber, 2006; Stricker & Fisher, 1990; Zur, 2007).

The standard is not determined by outcome:
Differentiating clinical intention from impact

Interventions by therapists, which do not violate the law or board regulations and utilize "good enough" clinical-ethical decision-making processes, are most likely to fall within the standard of care, even if the outcome is negative. For example, an unfortunate outcome, such as suicide, does not necessarily translate to substandard care (Simon, 2001; Zur, 2007). The same is true for self-disclosure. When therapists intentionally disclose personal information for sound clinical reasons, the fact that the client "took it the wrong way," got offended, or interpreted it as a "sexual come-on" does not necessarily put the treatment below the standard of care. If therapists' disclosures have reasonable clinical rationales, clients' negative interpretations or perceptions do not necessarily imply that the therapist provided substandard care.

The standard is not a permanent or static
standard: Historical shifts

The standard of care is a dynamic standard that continues to evolve over time. New state and federal laws and revised codes of ethics impact and change the standard. As more practitioners follow new psychotherapeutic techniques, methods, professional guidelines and practices, the standard of care changes accordingly. The coevolution of culture and psychotherapy practices is highly relevant to our understanding of the relationships between the standard of care and self-disclosure. As early as 1912, and consistent with the puritanical culture of this time, the analytic idea of the psychiatrist as a mere mirror was introduced. The rise of the humanist and feminist movement in the 1960s and 1970s advanced the argument that self-disclosure could be therapeutic and valuable (Brown, 1994; Greenspan, 1995; Jourard, 1971). Simultaneously, the 12-step programs used in many support groups, which are based on mutual self-disclosure, have proliferated since the 1980s. In the 1990s, with Oprah-type TV shows, we witnessed a cultural shift in which self-disclosure became almost fashionable (Farber, 2006). In the new millennium, so-called reality shows that promote uncensored voyeurism and uninhibited self-disclosure have proliferated. A societal change in attitude has manifested itself also in medicine and mental health services. In the managed care era of the 1990s patients or clients became consumers and physicians and psychologists became providers. Consumers have been empowered to become informed and to question their providers' experience, background, history, records, and expertise. Modern consumers feel entitled to access all kinds of information about their medical caregivers, and they can turn to medical boards, federal medical data banks, consumer protection agencies and numerous other resources. Finally, the Internet has brought about the most significant information revolution. Consistent with consumer requests for information, more and more psychotherapists are constructing consumer-friendly, personal Web sites featuring not only professional data but also significant amounts of personal information (Zur, 2008). As a result, in the 21st century there is much more openness and acceptance of therapist self-disclosure among most psychotherapists.

Self-disclosure in context

The meaning of self-disclosure, like any other clinical intervention, can be understood and assessed only within the context of therapy (Lazarus & Zur, 2002; Younggren & Gottlieb, 2004; Zur, 2007). Following are short descriptions of the different elements of therapeutic context and their relevance to self-disclosure.

Client factors

These factors include the culture, history, age, gender, presenting problem, mental state and type and severity of mental disturbances, socio-economic class, personality type or personality disorder, sexual orientation, social support, religious or spiritual beliefs and practices, physical health, prior experience with therapy and therapists, and so on, of clients.

Following are examples of certain groups of clients in whom self-disclosure is clinically significant. Self-help and 12-step programs employ the most common use of self-disclosure. Many of these self-help modalities have entered the therapeutic mainstream and include clinician-facilitated support groups for addiction, parenting, abuse, domestic violence, bereavement, or divorce (Mallow, 1998). Children and those with a diminished capacity for abstract thought often benefit from more direct answers to questions requiring self-disclosure (Psychopathology Committee of the Group for the Advancement of Psychiatry, 2001). Adolescents are often resistant to therapy as they frequently see adult therapists as authority figures. Self-disclosure is one way to make adolescent clients feel honored and respected rather than judged and patronized. Many clients who hold strong particular religious or spiritual beliefs place significance on knowing their therapist's spiritual orientations and values (Montgomery & DeBell, 1997). As was noted above, gay and lesbian clients present one of the most well-researched and convincing arguments for self-disclosure, as these clients often question therapists about their sexual orientation during the pretherapy interview (Isay, 1996; Liddle, 1997; Zur, 2007). War veterans with PTSD have also been cited often as a group of clients to whom self-disclosure seems clinically important (Stricker & Fisher, 1990) and so are clients of minorities who are often more comfortable with therapists who self-disclose or who were observed or perceived by clients as coming from the same or a similar minority group (Sue & Sue, 2003).

Setting factors

Setting factors put the focus on the exact environment in which therapy is taking place. This includes outpatient vs. inpatient and medical building vs. home office. It also includes different localities, such as large, metropolitan areas vs. small, rural towns or Native American reservations; or suburban settings vs. poor neighborhoods vs. university counseling centers.

As was noted above, certain communities or settings, such as college campuses, rural and other small communities, involve extensive "forced," unavoidable and inevitable self-disclosure (Schank & Skovholt, 2006; Zur, 2006). Similarly, working on a Native American reservation or in traditional ethnic communities often requires significant self-disclosure when it is held as a cultural value (Sue & Sue, 2003). Another setting that is likely to result in unavoidable extensive self-disclosure is the home office, which inevitably offers a wide range of self-disclosure about the therapist's personal life. This setting can readily convey information about the therapist's family, pets, economic status, hobbies, spiritual orientation, political affiliation, and much more (Nordmarken & Zur, 2005). Serving as a clinician on an aircraft carrier or remote small military base reveals an enormous amount of highly personal information to clients about their therapist (Johnson, Ralph, & Johnson, 2005). Adventure therapy settings, where the therapist may be backpacking or camping for many days with their clients, is another setting in which extensive self-disclosure is part of the therapeutic milieu (Zur, 2007).

Therapeutic orientation factors

The factor of therapeutic orientation takes into consideration modalities such as individual vs. couple vs. family vs. group therapy and short term vs. long term vs. intermittent long-term therapy. It is also relevant to populations (i.e., child vs. adult psychotherapy), frequency or intensity and theoretical orientations. Obviously, the attitude toward therapeutic self-disclosure is closely related to the therapist's primary theoretical orientation. Generally, therapists who disclose a lot view the psychotherapy process as an interconnection between the therapist and the patient, whereas less disclosing therapists focus on working through patients' projections (Stricker & Fisher, 1990). Different therapeutic orientations have obviously different takes on self-disclosure. Traditional analysts have followed Freud's instructions to serve as a mirror and a blank screen for the client and also the words of Simon (1994), who advocates that psychotherapists "maintain therapist neutrality. Foster psychological separateness of the patient. ... Preserve relative anonymity of the therapist" (p. 514). In contrast, as was noted above, the interpersonal focus of several modern psychodynamic psychotherapies has emphasized the importance of self-disclosure in relational and intersubjective perspectives (Bridges, 2001; Stricker & Fisher, 1990). Humanistic and existential psychotherapies have always emphasized the importance of self-disclosure in enhancing authentic therapeutic alliance, the most important factor in predicting clinical outcome (Jourard, 1971; Williams, 1997). Group psychotherapy is another orientation that has stressed the importance of self-disclosure (Stricker & Fisher, 1990), and behavioral, cognitive and cognitive-behavioral, and rational-emotive therapies have emphasized the importance of modeling, reinforcement, and normalizing in therapy (Tantillo, 2004). Feminist therapy values therapist self-disclosure for its role in fostering a more egalitarian relationship and solidarity between therapist and client, promoting client empowerment, and allowing them to make informed decisions in choosing women therapists as role models (Brown, 1994; Greenspan, 1995). Self-disclosure is viewed in feminist therapy as the ultimate way to equalize the power differential between therapists and clients and the most effective way to transmit feminist values from therapist to client. Self-help-based therapies use self-disclosure extensively (Mallow, 1998) and narrative therapy also places a high value on what is called therapists' transparency (White & Epston, 1990). Similarly, family therapy, Ericksonian therapy, and Adlerian therapy use self-disclosure for the purposes of modeling and therapeutic alliance (Stricker & Fisher, 1990).

Therapeutic relationship factors

The factor of therapeutic relationship takes into consideration the quality and nature of the therapeutic alliance (i.e., secure, trusting, tentative, fearful, or safe connection) and whether it is based on idealized-transferential relationships rather than familiar and more egalitarian relationships (Greenspan, 1995). Obviously, more egalitarian relationships are likely to lead to more clinically appropriate self-disclosures than a neutrally driven transference-based relationship. Most long-term or intermittently long-term relationships are also likely to yield more familiarity than short-term ones (Zur, 2007). Also, toward the end of treatment with some clients it is clinically beneficial for therapists to be more self-disclosing.

Therapist factors include gender, age, and sexual orientation as well as education, training, and scope of practice. Therapists' culture, personality, style of communication, and sense of privacy are likely to be very significant in the type and extent of self-disclosure they employ in therapy. Similarly, those who were trained and supervised by humanistically oriented therapists are more likely to clinically employ self-disclosure than those who have undergone psychoanalytic training. Rosie's (1974) finding that more experienced therapists are more likely to self-disclose is consistent with Williams's (1997) observation and Borys and Pope's (1989) findings that older therapists are more comfortable with boundary crossing in psychotherapy than less experienced ones.

Ethical decision making and self-disclosure

Although the codes of ethics of all the professional organizations do not refer directly to self-disclosure, there are several sections in the codes relevant to self-disclosure. As with any decision regarding boundary crossing, the decision to self-disclose is based first and foremost on the welfare of the client. Intentional and deliberate self-disclosures are made under the general moral and ethical principles of beneficence and nonmalfeasance—therapists intervene in ways that are intended to benefit their clients and avoid harm to them (APA, 2002). Applying these principles to self-disclosure means that intentional self-disclosure should be client-focused and clinically driven and not intended to gratify the therapist's needs. When self-disclosure is unavoidable, as often is the case in small communities, therapists must evaluate whether such exposure is likely to benefit, interfere with, or affect the therapeutic process in any way and intervene accordingly. When self-disclosure is unavoidable and is likely to interfere with the clinical work, therapists should discuss the complexities with the clients and, when appropriate, refer out or seek consultation.

The most common concern cited in regard to self-disclosure is that it is done for clinical-therapeutic purposes or for the client's benefit rather than for the therapist's. Thus the intent of the therapist is extremely important, as it should be focused firmly on the client's welfare and should not be fueled by the gratification of the therapist's needs or desires (Barnett, 1998; Bridges, 2001; Mallow, 1998; Zur, 2007). Several writers have raised the concern that the therapist's self-disclosure, when possible, should neither burden the client nor be excessive nor create a situation where the client needs to care for the therapist. Most scholars and ethicists agree, generally, that therapists should not share their sexual fantasies with their clients (Pope et al., 1987; Stricker & Fisher, 1990; Zur, 2007). The ethical decision-making process must include risks and benefits of both disclosures and nondisclosures. Although the risks and benefits of disclosures have been widely discussed and the benefit of nondisclosures has been the focus of traditional psychoanalytic theory, the risks of nondisclosure have been often ignored. Rigidly nondisclosing therapists may seem cold, aloof, and uncaring, and rigidly nonresponsive therapists may confuse clients and harm the therapeutic alliance, one of the best predictors of therapeutic outcome.

Guidelines to self-disclosure in psychotherapy and counseling

General guidelines

- Psychotherapists must realize that self-disclosures encompass much more than just deliberate or verbal disclosures. They must be aware that self-disclosures can be intentional, unintentional, or accidental; verbal or nonverbal; avoidable or unavoidable; and witting and unwitting.

- Clinicians should take into consideration that although therapists initiate some disclosures, others are initiated by clients or a third party. Then, most self-disclosures are part of normal everyday life and are not initiated by anyone in particular.
- Psychotherapists must explore their own attitudes, thoughts, and feelings toward self-disclosure and how these fit with their personal style of psychotherapy, theoretical orientation, and philosophy of treatment. Then they need to adjust to each client, setting, and form of therapy.
- The meaning of self-disclosure can be understood only within the context of therapy. Self-disclosures that are clinically appropriate in one context may not be in another. Some treatment plans may call for extensive self-disclosure, whereas others may call for minimal self-disclosure.
- Intentional self-disclosures must be constructed to enhance the treatment plan and must be considerate of the clients' welfare.
- Psychotherapists must conduct a risk-benefit analysis before making significant disclosures or when deciding on a strict policy of nondisclosures. It must be taken into consideration that inaction, such as rigid avoidance of any self-disclosure, may appear cold and unempathetic to clients and may be counter-clinical and even harmful.
- Clinicians must make sure that the self-disclosures are not done to fulfill their needs but rather the clients'.
- Psychotherapists should consult with clinical, ethical, or legal experts in complex cases and document the consultations.
- When conducting therapy in settings that involve extensive, unavoidable, or "forced" self-disclosures, psychotherapists should take into consideration how this may affect the clinical work. If necessary and appropriate, discuss these issues with the client and consult or offer referrals to other practitioners.

Guidelines regarding Internet disclosures
- Therapists should always assume that *everything* that they post online, whether it is on their own Web site, private or public blogs, Listservs, chats, social networks, and so on, *may be read* by their clients.
- Therapists should be very careful in discussing case studies online and make sure that they either get permission from clients to discuss their cases or make sure that they de-identify the information.
- When therapists find out that a client, or potential client, has acted in an intrusive manner in regard to online searching, they must think about the clinical, ethical, and legal ramifications. Depending on the

level of intrusion of the acts, therapists' responses may vary, from a clinical discussion with the client of the meaning of the actions, to boundary setting interventions, to reporting a crime.

- Therapists must search themselves online periodically so they are aware of what their clients may be privy to.
- If in their searches therapists find that private information or misinformation about them is posted online that they do not want to be public, they can try to correct it. It is advisable that they consult with experts on the different ways that they can try to delete or amend such postings.

Summary

Self-disclosure is a broad term that includes therapists' intentional and unintentional, avoidable and unavoidable disclosures about their personal lives. Digital technologies have significantly increased therapists' transparency, which may have clinical or ethical significance, as anything they write online must be viewed as if it is being tattooed on their foreheads. The meaning of therapists' self-disclosure can be comprehended only within the context of therapy. Self-disclosure that may be appropriate and clinically useful in one context may be inappropriate and harmful in another. Clinically driven self-disclosure that is done for the welfare of the client can be very beneficial for treatment and can enhance therapeutic alliance, the best predictor of therapeutic outcome.

References

American Counseling Association. (2005). *ACA code of ethics*. Alexandria, VA: Author.

American Psychological Association. (2002). Ethical principles of psychologists and code of conduct. *American Psychologist, 57*, 1060–1073.

Barnett, J. E. (1998). Should psychotherapists self-disclose? Clinical and ethical considerations. In L. VandeCreek, S. Knapp, & T. Jackson (Eds.), *Innovations in clinical practice: A source book* (Vol. 16, pp. 419–428). Sarasota, FL: Professional Resource Exchange.

Bersoff, D. (1999). *Ethical conflicts in psychology* (2nd ed.). Washington, DC: American Psychological Association.

Borys, D. S., & Pope, K. S. (1989). Dual relationships between therapist and client: A national study of psychologists, psychiatrists, and social workers. *Professional Psychology: Research and Practice, 20*, 283–293.

Bridges, N. A. (2001). Therapist's self-disclosure: Expanding the comfort zone. *Psychotherapy, 38*, 21–30.

Brown, L. S. (1994). Boundaries in feminist therapy: A conceptual formulation. In N. K. Gartrell (Ed.), *Bringing ethics alive: Feminist ethics in psychotherapy practice* (pp. 29–38). New York: Haworth Press.

Caudill, C. O. (2004). *Therapists under fire.* Retrieved June 1, 2004, from https://www.cphins.com/DesktopDefault.aspx?tabid=39

DeJulio, L. M., & Berkman, C. S. (2003). Nonsexual multiple role relationships: Attitudes and behaviors of social workers. *Ethics and Behavior, 13*(1), 61–78.

Doverspike, W. F. (1999). *Ethical risk management: Guidelines for practice, a practical ethics handbook.* Sarasota, FL: Professional Resource Press.

Farber, B. (2006). *Self-disclosure in psychotherapy.* New York: Guilford Press.

Galeazzi, G. M., Elkins, K., & Curci, P. (2005). Emergency psychiatry: The stalking of mental health professionals by patients. *Psychiatric Services, 56,* 137–138.

Greenspan, M. (1995, July/August). Out of bounds. *Common Boundary Magazine,* 51–56.

Gutheil, T. G. (1998). *The psychiatrist as expert witness.* Washington, DC: American Psychiatric Press.

Gutheil, T. G., & Gabbard, G. O. (1993). The concept of boundaries in clinical practice: Theoretical and risk-management dimensions. *American Journal of Psychiatry, 150,* 188–196.

Isay, R. A. (1996). *Becoming gay: The journey to self-acceptance.* New York: Pantheon Books.

Johnson, W. B., Ralph, J., & Johnson, S. J. (2005). Managing multiple roles in embedded environments: The case of aircraft carrier psychology. *Professional Psychology: Research and Practice, 36,* 73–81.

Jourard, S. M. (1971). *The transparent self.* New York: Van Nostrand Reinhold.

Knox, S., Hess, S. A., Petersen, D. A., & Hill, C. E. (1997). A qualitative analysis of client perceptions of the effects of helpful therapist self-disclosure in long-term therapy. *Journal of Counseling Psychology, 44,* 274–283.

Lazarus, A. A., & Zur, O. (Eds.). (2002). *Dual relationships and psychotherapy.* New York: Springer.

Liddle, B. J. (1997). Gay and lesbian clients' selection of therapists and utilization of therapy. *Psychotherapy, 34,* 11–18.

Mallow, A. J. (1998). Self-disclosure: Reconciling psychoanalytic psychotherapy and Alcoholics Anonymous philosophy. *Journal of Substance Abuse Treatment, 15,* 493–498.

Montgomery, M. J., & DeBell, C. (1997). Dual relationships and pastoral counseling: Asset or liability? *Counseling and Values, 42,* 30–41.

National Association of Social Workers. (1999). *NASW code of ethics.* Washington, DC: Author.

Nordmarken, N., & Zur, O. (2005). *Home office: Ethical and clinical considerations.* Retrieved August 8, 2005, from http://www.drzur.com/homeoffice.html

Pope, K. S., Tabachnick, B. G., & Keith-Spiegel, P. (1987). Ethics of practice: The beliefs and behaviors of psychologists as therapists. *American Psychologist, 42,* 993–1006.

Psychopathology Committee of the Group for the Advancement of Psychiatry. (2001). Reexamination of therapist self-disclosure. *Psychiatric Services, 52,* 1489–1493.

Renik, O. (1996). The ideal of the anonymous analyst and the problem of self-disclosure. *Psychoanalytic Quarterly, 65,* 681–682.

Rosie, J. S. (1974). The therapists' self-disclosure in individual psychotherapy: Research and psychoanalytic theory. *Journal of Consulting and Clinical Psychology, 42,* 901–908.

Schank, A. J., & Skovholt, T. M. (2006). *Ethical practice in small communities: Challenges and rewards for psychologists.* Washington, DC: American Psychological Association.

Simon, R. I. (1994). Transference in therapist–patient sex: The illusion of patient improvement and consent: Part 1. *Psychiatric Annals, 24,* 509–515.

Simon, R. I. (2001). *Concise guide to psychiatry and law for clinicians* (3rd ed.). Washington, DC: American Psychiatric Publishing.

Stricker, G., & Fisher, M. (Eds.). (1990). *Self-disclosure in the therapeutic relationship.* New York: Plenum Press.

Sue, D., & Sue, D. (2003). *Counseling the culturally diverse: Theory and practice* (4th ed.). New York: Wiley.

Tantillo, M. M. (2004). The therapist's use of self-disclosure in a relational therapy approach for eating disorders. *Eating Disorders, 12*(1), 51–73.

White, M., & Epston, D. (1990). *Narrative means to therapeutic ends.* New York: Norton.

Williams, M. H. (1997). Boundary violations: Do some contended standards of care fail to encompass commonplace procedures of humanistic, behavioral, and eclectic psychotherapies? *Psychotherapy, 34,* 238–249.

Woody, R. H. (1988). *Protecting your mental health practice: How to minimize legal and financial risk.* San Francisco: Jossey-Bass.

Younggren, J. N., & Gottlieb, M. C. (2004). Managing risk when contemplating multiple relationships. *Professional Psychology: Research and Practice, 35,* 255–260.

Zur, O. (2006). Therapeutic boundaries and dual relationships in rural practice: Ethical, clinical and standard of care considerations. *Journal of Rural Community Psychology, V. E9/1.*

Zur, O. (2007). *Boundaries in psychotherapy: Ethical and clinical explorations.* Washington, DC: American Psychological Association.

Zur, O. (2008). The Google factor: Therapists' self-disclosure in the age of the Internet: Discover what your clients can find out about you with a click of the mouse. *The Independent Practitioner, 28*(2), 82–85.

section two

Case examples by clinical orientation and clientele

chapter four

Self-disclosure as a turning point in psychotherapy

Judith Ruskay Rabinor

> If therapist disclosure were to be graded on a continuum, I am certain I would be placed on the high end. Yet I have never had the experience of disclosing too much. On the contrary, I have always facilitated therapy when I have shared some facet of myself. (Yalom, 2002, p. 90)

I was trained as a psychologist in the 1970s. Unfortunately, I did not have an Irv Yalom in my life at that time, and in fact, at that time, self-disclosure in psychotherapy was somewhat taboo. Writing this chapter has offered me the opportunity to sift back over my 30 years of clinical practice. In looking back, I am struck with the awareness that my own personal disclosures—intentional and inadvertent—have deepened not only the ways I work as a therapist but also who I am as a person. Often they have been turning points for me as well as for my patients; thus it is with gratitude to my patients, who have inspired me to take risks, that I write this chapter.

It is said that if you approach a rabbi with an important question, instead of an answer you will hear several stories. In what follows, I present several stories about self-disclosure in clinical practice, each of which addresses another step in my journey of becoming a psychotherapist. I hope these stories will widen your lens, raise new questions, and perhaps inspire some new questions about when and why you self-disclose.

Getting started

"Do you remember me, Dr. R?" Standing at a red light on a busy Manhattan corner, I immediately recognized Jenny although we hadn't met in over 20 years. As we stood on the windy corner catching up, the image of her as an emaciated teenager tugged at my heartstrings. Now Jenny was 36, an attorney, married with twin 8-year-old daughters. Recently she'd made partner at a prestigious New York law firm. And her eating disorder was "a thing of the past."

"I still feel fat sometimes," she added, "but now I can usually figure out what's really bothering me." I imagine I beamed, for recovering from anorexia nervosa is an incredible victory. Jenny had been one of my first patients and her treatment had been incredibly nerve-racking and challenging.

"Thank you for everything. I'll never forget our sessions."

"What do you remember most?" I asked. In the split second between my question and her response, my mind flashed back to the work we did when her parents' divorced, her mother moved across the country, and her brother's sexually abusive behavior came to light. How hard we had worked to figure out what was tormenting her beneath the starving, binging, and exercising, eventually uncovering unbearable feelings of grief, rage, and abandonment.

Interestingly, none of this was mentioned by Jenny.

"The thing I remember most?" She tilted her head and looked down and over at me. "I see you still wear the same kind of long skirts and boots you always wore—I especially remember your black velvet skirt. And ... oh yes, do you remember our walks to Ben's bagels store?" She still remembered the delicious warm cinnamon raisin bagels we shared!

Within a moment, the light changed and Jenny was off. I stood on the corner, stunned. What I had remembered was feeling daunted by her life-threatening symptoms and the traumas buried beneath them. But what she remembered was what I wore and the food we shared!

In the beginning

As I stood on the corner, I recalled the first time I left my office for the bagel store with Jenny. I remember feeling like an outlaw, like I'd broken one of the basic rules of Good Therapy 101. The year was 1979. I was an inexperienced therapist, just recently having completed my PhD, when 16-year-old Jenny and her father Richard sat down in my office. Richard turned to me and said, "It's not just that my Jenny is unhappy, another thing that bothers me is she hardly eats. I read something in the local papers about girls who don't eat. I think they called it anorexia nervosa. Ever heard of it?"

His question unnerved me. Anorexia nervosa had never been mentioned in my 7 years of graduate training. Droplets of sweat began to gather on my brow. My professional credibility was on the line. Should I admit to being unfamiliar with the very problem he sought help for? As he stood waiting at the door, suddenly I heard my Grandma Sophie's voice. I'd always loved how easily she quoted people she admired. One of her favorite quotes, from Winston Churchill, popped into my mind: "There is a time in a person's life when he is tapped on the shoulder. It would be sad if he was unprepared or unwilling to do something that could lead to his finest hour."

"I don't really know much about anorexia," I told Jenny's father, "But I'm going to look into it." I hoped my voice was sturdier than I felt inside.

Within a week of our first session I joined a study group focusing on this new epidemic sweeping the nation. Next I found a supervisor. There was no way I could have imagined I would become a specialist and spend the next three decades working with eating disorders.

Therapy with Jenny

We'd been meeting twice weekly for about a month when I realized regardless of how I listened or responded, Jenny remained silent, uncommunicative, and committed to keeping her "enemy"—food—at bay. And she continued to lose weight. My empathy, interpretations, and insight-oriented questions failed to arouse her curiosity. If Jenny refused to talk and eat—how could we make progress? I felt lost; surely a better therapist would help her gain insight about her self-starvation.

Struggling to find a way to connect, one day I asked, "Would you be willing to try an experiment?" In response to her nod, I added, "I'm not trying to force you to eat, but I'm curious what happens to you when you think about—or face—your enemy." To my surprise, Jenny lit up when I suggested bringing in an apple to our next session.

"You don't have to eat any of it," I said, attempting to be reassuring as I cut it in slices. "I'm just wondering what kind of feelings come up for you as we sit here together with this apple." Jenny remained silent. "Is it OK with you if I eat a few slices?" I asked, explaining I hadn't eaten anything since lunch and was hungry. Jenny nodded, and to my surprise, asked if she could have a slice—a small one! And thus we began with sharing an apple.

I was amazed at how curious Jenny became—first about my eating and then about her own. What else did I like to eat? Next we shared a banana, eventually a pear. With the goal of introducing her to her inner hungers, often I'd ask, "What are you *really* hungry for?" For the most part, Jenny shrugged. "What else did you eat before you restricted yourself to eating only fruits and vegetables?" I asked. Again, my question was met with a shrug. But at the next session she came in asking if I was familiar with the bagel store around the corner. She had loved going there as a kid and could still remember the smell of the fresh bagels. Hesitantly I asked her if she would like to take a walk with me … and we embarked on what became a new ritual: walks to the bagel store.

The part of this story that is most relevant here relates to the theme of this book: self-disclosure. When I told a colleague about our walks, her reaction was memorable. On the one hand, she heard my excitement. And it did seem clear that Jenny was engaged...and eating! On the other hand, my colleague cautioned me to certainly not disclose what were clearly boundary violations—eating and taking a walk with my client—to my supervisor. Just hearing my colleague use the term "boundary viola-tion" caused my stomach to drop. Unfortunately it would take me more than a decade to read the work of Zur (2002, 2007) who made a distinc-tion between unethical boundary violations and boundary crossings that could actually be eminently therapeutic and ethical.

My colleague's admonition sat with me. The dominant theme in my training had emphasized neutrality and anonymity as the *sine qua non* of a healing therapeutic climate. At this point in time offering suggestions and advice and revealing personal information were considered danger-ous and damaging "errors of intrusion." "Errors of distancing"—long periods of silence—were barely acknowledged. I myself had been a psy-choanalytic patient for 6 years in treatment four times a week where my analyst only rarely—and only under severe crisis conditions—deviated from the rule of strict analytic anonymity.

My experience with Jenny moved me. I was unable to ignore my gut experience of feeling hopeful and optimistic in the midst of our challeng-ing work. It was clear to me Jenny had become more comfortable, open, and accessible since we'd begun our ritual of eating together. She had even admitted how surprised she was that she actually looked forward to coming to our sessions. How was I not going to discuss this exciting and challenging case with my supervisor?

In retrospect, my impetus to be truthful may have been inspired by a stimulating professor I'd been lucky enough to have early in my training, Dr. Erwin Singer. Singer, a highly esteemed professor at City College as well as an interpersonal analyst at the William Alanson White Institute in Manhattan, was one of the first analysts to challenge orthodox beliefs. As a professor, he had always encouraged students to value their experience with patients over abstract theoretical constructs. As a supervisor, he was particularly interested in exploring authenticity in the therapeutic rela-tionship and how the "real" relationship could enliven analytic work. I'd been particularly impacted by his courageous essay, "The Patient Aids the Analyst" (1971), in which he discussed how disclosing his wife's terminal diagnosis facilitated his patients' growth. Although I didn't know it then, three concepts from Singer would stay with me a lifetime: authenticity, transparency, and the importance of processing everything.

Fortunately, I ignored my colleague's warnings. To my surprise, when I began talking about my desire to reach Jenny on the concrete—as well as the symbolic—level, my supervisor disclosed that his sister had died of anorexia. He was curious, enthusiastic, and supportive of my work with this challenging patient, and thus my first eating-disordered patient introduced me to an experiential approach that by its very nature included a self-disclosing component.

From the first, eating together offered us a unique bond, for the very act of eating taps into our earliest relationships and most primitive needs. Eating together and processing that experience offered me a way to encourage Jenny to think about how her emotional needs were both masked and expressed by her nutritional needs, a core dynamic for all people with eating disorders (Bloom, Gitter, Gutwill, Kogel, and Zaphiropoulos, 1994; Bruch, 1978; Rabinor, 2002; Zerbe, 1995). Eventually we developed rituals that took us deeper into her inner world: when we planned our snacks and when we sat down to eat, I'd ask the question, "Are you hungry—and what are you hungry for? Just take a moment and think about what it is you really need and desire." This question paved the way for her to repeatedly reflect upon how the way she handled food might metaphorically express how she dealt with her emotional needs as well.

Dry bagels became an entrée into her constricted cognitive world. From identifying her hesitancies moving from plain to onion to sesame and finally to cinnamon raisin bagels, we opened to other domains, such as her decision-making process and risk taking. From discussing her fears about needing to be "right" and perfect and avoiding taking risks in the bagel department, we eventually slid over to other risks she avoided, involving friends, schoolwork, and family issues. By talking to her about her concerns in her language (food and fat) and validating her fears (at first condensed in the fear of weight gain and fat) I hoped to build a relationship where eventually we would have the opportunity to dig deeper and examine how issues of food, weight, and dieting masked other deeper issues. Which is exactly what happened: as therapy deepened, we explored her other hungers, appetites, and desires, her shame of taking up too much space, desiring more, and being sexual.

One day I told Jenny I was a bit bored eating dry bagels (without butter, jam, or anything else). I was considering adding a slice of turkey and wondered if she wanted to join me. Instead of answering me, she asked, "How do *you* feel about adding the turkey?" I spontaneously told her I loved turkey and would look forward to it.

"You'd eat turkey on a bagel even though you have already eaten lunch?" she asked. I told her if we were going to expand into eating sandwiches at 4 p.m. (her appointment time), I'd probably eat something light for lunch. She took a breath.

"Do you worry about gaining weight?" she asked me.

"Even though I know I'm normal weight, yes, sometimes I do worry about eating too much," I said, hoping my self-disclosure would minimize her sense of pathology and normalize and validate her personal struggle, one that is shared by most girls and women in America. She glanced up at me and smiled and as our eyes met, I thought I detected a nod that told me, "This seemingly insignificant tidbit of information means the world to me!"

In answering questions like these, over and over, I hoped to model the realistic vulnerability that most women in our culture are damaged by media images glorifying thinness. "Body image dissatisfaction is, sadly, the norm," I told her. My openness and vulnerability invited more questions: Did I do what I told her to do: eat when I was hungry? Did I eat with all my clients? Did I ever worry about feeling fat? Getting fat? Did I feel fat after eating a bagel at 3 p.m.?

Although I had been taught to avoid these kinds of self-disclosures and turn the question back on my patient, a small voice inside encouraged me to sidestep this taboo. That voice reminded me that Jenny was disconnected from her hungers—emotional as well as nutritional—and by using myself and our concrete connection around food we might develop a deeper dialogue about her internal world as well as about our relationship. So over time I told her things like:

"I try to eat when I'm hungry and stop when I'm full—most of the time...and sometimes I eat too much. When I do, I try to forgive myself."

"I hate being judged by my appearance, but that's how it is too often."

"I certainly do care about looking good."

"I hate feeling that I'm not perfect, but I'm not."

A prerequisite for engaging in this kind of dialogue was my being comfortable with my own (imperfect) size, shape, and appetites, nutritional as well as emotional. Had I not been at peace with my own eating—and with my own insecurity and discomfort at times with my own body—her questions might have terrified me. Although now it is common for therapists to educate clients about the ways we have all internalized unrealistic media images (Kilbourne, 1994; Kearney-Cook & Striegel-Moore, 1997), this kind of self-disclosure was not yet part of the therapeutic dialogue, thus I felt insecure about my own educative and authentic style.

In retrospect, entering the field of eating disorders in the 1970s offered me the opportunity to expand the traditional boundaries that often separate patients and therapists. What I was discovering to be good therapy was new and innovative at that time, yet has been borne out by the research and theory that evolved over the next three decades. Clinically driven eating of meals with clients is now an accepted component of eating disorders therapy (Hornyak & Baker, 1989), as is developing an authentic relationship that includes judicious self-disclosure (Tantillo, 2004). Through eating together and talking about our experience, I learned that sometimes, bringing myself into the relationship as a real human being—who eats, has feelings and insecurities about her body, and yet can role model a healthy relationship with food and the body—made for good therapy. What I learned was in answering questions honestly, and using my own life experience as a helpful guide when it was called for, I was helpful to Jenny. As a result of my successful relationship with Jenny, I became more willing to trust my intuition when considering what each client needs to make their therapy work, which included exploring the details of my own life when relevant to offer a sense of mutuality.

A funny thing happened when I was leaving your office: A story about inadvertent self-disclosure

Carolyn came to therapy in the throes of anorexia, unable to eat. Now, after three years of working together, she had learned a great deal about nourishing herself, emotionally as well as nutritionally. She was leaving therapy to move across the country with her new husband. Because the process of healing is so mysterious, I asked the question I often ask:

"What do you think helped you the most: Our individual sessions? Joining the group? The family sessions—or perhaps the antidepressant medication? Anything in particular come to your mind?"

A wide smile spread across Carolyn's face. Without a moment's hesitation, she replied that her turning point had occurred when she was leaving my office one day and happened to catch sight of my daughter's camp trunk.

"My daughter's camp trunk?" I was mystified.

It was more than the trunk: it was my daughter's name taped to the trunk. I was still bewildered.

"Your daughter's name is Rachel, right?" She recalled how the name Rachel had bothered her all that day. "I found myself walking around in a blur, whispering her name. Rachel, Rachel."

"Say it again," I suggested, and she whispered her name, "Rachel, Rachel."

"Louder, louder," I said.

And as she repeated Rachel's name, a trickle of tears began. I wondered what was happening to her. She responded with a shrug, "I'm clueless."

Suddenly I remembered that her maternal grandmother, who had died in the Holocaust, was named Rachel.

"Your grandmother," I said, softly, "She was also a Rachel," and although we had worked together intensively for three years, it was clear that now, in this final phase of work, something new was emerging.

"I touched something deep," I said, and Carolyn began to sob.

"Do you know why my parents named me Carolyn?" The name Carolyn had been chosen specifically—to disguise her Jewish roots. The Holocaust experience had wiped Carolyn's parents' entire families. Twenty-one relatives—mothers, fathers, brothers, sisters. Gone. When the camps were liberated, her parents, barely teenagers themselves, met, married, and relocated to the United States, carrying with them the internalized scars of fear, oppression, and prejudice. When their first child was born, they chose Carolyn's name with a specific goal: to conceal her Jewish identity.

"You named your daughter Rachel—the name I should have had," she said softly, and with these words, I suddenly remembered my initial impression upon meeting Carolyn: She had reminded me of a concentration camp victim.

"You asked what I felt helped me to get better. It was the fact that you had the courage to name your daughter Rachel. You weren't afraid of being Jewish. That's what helped me get better."

And within moments, she stood and left my office.

Left my office but not my heart. As the years have ticked by, I have retold this story in clinical conferences. Feedback from colleagues has enriched my thinking, widened my lens, and yet provided no firm answers, for our field is a wilderness without a clear map. What wounds and what heals remain, at best, unclear and mysterious. Perhaps the "fact" that I had named my daughter Rachel told her I was a liberated spirit and gave her permission to free herself from the "prison" of her own "starving madness." I recalled a line from Judith Herman's (1997) book, *Trauma and Recovery*: "A whole life can be constructed around a trauma, remembered or not." Had my daughter's name on her camp trunk stimulated her unconscious memory in a way that allowed her to break free from the trauma and oppression that had, destroyed her family and had, perhaps, been unconsciously passed from generation to generation in symbolic enactments encoded in the body?

Other ideas have surfaced, of course. What about the idea that to my patients, I am always a mother figure? Perhaps the camp trunk reminded Carolyn of the mothering she longed for, for we are all loved by imperfect parents, who leave us feeling somewhat unloved. Even with the best of intentions, parents pass on their own frailties, limitations, and wounds. What is noteworthy here is that something about me that happened to be very important to my client was inadvertently self-disclosed simply because my office was in my home and more of myself was visible. The story provides an excellent example of how what becomes known about us may have healing potential.

Coming of age in the era of self-disclosure: Revealing the personal

Therapist self-disclosure is not a single entity but a cluster of behaviors. The previous stories focused on disclosures in the here and now of the therapy experience (eating with and processing the experience) as well as inadvertent disclosure. With the larger goal of offering a sense of mutuality, validation, and empathy, many years later I found myself struggling with the decision when to reveal the personal details from my own struggles.

The group therapy session was about to end when Reena, a 26-year-old nursing student, burst out crying, "I can't leave without talking about this—I'm eating myself into a coma!" Reena was struggling with her first professional presentation. She worked in a burn unit in a hospital and had been invited to discuss her clinical work on a panel. At first she had been excited, but now the thought of facing the entire hospital staff—500 colleagues—terrified her. And with the dread of public speaking had returned her old friend, bulimia. Just last night she had thrown up for the first time. Now, in addition to coping with her public speaking anxiety, she was obsessing about food, fat, and her failure to overcome her battle with bulimia.

In response to Reena's plea for help members mobilized, validating her entitlement to take up space and find her voice, on this panel and in the world at large. One member reminded her of her poise and tactfulness in handling difficult doctors at the hospital. Another suggested Reena more carefully monitor the events and situations that triggered these devastating feelings. Another member suggested alternative self-regulation strategies—rather than eat, she could take a bath, write a letter, or call a friend. Learning to identify, feel, contain, and live with her feelings—basic steps of recovery—were discussed. Identifying with Reena's struggle, group members reminded her of their own struggles, and that relapses were an expectable part of recovery. And yet, as the group was coming to a close, it was clear that Reena was unable to override her negative self-talk—she was certain she would be unable to be comfortable speaking to this professional audience.

At that moment, an outspoken member of the group spoke up. "Judy, you do a lot of public speaking. Do you ever get nervous?"

My initial impulse was to avoid this question. My traditional training kicked in: answering personal questions can interfere—even jeopardize the therapy. Just as I was about to flip Rosanne's question back to her, and do the traditional nondisclosing thing: ask her whether she imagined I had anxiety about speaking publicly, or explore how she imagined I would handle my anxiety, a message from my right brain, the seat of intuition, kicked in. An image of Jenny and me standing in the bagel store appeared as if to remind me that some of my most important breakthroughs had occurred by not adhering to rules that didn't work in the present context. Suddenly another memory emerged.

I remembered an early experience of my own, one of my first professional presentations. My fear of public speaking had been overpowering. After I put much effort into trying to understand the roots of that fear, what ended up staying with me was a suggestion I'd never forgotten: "Just focus on one kind face in the audience." As I remembered how much this advice had helped me, I decided to deviate from the analytic tenet of nondisclosure. I took a breath. While sharing a brief story about how that suggestion had helped me, I tracked Reena's face. Within moments, I knew: my story had bombed.

"Dr. Rabinor," Reena said in a low voice, "That might have worked for you, but it wouldn't work for me, because if I were to look out into a roomful of people, I wouldn't find kind eyes. I would probably feel alone and yucky."

As she spoke, my palms began to sweat. My self-disclosure had flopped. I needed to normalize our disconnect. I hadn't realized that, like most people struggling with eating disorders, Reena might easily anticipate feeling rejected rather than connected. Instead of offering her a sense of support, my story seemed to highlight her sense of inadequacy. I wondered if she felt disappointed in herself for not having the capacity to imagine a kind and loving "other," badly for disappointing me, or angry that I'd challenged her. I apologized for my misattunement, and afterwards, sat in the uneasy silence, feeling my anxiety mounting, wondering what to do. Eventually, a little voice kicked in, reminding me to manage my own response and to help the group shift into a better place.

Knowing that deep breathing usually calms me down and has that effect on most of us, I said to the group, "Let's take a moment and just breathe. Take a moment and dip down, deep down, way down deep inside. Allow yourself to breathe, in and out, no place to go, nothing to do, just breathe," I said. And in sitting in the silence, just noticing the sound of all of us breathing together, I became aware of feeling reconnected to myself and to the others. My hope was to gracefully move on from that mistake. "Breathe relaxation in, and tension out," I suggested and as I spoke slowly, absorbing the cadence and rhythm and tone of my own words in the stillness of the room, suddenly, I knew that even though my self-disclosure hadn't had its intended effect, I knew that the present moment offered an important opportunity where I was modeling living with failure and recovering from an unexpected disappointment.

In addition, it occurred to me that while my self-disclosure didn't help, someone else in the group might have some useful advice for Reena, for one of the benefits of group therapy is that members always have strengths to offer when things get stuck or off-track. Imagining others in the group would identify with Reena's feelings of inadequacy, I suggested to the group, "Think about a time when you were faced with a really tough problem. Remember a difficult situation, a time when you had to face something that may have seemed insurmountable." After giving the group members time to think, I directed the members to speak directly to Reena, rather than to me. I suggested that Reena remain quiet, just noticing her internal experience as members recalled personal dilemmas and the inner qualities that helped them deal with the obstacles faced:

Member #1: "Do you all remember last year at this time? I was so frightened about going home for Thanksgiving. It took me so much courage to go home. And I'm so glad I did—that was the beginning of reconciling with my mom."

Member #2: "I was sure that going home for Thanksgiving would be a disaster, so I didn't go. That took a lot of strength. And I decided to join up with a group from my dorm who were making dinner, and we made our own Thanksgiving. That was a turning point for me and it was the happiest Thanksgiving I ever had."

Member #3: "I had to dig deep to find all the self-confidence I needed to quit the job I hated. I didn't really feel confident, but I acted like I was—and it paid off. Acting confidently helped me finally get the job I deserved!"

Group members continued, recalling moments of emotional strength and pleasure in overcoming difficulties and making painful decisions:

"I asked for a raise."
"I threw away my scale."
"I told my sister to keep her hands off my clothes."
"I told my mother's boyfriend to keep his hands off my little sister and me."
"I told my boyfriend to stop cursing."

When Reena tried to interrupt, I gently requested she just listen, rather than slide into her automatic "Yes, but" response. When the group finished, I asked Reena to look around the room and make eye contact with all the members and to simply breathe in their energy, their words of support.

"Take what you need and leave the rest behind," I said, words that frequently close my groups. The next day, after completing her presentation, Reena left a message on my answering machine. She told me her presentation had gone very well, and then she made a statement I've never forgotten. Her voice communicated excitement and new energy.

"Last night, you were all with me at the auditorium. I took the group in my pocket, sat you down in the front row and there you were, smiling at me as I gave my presentation. Thank you."

Reena's message left me shivering and filled with a sense of awe. So often insights and skills learned in therapy sessions are forgotten when people leave our offices and face the challenges of everyday life, but something important had occurred in the group: Reena had internalized the support of the group and had blazed a new pathway. The care of the group had registered. Not only had care been given: It was received. Clearly, the group had impacted her—and her response would, I imagined, help the members feel vital, useful, and empowered. How ironic—what I had defined in my own mind as an unsuccessful self-disclosure had been, in the end, useful. The group had offered up and connected with her around their own struggles and their moments of courage and strength, and she was able to take their words, support, and kindness with her. How brilliant. Even though she had initially rejected my suggestion of finding a supportive face in the audience, she had integrated the deeper message and internalized the strengths of our group.

This incident reinforced once again the mystery of therapy. What seems like a brilliant intervention may not be effective while what seems like a mistake might end up being helpful. Reflecting back, it was good that I kept the group process going in the intended direction even when I believed that my particular disclosure, offered with the best of intentions, had not been helpful.

The following week I began by congratulating the group for being attuned and supportive to Reena in such a profound way—and for bailing me out of my blunder. To my surprise, many members hadn't experienced my self-disclosure as a blunder. This offered the opportunity to talk about the process of risk taking and the inevitable possibility of failure. Members expressed relief that I'd been able to acknowledge my fears of public speaking and I was reminded that too often the anonymous therapist is idealized and deemed to have unachievable strengths and skills. What is really needed is for members to know that therapists and clients alike struggle to overcome their own weaknesses and vulnerabilities. Perhaps what all of us need are role models—therapists as well as clients—who normalize the trials of everyday life and remind us of our strengths, resources, and capacity for resilience and generativity.

"I took the group in my pocket." Not only do our patients take us with them, but we take them with us as well. Reena's words reminded me of a few of the basic tenets that guide my life and my work as a therapist: authenticity begets authenticity, vulnerability promotes vulnerability, and self-disclosure begets self disclosure. In stepping out of my role as a "silent expert" and in admitting that public speaking scared me, I acknowledged and validated the problem Reena faced, and in doing so I probably normalized her sense of shame. In addition, although I took a risk that initially didn't pay off (she dismissed me) I survived, stayed related and engaged, and found a new way to reach Reena and the group. When my experience was dismissed and my input wasn't helpful, I didn't fall to pieces in shame about it but rather managed and discussed my feelings about that and continued relating to the group, hopeful that new input could be useful. Instead of labeling her as resistant, because she didn't find my input helpful, I looked for a new way of making contact with her and demonstrated that everyone makes mistakes and that even when we err, things can work out. And although my personal story didn't, according to Reena, relate to her, it seemed that she took a seed from it, which blossomed into exactly what she needed.

The final word: The patient speaks

Several years ago I received an unusual referral. Alyssa had just completed her sophomore year of college and requested a few sessions before she went off to Europe for a 2-month summer school session. "I need a few sessions, a checkup" was how she introduced herself. She'd recovered from bulimia but was still prone to "fat attacks" where she worried about her weight and became phobic about certain foods. And so we began our work.

By the fourth session, Alyssa was elated, amazed with our progress. She'd been in previous therapy but had never understood how being scapegoated in high school had devastated her and ultimately triggered her bulimia. "You really zeroed in on the scapegoat incident," she said, wondering how I could have been so sensitive to her trauma.

As she spoke, I knew why I'd been so sensitive to her trauma: because our own pain is a window to others' suffering. I'd been a therapist for more than 20 years, and was quite comfortable with certain aspects of self-disclosure, yet now, I felt shaky. In the last year of junior high school, I'd been singled out by the ringleader of a vicious group of girls in my class.

"They made my life hell," I told Alyssa. "You'd have thought that now, decades later, I would have forgotten all that—but not so." I told her that just the previous year, I'd been sitting in the balcony of a huge theater. Just before the curtain rose, I looked down—and to my surprise, I spied my old junior high school tormenter. Suddenly she looked up at me intensely and waved. My stomach dropped and I felt as if a 40-year-old wound burst open. The house lights went down, the play started, but I was in junior high again and was unable to concentrate on the theater before me. My mind was filled with images of that miserable year in school. I felt so many different ways—nervous, powerless, bitter, and vengeful—all at the same time.

"I couldn't believe that those old emotions were still raw," I told Alyssa. "I guess that's how I understood your pain," I said. "Painful experiences stay with us, live on in our bodies."

The following session Alyssa had arrived and within minutes began crying. "Dr. R, I've lied to you...or at least, I haven't been 100% truthful." She paused to catch her breath. "There's something I didn't tell you. I still vomit. I'm bulimic. I told everyone I recovered but that's not really true— and no one knows. And now I'm leaving for Cambridge for the summer and I'm scared. What should I do?"

"Thank you for trusting me," I told her and she burst into tears. And the next chapter of Alyssa's therapy began where we could begin to address the reality of her life.

Years later, when I was writing a book, I contacted Alyssa requesting permission to tell her story. In response to the draft of the chapter I'd written about our work together, she wrote the following letter, which she has given me permission to include here:

> Dear Dr. R,
>
> Thank you for sending me the chapter. Of course I recognize myself and reading this made me think about all I've learned in my Psychology class this semester. I know that many professionals frown upon a therapist revealing parts of his/her life to a patient. However, I think that by allowing the patient into your life, you set up a much more comfortable situation for the patient. Speaking from personal experience, the first psychologist that I went to, before I saw you, made me very uncomfortable. Looking back now, it is very clear to me as to why I dreaded going into her office once a week. I always felt like she was judging me, looking at me as just a patient with a problem rather than as a real person. There is much more to my life than just the eating disorder, but none of that concerned her. She was also very secretive about herself. I didn't know

anything about her, and so I was uncomfortable revealing so much to someone who I didn't know anything about. Most things in life are give and take, and I think I was uncomfortable in giving away so much private information about myself, and not really receiving anything in return ... I didn't want her life story, I just wanted for her to maybe relate something that I was saying to an experience of her own ... I wanted to be treated like a real person with real emotions, but instead I felt like this object she was trying to analyze and fix. Your technique is very different from hers, but when I first started seeing you, I definitely didn't realize that my relationship to you was going to be so different than mine was with the other therapist. You do not demand information, and you do not set up a wall dividing yourself from your patients. As a result, I felt much more comfortable confiding in you and asking for help. I realized it wasn't about being judged, analyzed, and as a result being cured. Basically from our first session together you assured me that therapy was a lengthy process, and that there was no timeline or calendar that we were trying to adhere to. Knowing that you weren't expecting instant results from me took off so much of the pressure, and allowed me to be honest with you each session, instead of beating around the bush or just lying.

Final thoughts

We don't ever know exactly what it is that promotes growth in psychotherapy. Sometimes it appears that change results from something we deliberately do or reveal, whereas at other times, an inadvertent remark or revelation appears to catalyze the change process. Often we are unable to identify exactly what events or processes contribute to the process of change. While not knowing can be frustrating, this ambiguity also contributes to the challenge I have come to feel safe knowing awaits me most days in my office.

Because therapy is not and cannot be scripted, every moment in my office offers rich possibilities for becoming. At any given moment I am relying on the rich interplay between all I have learned about human nature, developmental theory, and everything about the process of therapy I have internalized from my own therapy, and my years of working with patients and working on myself. My work has not only helped my patients find themselves, but has helped me become familiar with parts of myself I may never have known if not for being a psychotherapist. Witnessing our patients' daily struggles reminds me that growth—my own as well as my patients'—is a never-ending process. All that is necessary are a few crucial ingredients: the capacity to tolerate living in the unknown, take risks, and know that my own struggles as a therapist offer me the opportunity to develop new resources and learn unexpected lessons about therapy and life.

References

Bloom, C., Gitter, A., Gutwill, S., Kogel, L., & Zaphiropoulos, L. (1994). *Eating problems: A feminist psychoanalytic treatment model.* New York: Basic Books.

Bruch, H. (1978). *The golden cage: The enigma of anorexia nervosa.* Cambridge, MA: Harvard University Press.

Herman, J. (1997). *Trauma and recovery: The aftermath of violence: From domestic abuse to political terror.* New York: Basic Books.

Hornyak, L., & Baker, E. (1989). *Experiential therapies for eating disorders.* New York: Guilford Press.

Kearney-Cook, A., & Striegel-Moore, R. (1997). The etiology and treatment of body image disturbance. In D. M. Garner & P. E. Garfinkel (Eds.), *The handbook of treatment for eating disorders* (2nd ed., pp. 295–306). New York: Guilford Press.

Kilbourne, J. (1994). Still killing us softly: Advertising and the obsession with thinness. In P. Fallon, M. Katzman, & S. Wooley (Eds.), *Feminist perspectives on eating disorders.* New York: Guilford Press (pp. 395–418).

Rabinor, J. (2002). *A starving madness: Tales of hunger, hope and healing in psychotherapy.* Carlsbad, CA: Gurze Books.

Singer, E. (1971). The patient aids the analyst: Some clinical and theoretical observations. In B. Landis & E. Tauber (Eds.), *In the name of life: Essays in honor of Erich Fromm.* New York: Holt, Rinehart, and Winston.

Tantillo, M. M. (2004). The therapist's use of self-disclosure in a relational therapy approach for eating disorders. *Eating Disorders, 12*(1), 51–73.

Yalom, I. (2002). *The gift of therapy.* New York: HarperCollins.

Zerbe, K. (1995). *The body betrayed.* Washington, DC: American Psychiatric Press.

Zur, O. (2002). Out-of-office experience. In A. A. Lazarus & O. Zur (Eds.), *Dual relationships and psychotherapy* New York: Springer (pp. 88–97).

Zur, O. (2007). *Boundaries in psychotherapy.* Washington, DC: APA Press.

chapter five

To share or not to share

Self-disclosure in the treatment of borderline personality disorder

Linda Filetti and Stephanie Mattei

Introduction

Dialectical behavior therapy (DBT) is a modified form of cognitive behavioral therapy (CBT) that was originally developed by Marsha Linehan, PhD, to help chronically suicidal clients. These clients, often meeting criteria for borderline personality disorder, were difficult to treat effectively. She noticed that the clients being treated with typical cognitive behavioral therapy (CBT) were either dropping out of treatment, not acquiring the skills they needed to make changes in their lives, or engaging in the kinds of relationships with their therapists that were getting in the way of effective treatment (Dimeff & Linehan, 2001).

In the service of targeting these problem areas, adjustments in the treatment and theory were made. As far as theory, the goal in CBT was to help clients identify their automatic and dysfunctional thoughts, challenge them so that they were thinking more "rationally," and then encourage new interactions in their environment based on the new learning. Linehan, however, recognized the need for the client's experience to be "validated," not challenged. These clients were already entering into the therapy room invalidating themselves and their emotions; they didn't need any more reinforcement to continue. Also, the idea of focusing on pure change strategies was altered to balance acceptance with change. Clients were encouraged to accept the emotions and thoughts that they were having about their world *and* make changes in their lives.

Changes were also made to the actual structure of treatment. One change that was made was the expectation that clients would attend a separate "skills group" on a weekly basis. In this environment, clients would learn the various interpersonal, mindfulness, emotion regulation, and distress tolerance skills in a structured classroom setting. No longer would clinicians have to struggle with teaching these basic skills within the 50-minute hour, as they would get them in another forum.

Clients would be encouraged to generalize the skills into their natural environment through "skills coaching." This would involve phone calls outside the therapy hour to the individual therapist to get in vivo coaching on how to use the skills. It's important to take note that when you invite clients to contact you when they are in "crisis," the door opens up for some kind of self-disclosure. Additionally, DBT therapists would come together as a team to help each other work more effectively with their clients. This addition would be an opportunity for more than just supervising the nuts and bolts of the treatment. This environment would be a place for support, coaching, and validation for the therapist (Linehan, 1993).

Self-disclosure and DBT—How they fit together

The feature that initially drew us toward DBT as a treatment approach was its focus on the relationship between client and therapist as a vehicle for behavior change. This feature makes therapy less like a stiff, doctor-patient meeting, and more like a real, human interaction—not completely unlike those the client will presumably encounter outside the therapy room. To us, this makes therapy seem more relevant to the client's needs, as many of the issues presenting challenges to most of our clients are interpersonal in nature.

In fact, in DBT, the second goal in the hierarchy of treatment targets is any behavior that interferes with the process of therapy. So, any behavior on the part of the therapist or client that interferes with the forward movement of therapy rises to the forefront of issues to address, preceded only by suicidal or life-threatening behaviors. Therapy-interfering behaviors might include the therapist beginning every session 10 minutes late, or the client refusing to complete diary cards, or the refusal to call for skills coaching when they are feeling suicidal.

In our experience, addressing these behaviors almost always requires a focus on the therapeutic relationship. As you could imagine, it would be feasible that the relationship would enter into the discussion, from the therapist disclosing that it is frustrating and difficult for her to help the client without knowing about symptoms that occurred during the week, to the therapist praising the client profusely upon an on-time arrival.

In DBT, self-disclosure is encouraged, as long as a clear therapeutic goal is being addressed, and as long as the therapist has oriented the client to the use of self-disclosure in DBT. Some other therapeutic approaches view self-disclosure as an ineffective strategy, so it is important that clients understand the rationale for using self-disclosure in

DBT. This will minimize confusion on the part of clients. In addition, DBT therapists are encouraged to be skillful in their use of self-disclosure, and more specifically, are encouraged to utilize the skills they are teaching to clients. Mindfulness, emotion regulation, and interpersonal effectiveness skills increase the likelihood that therapists will self-disclose appropriately.

With that said, there are a few typical reasons why a therapist might make the choice to self-disclose within a DBT framework. Self-disclosure might be validating to the client. So, through self-disclosure, we may communicate that a particular situation would be difficult for most people, ourselves included, or we might want to validate their emotional experience by saying we might have a similar emotional reaction. Through this validation, our clients learn to not only trust their own interpretations, but their own emotions as well. Self-disclosure may also help to ease the power differential in therapy. It is inherent in DBT that the therapist is the expert on emotion regulation, but is not necessarily better than the client or more important in any way. Self-disclosure helps to communicate this philosophy by establishing a more level playing field. Finally, clients often ask questions of the therapist that would be considered normal in most relationships but can become pathologized in a therapeutic relationship. Questions such as "Do you have any children?" demonstrate normal discourse on the part of the client, and a DBT therapist would want to encourage rather than discourage normative responses such as these. DBT therapists must always think of how they are managing contingencies, and whether their behavior is encouraging or discouraging effective behavior on the part of the client.

Self-disclosure and individual DBT

Below is an example of an interaction between one of the writers and her client during an individual outpatient therapy session, in which self-disclosure was utilized as a means of validation:

> T: How have you been feeling about your sister leaving this week? (Orienting to experience of sadness/anger, which the client avoids)

> C: Oh, it's the same. Nothing's ever going to change with me anyway. This is all just a waste of time. (Avoids talking about feelings)

> T: Remember how we talked about observing that thought, and how it functions to protect you from painful feelings? (Redirects back to emotions)

C: (Remains silent; stares at therapist)

T: So, what's your reaction to that? (Questions to expose feelings, model effective problem solving)

C: (More silence) It doesn't matter what I say because I feel like you're not listening anyway...

Uh-oh. At this point in the session, I realized I needed to be mindful of my own emotions. I noticed that I had not really been listening to her. I had an agenda and a plan for the session, and I wanted to stay on track. This had probably prevented me from being present for her. Judgments of myself as a therapist immediately passed through my mind: "What was wrong with me?" "Wasn't that 'Listening Skills 101'?" "Maybe another therapist would better serve this client." As these thoughts went through my mind, I noticed them. This is where mindfulness practice helps. I told myself that they were just mental events, and not facts. I could let them go and return to the matter at hand. It felt like a choice point. I could play it safe (i.e., not self-disclose) and remind her that this thought often goes through her mind. (Or would it be safe? Maybe it would be invalidating.) I could validate that it made sense based on her history (Level 4 Validation). On the other hand, I could self-disclose my own experience in the moment. I could be radically genuine (Level 6 Validation), and treat her like a real human being, without treating her as fragile. My worry with this choice was that she would be so hurt or angry that she would no longer be able to stay present in the session. I told myself that the most likely scenario would be that she would feel validated, and would therefore become more emotionally regulated in the moment. And, she would have the added benefit of feeling like I would be honest with her. I opted for radical genuineness:

T: (Realizing client is right and needs validation) OK—I can understand that . . . I do sort of have a goal in mind to bring you back to your emotions. Sometimes when I'm focused like that, I know I'm less mindful of what you're telling me in the moment (therapist self-disclosure in service of validation). You're getting upset, aren't you? (Observes tears in client's eyes)

C: (Begins to cry) Right.

T: OK. So, let's slow down and talk about what you're feeling right now. (Coming back to experience of emotions)

So, the impact in the moment was that the client did feel validated. She was able to tune in to her emotions rather than avoiding them or invalidating them, and she was eventually able to use them effectively. Her feedback to me later was that she appreciated my honesty. She stated that it helped her to feel safe, to know that I would be truthful with her, and that it was one of the things she really appreciated about me as her therapist.

We might also use self-disclosure in individual therapy as a form of contingency management. In other words, we use our relationship with our clients to increase the likelihood that a desired behavior will occur, or decrease the likelihood that undesirable behaviors will occur. The relationship is used as a tool in helping clients work toward long-term goals and is often the most important tool at the therapist's disposal. We might tell our client about our experience with them when they are being skillful, or what interpretations we have when they engage in particular behaviors. These self-involving self-disclosures often inform the client that we are "in" the relationship with them as real and genuine people with limits, boundaries, and beliefs (Linehan, 1993).

The following is an example of an experience that one of us had during an individual session that involves a self-involving self-disclosure. In the following segment, the client has entered into session after having had a fight with a friend. This 33-year-old friendship ended when the client decided that she didn't want to be in the relationship anymore because she felt disrespected and discarded. When asked about how she made the decision to end such a long-term friendship, the following took place:

> C: So why can't you just admit that if you weren't my psychologist that you wouldn't be my friend? You would never want to spend time with someone like me. I've got so many problems and you're so perfect.
>
> T: It seems really important to you that I acknowledge how defective you think you are. (Validation)
>
> C: I am. Why can't you just admit that I'm awful and horrible? Things are never going to be different for me, and you have such a terrific life. People don't treat you the way they treat me. You've never suffered like I suffer and you just sit there pretending to understand how awful it is for me.
>
> T: I imagine it is awful for you. Life the way it is right now *is* difficult. I know you're upset about the fight with Rachel. It is so important to you

to have relationships (validation). I'm curious about your fight with her, and I'm aware that you sound really angry with me. Are you mindful of any other emotions or interpretations you're having? (Encouraging the use of emotion regulation skills)

C: You keep turning this back around on me. I'm talking about you. You don't really care. You just pretend because I'm paying you to care. You always say that you don't think horrible things about me, but you have to. Are you that naïve that you don't see what a piece of dirt I am? You are so high and mighty in that little life of yours where everything is just perfect. And of course I'm angry with you. You're lying to me (client stands up and points her finger at therapist). I don't know if I can trust someone who lies to me. I might need to go look for another therapist.

What can be so difficult about a self-involving disclosure, especially at a time like this, is that first I had to figure out what I was feeling and then decide how much of it would be effective to share. At this particular juncture, I was experiencing so many thoughts and emotions that it was difficult to discern what they all were. I noticed my heart beating quickly, and my face getting hot. For a minute, I wasn't mindful of my own emotions at all. I did, however, notice the action urge to say something like "Hey, who do you think you're talking to?" or "What, do you actually think another therapist will put up with this?" Mindfulness, however, is not just a tool for our clients, so with a little of it, I was able to be mindful of my own anger, interpretations, and judgments. I was angry…really angry, and part of me wanted her to know it. I wanted her to know that this was the reason that she has no friendships in her life. I wanted her to know that she lashes out without thinking, and that it hurts. I was also aware that I wanted her to be grateful that I was there helping her. I didn't want her to be angry with me for something that I thought had nothing to do with me. I wanted her to get that she couldn't do this and have things in her life be OK. I wanted the moment to be something other than what it was. I was struggling to notice how much *she* must have been suffering to push the only safe relationship she has away. I was aware that she couldn't possibly know any other way to express her intense emotion, or she would. I noticed all of this in a split second. I knew what my interpretations were, and I wondered about her interpretations. So I asked.

> T: So your interpretation is that I'm not being truthful when I tell you that I'm not thinking awful things about you. What is making you vulnerable to that thought?

> C: Because you're one more person in my life that doesn't really care, and I'm pissed about it. I'm tired of people pretending they like me and then going off and thinking horrible things. Admit it, you'd never be my friend. You don't even have the decency to tell me to my face.

> T: It's difficult for you to imagine that people don't think bad things about you.

> C: You just don't get it. You're like this privileged person whose life is just perfect. You're just so naïve and perfect. You have no idea. You're clueless. You think that because you're a professor that you're so much more intelligent than those of us who aren't. You don't know anything.

So here were her interpretations, *and* I was still angry. Why? Why was I still feeling so hot under the collar? Well, she was still putting me down, putting her finger in my face and still yelling at me, all while I was trying to help. So, now that I'm clear about the prompting event for my anger, how much do I share? Do I share with her that I'm ready to walk out? Do I tell her that the way she chooses to express her anger has interpersonal consequences? Do I tell her that if she ever speaks like that to me again I will break our commitment to work together? How can I explain to her that her lack of interpersonal skill is once again pushing someone away? Do I treat her as fragile and not say anything? Could she handle it if I shared it with her? How much of this would be effective for her to know? Am I taking care of myself? Of her? Of our relationship? Could I use my skills?

I can observe all of these thoughts travel through my mind as thoughts on a conveyor belt as I decide how to respond. I feel my face get hot as I search for the words to explain what I know I need to say. I can't be of any help to her if I can't find a way to share this experience. It's at that moment that I am thankful for the DBT skills of "DEAR MAN," "GIVE" and "FAST." So, out come the interpersonal effectiveness skills in the service of stopping this therapy interfering behavior.

T: If feels like you are trying to hurt my feelings by putting me down and making this about my life and me. When you do that, it interferes with our relationship. I have to tell you, I'm not OK with you attacking me like this (self-disclosure to address therapy-interfering behavior).

C: Why, am I hurting your feelings? Now you know what it's like. It's horrible. This is how I feel every day.

T: You know, I'm aware that in your past, you've had the experience that people treat you badly. I also know that it makes you leery of entering into relationships because you're not sure if you can trust other people. When you trust people, you make yourself vulnerable, and that feels uncomfortable (validation). On the other hand, I'm also aware that right now you're yelling at me, attacking me, and not really treating me with the respect that I think I'm showing you. I appreciate that you're upset with what has been occurring in your life right now. It's hard to lose a friend after 33 years. However, when you yell at me and put me down, I notice that I get frustrated and angry. I am not thinking clearly and it's difficult for me to be at my best in helping you with the problems you are having (self-disclosure to address therapy-interfering behavior and highlight interpersonal consequences of behavior).

C: I'm so sorry. I didn't realize I was hurting your feelings. I didn't really mean to hurt you. You must hate me. Do you want me to leave now? Should I find another therapist?

T: What I want is to help you understand what just happened, both in here and in your fight with Rachel this week. Let's go back and see if we can figure out what prompted this interpretation that I'm not being truthful and what skills you could have used with both of us. I imagine that if we can figure some of this out, you will not only feel some relief at understanding what happens in interpersonal relationships, but a bit more skillful the next time you feel such intense feelings.

Self-disclosure and skills coaching

We might also use self-disclosure when we are teaching skills. In this situation, be it in skills groups, individual therapy, or telephone coaching, we might use examples from our own life in the service of teaching. These personal self-disclosures may include various forms of problem solving that were effective and sometimes even ineffective. We have found that often the disclosure of ineffective skill use or problem solving not only gets our client's attention, but also prompts conversation about how to avoid pitfalls and how to cope ahead for similar situations. When we are coaching clients on the phone during the week, personal self-disclosure might be different. Clients might overhear our children in the background, or the traffic whizzing by while we are on our cell phone. These are times when our personal lives might bump up against our clinical lives, and we might need to ask our clients to recognize that we are people too. One example of this is when a client called one of us for phone coaching after using skills to distract from the urge to take a bottle of diet pills. The interaction went something like this:

> C: I hate to bother you, but I'm just so close to taking the whole damn bottle. It took just enough strength to call first. I'm so sorry ... are you too busy?

> T: I'm really glad you called. You seem to be so willing to use your skills. I want to hear about what skills you've employed already so that we can see what's been effective. I'm also aware that I am in the middle of something and I can't give you my undivided attention. (Therapist self-disclosure to communicate limits) I would be willing to call you back in a few hours, but you would need to commit to using skills during that time. (obtaining commitment for skills practice)

> C: Why can't you talk now? I've worked so hard to
> use my skills. You said I could call you if I was
> skillful.

The truth was, I was busy. It was a Sunday evening, and I had a
wonderful dinner planned with my family. This was important because I
had been busy working all week and hadn't given my family or myself
the time that I wanted. It was Sunday, and it was a value for me to have
this sacred time together, and I didn't want to stay on the phone at this
particular time. I also have to say that I was really glad she called. She
had been struggling with this issue of buying more pills for the past few
weeks. She had given all the pills to me, had indicated she had no more
access, and had committed to not buying any more. So, with that said, I
was glad that she called instead of taking the pills she had just purchased,
and I wanted to reinforce that she was doing the right thing by using her
skills and reaching out.

> T: You're right, I did, and I'm really glad that you
> were willing to use your distress tolerance skills
> instead of choosing a problem-solving strategy
> that will only lead to more problems for you in
> the long run. (contingency management)
>
> C: I know it will. They're like poison.
>
> T: I want to be able to give you my full attention
> and want to help you think about how to get
> through until your appointment tomorrow. I
> will be busy for the next few hours and then I'll
> be able to call you back between 9:30 and 10:00
> tonight. Can you commit to refraining from
> pill-taking until then?

I was experiencing the dialectic and I needed to see if she was willing
to hang on before I could decide what was wise.

> C: I don't know.

I was afraid she'd say this. I didn't know what "I don't know" meant.
There were a few interpretations that came to mind. It could mean, "No,
I'm mad at you," or "I'm not sure if I'm willing," or "I'm so drained from
trying this long, I don't know if I can hold out." So, with that in mind, I
wanted to offer her some activities and comparisons (distress tolerance
skills) that she could use in the meanwhile.

T: I would like you to make a list of skills you have
     used, and which ones have been effective. Also,
     think about what skills and strategies you've used
     in the past. That might be a good place to find
     some new skills that you haven't thought of yet.
     When I call you back later, that's the first thing I'm
     going to ask you for. Then, I'm going to ask you to
     pick two more you might be willing to chain with
     them for maximum effectiveness. Would you be
     willing to do that as an activity until we speak?

C: Yeah, that might help me distract some more,
     but in a skillful way. Yes, I'll try. Can I call you
     back if I need more help?

T: Yes. In fact, why don't we say this, if you're skill-
     ful, I'd appreciate it if you would be willing to
     leave me a voice mail letting me know what you
     did. I would be really glad to know which skills
     were effective, and how it is that you were able
     to do it. Talk to you later. (Reinforcing indepen-
     dent skill use)

Self-disclosure and the consultation team

Another important place where we might use self-disclosure is with the
DBT consultation team. Since the primary goal of the consultation team is
to provide therapy for the therapist, it is nearly impossible to do so without self-disclosure on the part of the therapist seeking consultation. The
consult team helps the therapist adhere to DBT protocol, provides validation of the therapist's experience, and assists the therapist with identifying therapy-interfering behaviors that may be occurring with clients. One
example of this process is illustrated below:

T1:   So I know I need some time to talk about my
      client because I'm aware that I'm feeling really
      frustrated about her (therapist observation of
      own emotions that could be interfering with
      effective treatment).

T2:   OK, so what's happening with her?

T1:   Well, I had a conversation with her on the
      phone, and I was coaching her to use her

emotion regulation skills, and be aware of interpretations about my behavior. She just couldn't seem to hear what I was saying. I felt like she was attached to her own beliefs and no matter what I said, she couldn't hear me.

T2:   Oh—that's so hard. It really does get challeng-ing when you come up against a strongly held belief, doesn't it? (Validation)

So, as the therapist looking for help, I noticed the relief that came with being understood and validated by my colleague. It felt like a weight was lifted from my chest, and I imagined this was probably the experience of my clients when they receive validation from me. In that moment, I made a mental note to be more diligent with validating my clients, since it felt so effective to be on the receiving end. I noted to myself that there is nothing like experience as a teacher. I used my mindfulness skills to return to the problem with my client and explore it more, feeling freer to do so than before being validated. I was starting to become more aware of the familiarity of the feelings, as I allowed myself to stay mindful and not push the emotions away. At this point, I made a choice to explore my emotions more. It felt risky. Was I stepping outside the role of therapist too much? Would my colleagues think I was too needy? Or worse, incompe-tent? I thought about going back to problem-solving and rational mind. Safe territory. I noticed my judgments in that moment, and decided that I was willing to make the best use of my time in consult group. If I could get clearer on my emotional mind, and its impact on my interactions with this client, I knew I could be much more effective. That is what I needed as her therapist.

T1:   Yes—*so* frustrating. And as we're talking about this, I'm realizing that the feeling that I have with her is familiar. It reminds me of a feeling I would have in my family in which I wasn't listened to (therapist self-disclosure to explore therapy-interfering behavior on part of therapist).

T2:   So, what's your interpretation when your cli-ent holds onto her belief like she does?

T1:   That my opinion doesn't matter. That no mat-ter what I say, it's falling on deaf ears. That my opinion is unimportant.

> T2:   OK, so what if you pause for a moment at those times, and try to observe your own feelings and interpretations. Take a deep breath, slow down, and validate yourself. Remind yourself that your client is pushing one of your buttons (coaching therapist).

It can be so easy to see this with clients, but so difficult to see it with ourselves in the heat of the moment with clients. I made a mental note to myself to remember how hard it is to be mindful when emotions are intense. Several clients flashed through my mind, and I considered ways to help them use mindfulness at emotionally dysregulated times. It always amazes me how the consultation group makes me a much more skilled and effective (not to mention happier) therapist.

> T1:   Right. I think that would really help me be nonjudgmental with her, if I pause, stay mindful, and validate myself.
>
> T2:   Yeah, and that would then allow you to work with her more effectively...

As it turns out, I *was* much more effective with my client after this consult group. My client even called me after her session and said it felt like I was more present, validating, and helpful to her. I, as her therapist, felt more centered and clear about where my own emotions were coming from; therefore, it was much easier to help her with her own. I was no longer in emotional mind, and was able to stay grounded in wise mind.

Conclusion

As our examples illustrate, self-disclosure is an important tool in the delivery of DBT. Whether it is in individual therapy, skills coaching, or consultation team, self-disclosure is a vehicle for delivering a robust, authentic, and effective treatment. Our conclusion is that self-disclosure is not merely a helpful technique, but is actually an essential feature of DBT. Without it, DBT would be much less effective than it could be and would be so altered that it would no longer be DBT.

References

Dimeff, L., & Linehan, M. (2001). Dialectical behavior therapy in a nutshell. *The California Psychologist, 34,* 10–13.

Linehan, M. (1993). *Cognitive behavioral therapy of borderline personality disorder.* New York: Guilford Press.

chapter six

I second that emotion! On self-disclosure and its metaprocessing

Natasha Prenn

> I assert not only that the analyst's self-revelation is permissible but that it is a necessary part of the clinical process. (Bromberg, 2006, p. 132)

> In thwarting our patients in their quest for an emotional response from us, have we unknowingly been withholding that which could be most therapeutic? We might be tempted to rationalize our lack of overt emotional expression, on the old grounds that we will detract from the patient's experience, but this fails to address the change process. (Maroda, 1999, p. 84)

Not enough has been written about self-disclosure, and I think I know why: to write about self-disclosure involves self-disclosing! I feel my anxiety rise as I contemplate revealing myself. I feel like a new patient trying to decide how much or how little I want to say to you. I am back in a classical analysis: I am not sure how you are reacting as I write, and so I am anxious. This may be a little much for you already—we are just meeting. Can we track it together? I am wondering if I can write about my own tears and struggles as a patient and as a person. I am wondering how much I can dare to tell of my own thoughts and feelings as a therapist. It seems to be all right and accepted to talk about anger and hatred and frustration, but love and caring and closeness are less safe. So I feel like a patient, and I feel anxious. Maybe we can find a way to be in this experience of this chapter together. Maybe I can check in with you along the way to wonder how you are feeling as you are reading and I can tell you how I feel as I am writing.

Pivotal experiences

My first experience of psychotherapy was not as a therapist but as a patient. I know viscerally what it feels like to be sitting in the other chair or on the couch. I want to start by describing my two very different treatment experiences to illustrate what now so deeply informs my work as a psychotherapist. Karen Maroda writes that when she first started working as a therapist she could not understand why her patients felt humiliated by her not answering their questions. She was applying "right" technique. How come it felt so terrible? (Maroda, 1998). I know the humiliation personally: the shame of wanting to know and the double humiliation of being denied when I asked. In my first therapy, an analysis, I learned this "rule" the hard way, by feeling it, and, in the treatment itself, learned new areas of defensive exclusion (Bowlby, 1980).

Slinging my book bag across my shoulders, I stood up. "Are you going anywhere nice?" I asked casually. I was new to therapy. Mark, my therapist, was going away on vacation. He froze, put his hands in his pockets, and looked away from me. "What makes you ask that?" "Um … I don't know," I stuttered.

And so began a process of tentativeness and hesitancy on my part as I tried to avoid making this kind of mistake again and the shame I felt at having gotten it wrong. I lost my spontaneity in this exchange and many other interactions like it. I didn't ask Mark about the specifics of his life then and I didn't ask about his feelings either. But I watched him, and I imagined what he was feeling and thinking, and the transference blossomed, but I did not change, and in some new ways I felt more constricted. I remember crying and looking up to see him silently looking away. I don't think I have ever felt more alone or more ashamed.

Fast-forward to starting a very different kind of therapy. My new therapist, Claudia, had told me her schedule and I knew she was going to be away. She smiled, "I will see you in 2 weeks." I broke eye contact, looked away and then down. "What just happened?" she asked. "You looked away." I hesitated, but spoke up, "Can I ask you where you are going?" "Of course you can," and she proceeded to tell me specifically where she would be over the next 2 weeks. Tears welled up in my eyes, and I felt my body relax in relief. I would not have to constrict my "self" in this relationship. And then she said, "I see tears." "Yes, it is just such a relief to know, to have you answer me," I replied.

Not only was the disclosure hugely important, but so was the conversation about the feelings that accompany the disclosure. This interaction literally freed me up to be myself and to talk openly and emotionally about things I had not allowed myself to think about for years. If she would let me into her world, I could dare to let her into mine.

Fast-forward again to my own office. I am the therapist. It is the end of the session. I am going on vacation. "I will see you in 2 weeks then," I say. "Where are you going?" Ellie asks. "I'm going to London," I reply. "That's where you are from originally, right?" "Yes, it is." We look at each other and smile. "What is it like to know where I'll be?" "Oh, it feels good. I can imagine you there." Ellie stands up, buttons and belts her coat, throws her backpack over her shoulder. She hugs me. "All we are doing will stay with me," I say. "I'll think of you and you think of me," she says. "Yes, I will," I say. Ellie is young, 22, and she has never been in therapy before. Should I ask her why she wants to ask me such a "normal" question? Should I shame her by not answering? Should I teach her that there are things that cannot be discussed in a talk therapy? That just doesn't make sense to me.

Becoming an AEDP therapist

As I began my career as a therapist I knew how I didn't want to be as a therapist and I thought I knew how I did want to be. I feel incredibly fortunate that as I searched for a theory and a way of working that fit with me, I found AEDP (Accelerated Experiential-Dynamic Psychotherapy), an experiential treatment modality, the work of Diana Fosha (Fosha, 2000, 2003, 2006). AEDP not only approved of self-disclosure, but required it and provided guidelines on how to do it effectively.

> Establishing the trust needed for deep affect work requires that the therapist's sense of self be engaged... AEDP's clinical stance demands at least as much from the therapist as from the patient: the patient cannot be expected to rapidly open up to a therapist who remains hidden and shielded. The emotional atmosphere should be one in which the patient feels safe and the therapist brave. The patient's sense of safety within the therapeutic relationship is enhanced in part by the therapist's risk taking. (Fosha, 2000, p. 213)

In AEDP self-disclosing is only the first step of the intervention and is always or whenever possible followed by exploring the patient's experience or reactions to the self-disclosing: *metaprocessing* the disclosure. Metaprocessing (Fosha, 2000) helps patient and therapist collaborate and titrate disclosures together. How doubly fortunate I am also to have begun my career at a time when affective neuroscience and mother-infant research were hugely impacting how we think about adult treatment. My children's infancies and toddlerhoods were fresh and alive in me; I felt softer, more open, more connected to people and to the world. All of this informed how I wanted to work. Before I found AEDP I struggled through an analytic training program. My training paralleled my experiences in treatment.

Consider my first analytic supervisory experience: I am reading process notes to my supervisor. He tells me over and over again that "silence" is the best intervention. I should be silent? I think about what had worked and not worked for me in my own treatment, and I think and feel the rich mutual communication I have with my small children. And I read mother–infant research and Allan Schore (Schore, 1994), of course. And I think: silence? I remember the shame and mortification I felt at Mark's silence and lack of response to me. I liken the experience to what happens to infants and children in the "still-face experiment" (Tronick, Als, Adamson, Wise, & Brazelton, 1978). They are confused, they try a number of strategies (some more extreme than others) to get their mother to react, and finally they give up. What is important is not only how anxiety-provoking it feels for the children but also how painful it feels to the mothers who are asked not to respond to their children/ babies for just 3 minutes: a typical testimonial reads something like, "It was all I could do not to respond. I felt as if I were deserting my baby. I felt torn away from her, and I felt as if I were losing a part of myself. I felt sad, angry, and desperate in turns. I never want to do it again." They go on to say that it was a "relief to be 'real' again." In reuniting with their children/infants they often said: "Mommy is real again" (Brazelton & Cramer, 1990). Not responding does not feel good to patients or to therapists. Silence? How could that possibly be right? How could that help? I watched as my colleagues wrestled with themselves not to show their patients how much they cared about them. On more than one occasion I saw therapists crying because of their patients' suffering and distress and their desire to help. I thought, if our patients knew how much we care and are invested in them, wouldn't that help?

What a relief to start AEDP supervision. Robert, my supervisor, asks me how I feel about the patient in this moment. How do I feel? I feel delighted, I feel full of love, I feel protective of her. "Have you told her?" he asks. Wow! What a different experience.

Beyond the taboo—self-disclosure as a necessity

Can we check our Freudian superegos at the door, and look at disclosure not as a taboo but as a necessity? There is every reason to self-disclose to patients: "It stands to reason that if emotional exchanges, or lack of, create affective patterns that a person creates over and over again, that only new emotional exchanges could facilitate the altering of old affective patterns"

(Maroda, 1998, p. 83). There are no good reasons not to self-disclose. If we step back from Freud, if we think about mothers and infants and let that inform our work, then of course we would disclose. And this is just the beginning, the minimum requirement.

If we reframe our thinking about self-disclosure so that it is an essential part of the fabric of every treatment, which I believe it is, then we have to figure out how to do it well. To my mind, it does not matter so exactly what you do and don't self-disclose (I have disclosed all kinds of things); it is what you do next that matters. Self-disclosure is neither good nor bad; *it is the quickest way to have an experience between two people*. Then patient and therapist have an opportunity to process together what that experience was like: an experience they have had together. We are not "talking about" experience. A lot has been written about impingement, intrusiveness, and overstimulation (mainly by men and predominantly by analysts), but I contend that if we ask what the experience was like for the patient we can figure out together with the patient how much of what and when they need from us to facilitate the work together. This exploration of the experience of whatever has happened is called metaprocessing in AEDP (Fosha, 2000). It is an essential tool in the change process and a crucial way to measure with the patient how disclosing, for example, is experienced by the patient. It also cements the interaction transferring a right-brain emotional experience into left-brain language.

Therapists, with noteworthy exceptions, are afraid to self-disclose and they are afraid to talk and write about self-disclosure. This is for a number of reasons. The first and most forbidding is that it has been considered taboo and the beginning of a slippery slope into boundary violations and acting out: "There is a correct analytic stance and ... this [self-disclosure] is not it" (Bromberg, 2006, p. 132). The consequence of this taboo and the second reason therapists are afraid to self-disclose is that therapists have not learned to use it well or effectively. The third reason therapists get anxious about self-disclosure is that it is not one therapist activity, but rather a number of different behaviors (Yalom, 2002). Let me be clear about what I mean.

I think there are three main activities that fall under the umbrella of self-disclosure: (a) there is the most crucial kind of disclosure: the self-disclosure of affect and process as it unfolds in the session and session to session; (b) there is the self-disclosure of actual life experiences which are often extremely helpful for patients to know about: they help undo aloneness and increase what Yalom calls "universality" (Yalom, 1995, p. 6): we are all human and struggle with similar things; (c) there is therapist vulnerability, errors, and anything that decreases therapist omnipotence and creates a collaborating partnership: we are a team working on the patient. I have my psychological expertise, but you are the expert on you (Fosha, 2000).

Back to my first treatment

I arrive at the session with Mark. I have been needling him for weeks and I know it. I keep asking him if he is angry and he always replies, "Maybe you are angry." I read up on it: I am "projecting." But am I? Am I always? And what about him? Isn't he angry? How could he not be? I continue my needling. He finally erupts. "Fuck you," he splutters at me. I am simultaneously delighted and afraid. I am delighted because now I can relax: I have had enough of an impact on him for him to react like this. But at the same time, I am afraid because he was frightening; he was out of control. We take most of this session and the following sessions to regroup. But that moment is pivotal: I now know I exist for him. I exist enough to make him angry, but why was I provoking him? I was talking to him openly and emotionally every session, and I was getting no response from him. Did it need to be so hard and so extreme? I don't think so.

It is now some years later. I ask Claudia, my AEDP therapist, if she is angry. Yes, she is, she says, but she adds straight away, "I am angry with you, but I am not going anywhere." She lays out what she feels I am avoiding, and how painful it is for her to see me avoiding it. A very different scenario, but a similar feeling. It is not acted out, but it is talked through with some intensity.

Self-disclosure of emotions: Completing the affective cycle

These are two examples, big examples from my own experiences of what Maroda calls "completing the cycle of affective communication" (Maroda, 1998, p. 65). Why is the affective cycle so important? In a way, the first example is more illustrative because there was a huge intensity of feeling. It is in these times of affective exchange that change can take place. These are the moments of therapeutic action. Psychoanalysis calls the big moments *enactments*, and the writing on these is important. I want to add that the pressure of feeling that builds up by not being responded to is not only transference and not only enactment. The nondisclosing stance is in many ways pointing the finger and saying, "It is *you*." Mark swearing at me was such a relief because his anger told me, "It is *us*." Which it was all along, of course.

In my AEDP therapy not only did I feel I could read Claudia's emotions accurately, but her owning and disclosing her affect meant I wasn't shamed into thinking I was projecting, "It is all in your head!" I wasn't projecting, and I wasn't crazy; she was angry, and angry for a reason.

OK, not the end of the world. We had some stuff to deal with, and we did. This is also an example of "saying all of it" (Greenberg & Watson, 2005, p. 128). It is not enough to say we feel angry or sad or distanced by a patient; we need to "say all of it" and tell the patient why, what the content is, and what our process is.

There are lots of reasons for therapists to disclose actual life experiences and feelings embedded in life experiences. How very powerful to give an example of a feeling I have had and the context in which it happened for me. I often find that disclosure of some of my more "taboo" thoughts or feelings helps patients the most. This increases the sense that "we are all in this together" and nearly always creates momentum in the treatment. I think of this as introducing into individual therapy an aspect of the efficiency and effectiveness of group therapy where group members traditionally have had more latitude to disclose than individual therapists: "In the therapy group, especially in the early stages, the disconfirmation of a patient's feelings of uniqueness is a powerful source of relief. After hearing other members disclose concerns similar to their own, patients report feeling more in touch with the world and describe the process as a 'welcome to the human race' experience" (Yalom, 1995, p. 6). I notice as I write that I am hesitating to be specific about the kinds of feelings I have disclosed to patients. This is one of those moments when writing about self-disclosure feels risky and yet I can't help but feel that your knowing that I have felt full of love, bursting with pride, shaking with anger, and red-faced with embarrassment, just as you probably have, will make me a little more real as I write. Should I promote hiding?

This is not an easy task: I recently shared with a patient that sometimes I feel vulnerable and unsure. She lifted her chin and looked down her nose at me. "How can you help me if you feel vulnerable sometimes? How can you help me if you are weak?" was her initial response. We were able to really look at her feelings about me: her utter contempt for my "weakness" and disgust with weakness in herself. We were able to reframe her definition of weakness. I certainly don't feel my uncertainty is a weakness: I think of it as one of my strengths. Did she shame me with my vulnerability? Yes, at first she did. Did it deepen the work and help her in the long run? Absolutely.

Self-disclosure: Facilitating corrective emotional attachment experiences

Midway through writing this chapter, I became aware that I am still fighting for self-disclosure and against the disclosure taboo: Freud/ one-person psychology casts a long shadow. I realized while writing that AEDP is such a different way of working, and I found myself reflecting on how much I self-disclose, and why I do it. If we believe, as I do, that (a) emotions must be felt interpersonally before they can be felt intrapsychically (Maroda, 1998), (b) intolerable feelings need to be projected before they can be integrated, and (c) most patients need more help figuring out what they are feeling than anything else, then we have to pay careful attention to our minds, emotions, and bodies in session and between sessions and communicate what we notice happening within us in our process to our patients. I think of therapy as a series of corrective emotional experiences in a corrective emotional attachment relationship. I will quote Maroda again: "Only new emotional exchanges [can] facilitate the altering of old affective patterns" (Maroda, 1998, p. 85). I repeat: Self-disclosure is essential, but in some ways a minimum requirement.

AEDP translates and synthesizes attachment research, emotion theory, developmental models, and affective neuroscience into transformative therapeutic action. AEDP takes seriously and literally the plasticity and fluidity of the mind as well as its constancy and continuity. If we can change dramatically for the worse in trauma, why shouldn't we also be able to change rapidly in therapy (Fosha, 2006)? In AEDP self-disclosure is one of many interventions employed to create patient safety and to swiftly bypass defenses (Fosha, 2000). The feelings I disclose are real, the experiences from my life are real, and my uncertainty and need for help are real. The relationship is real from the very beginning.

I read over and over again that one must wait until the patient is ready and that the patient will let you know when that time is. In AEDP, which is not a time-limited or even necessarily a short-term treatment modality (although sometimes it is), one is constantly on the lookout for what is most active or alive emotionally in the patient. We want to be at the leading edge of where the patient is. As a result, the AEDP therapist is active and often directive. Moment by moment, patient and therapist work to negotiate their relationship, and this begins from the first moment of the first session. In fact, the first session is "a unique opportunity" (Fosha, 2000, p. 189).

> The relationship with the therapist evokes intense feelings: from the first minutes of the first session, the therapist declares that she wishes to relate to the patient. By focusing on the patient's feelings, asking for specifics, and responding empathically and emotionally to the patient, the therapist activates the patient's complex feelings about intimacy and

> closeness. … The emotionally charged atmosphere
> of the first minutes of the first session offers tremen-
> dous opportunities as the first set of dynamics that
> underlie the suffering the patient is seeking to rem-
> edy is exposed. (Fosha, 2000, p. 189)

My new patient arrives; she hangs her coat and arranges herself on the sofa. "What is it that brings you in today?" I want to capitalize on the precipitating event, the final straw that pushed her to find a therapist and dial my number. This is usually the most affectively alive in the patient. "How are you feeling telling me that?" I initiate our collaborative process from the very beginning. "I am feeling scared," she replies. "I am so glad you are telling me. It helps me a lot to know that. Can you tell me more about the scared feelings?" My stance is empathic, collaborative: I need her help, and I am appreciative of all she is doing. In this first session I want to be explicitly affirming: "You are doing a good job telling me; you are helping me." The focus on how well she is doing and how her efforts are helping me often leads to an affective experience of pride or mastery or hope (Russell & Fosha, 2008). In the rounds of work that follow, we begin to track our responses to each other, and I often use self-disclosure to open up patients' curiosity to their own internal experience. "I notice you came forward and then you seemed to withdraw or retreat a bit. Did you notice that?"

In AEDP the unit of intervention is not just the disclosure or intervention itself but rather the therapist's intervention *and the patient's response to it* (Fosha, 2002). The research is undecided about whether disclosing *per se* is essential in successful treatment or not, but what is essential to positive outcome is the therapeutic relationship; it is in the metaprocessing, the exploring of the intervention/interaction, that greater traction and intimacy in the relationship take place (Farber, 2006). Ehrenberg calls this place "the intimate edge" (Ehrenberg, 1992).

This is leading me to want to take what Maroda says about affective cycles and projective identification quite a lot further. If we put all of this into the framework of attachment, attunement, disruption, and repair, we are in the land of dyadic regulation of affect. Mothers and infants regulate their affect together: babies, toddlers, children, and adults need their mothers/therapists to calm them, to reflect them, to be excited with them. And the wonderful freedom of the cycle of attunement, disruption and repair means that we don't have to get it right all of the time; the moments that we get it wrong are as important if not more important than when we get it right.

This is very much so, working with depression.

Treating depression: Moving out
of comfortably numb

An active, involved, leading, self-disclosing stance helps depressed patients. They have lost their vitality and need ours. They need to know that their depression is about something, and that we will understand what it is about and work together so that they feel better. This disclosure in session nearly always has an emotional impact on a depressed patient, and is a great example of how self-disclosure about the process is *the fastest way to an emotional experience* between two people. Educating patients that depression is not a primary or categorical emotion can be hugely helpful. Depression is a secondary emotion: It lets us know something is awry, but like a panic attack, it is not the thing itself (Fosha, 2000; Greenberg & Watson, 2005; Greenberg & Paivio, 1997).

Here I want to give some examples from a therapy that relied on my being in touch with my embodied feelings and sharing my emotional life in sessions with my patient. Gradually with me leading the way, he started to listen to his body and his feelings as they told his emotional story. We did rounds and rounds of work focusing on the categorical emotions of anger, grief, joy, and sadness. When we processed his feelings to completion (Fosha, 2000), he felt better and when we did not get to the other side of the depressed mood, he continued to feel depressed. So for him very clearly his depressive moods were "about something," something coming up to be dealt with in treatment and something he needed me to feel before he could feel it himself. My feelings gave him permission to feel. I will call him Jay. (Patient is composite).

Jay arrives. He looks anxious. He is depressed. He tells me he can hardly get up off his sofa. He feels like he is free-falling into paralysis and inactivity. I feel connected to him and tell him so. I tell him I feel optimistic: He is in touch with his somatic sense of himself. I think I can help. We agree to roll up our sleeves and get to work together. We do. I am worried he will kill himself. I seek consultation. We start on a very interesting and at times for me uncomfortable treatment. He feels anxious and depressed or nothing much at all. We all have experiences like this in session: "How are you feeling?" "Dead." "What are you feeling right in this moment?" "Numb." "What are you in touch with inside?" "Nothing." "What do you notice?" "Nothing!" And, as I think often happens with patients suffering from depression, I felt a lot: I felt sad and angry and hopeless and angry and irritable and frustrated. I felt a lot with Jay. He would come in feeling nothing and not much else. It is simplistic to say that as I paid attention to my feelings and shared them with him, he learned to name his feelings and let himself have them, but this is a lot of what happened. Eighteen months later, equipped with a newly found emotional repertoire but no depression, he feels ready to graduate.

An early session

Me: How has your mood been?

Jay: I have been really depressed yesterday and today. This morning I could hardly get out of bed. I lay awake staring at the ceiling.

Me: Uh-huh. What has been going on?

Jay: Nothing I can put my finger on.

Me: What are you feeling now as you are talking?

Jay: Nothing.

Me: If you scan your body, are there places you feel more tension ... less tension?

Jay: I feel tight in my back.

Me: OK. Stay with that. What comes up inside as an image or sensation?

Jay: It feels as if I am being whacked.

Me: Stay with that. Let yourself focus there...

Jay: I feel as if I am being whacked. I got so angry at work this week. My boss asked me to stay late and I couldn't say no, and he was being such an asshole.

Me: Uh-huh...and you were angry?

Jay: Yeah, really angry.

Me: Are you feeling it now?

Jay: No, not now.

Me: What are you feeling as you are talking?

Jay: Nothing. Numb. Dead.

Me: And with your boss. How did you feel when he asked you to stay?

Jay: Furious. Mad.

Me: What did you say to him?

Jay: Nothing. I couldn't say anything.

Me: Oh, I feel so angry listening to this. He is always doing this. I'd like to tell him to leave you alone.

Jay: (silent)

Me: What is it like to have me feel so angry at him and want to stand up for you?

Jay: It's great. It feels good.

Me: What's it like inside ... physically?

Jay: It makes me feel bigger, filled out inside … filled
up. Bigger. I want to tell him to pick on someone
else.

On another occasion tears well up in me as he tells me about how
lonely he felt after his mother left his father when he was eight. He wrin-
kles his brow and tears come into his eyes. "Oh, it was sad. I am sad." He
feels it now. In the metaprocessing, he says, "Your tears give me permission to have my own tears."

Very often patients feel that there was a manual given out to other
people about how to live their lives and how to feel their feelings, and
with no training from their parents they feel that they didn't get the manual. I think it is essential for them to know that there is no manual and
that in many ways we are all in the same boat. For this reason, I very often
disclose that I have been in my own therapy, and the different ways I
know firsthand what it is like to be in the other chair.

Jay has asked to reschedule. He arrives at exactly the moment I am
saying good-bye to my previous patient. He is unable to articulate what
is wrong for the first half of the session. All attempts I make to figure
out what is going on go nowhere. Finally I start to guess out loud what
he might be feeling, including wondering if his rattledness could have
anything to do with seeing a patient leave as he arrived for his session. At
this, he let out a huge sigh and says maybe it was something to do with
that. End of discussion. He cannot make eye contact and becomes more
and more distant. He says he is feeling numb but that is about it. He is
having a reaction to something, not wanting to have the reaction to it,
feeling ashamed by having the reaction. I am asking him to talk about a
reaction that is raw and alive and shaming. I decide to self-disclose about
a time when I was in my own therapist's waiting room when another
patient came out of her office. I talk about my fear that my therapist liked
this patient better than me and how intense and important those feelings
were. I wonder out loud if anything like this could be going on for him. I
tell it like a story in a slowed-down, right-brain to right-brain kind of way.
I say that if this doesn't fit or isn't helpful, he can disregard it, but that he
can take anything that resonates and help me fill in the rest. I talk about
my feelings and what I can imagine about his feelings. Dan Hughes calls
this: "speaking for" a patient (Hughes, 2007, p. 202). He starts to cry. He
has not thought these feelings were all right to have. Telling him about my
intense feelings for my therapist allows him to have his about me.

I love you

Jay phones late at night. He is suicidal. He has talked for a long time about
hating himself, feeling helpless, hopeless, desperate. Nothing is ever

going to change: "No one loves me; no one cares about me; I don't make a difference. No one would miss me if I was gone." How am I to respond? To his "I hate myself," I have empathized and heard his pain: "I hear how you hate yourself right now." There is a lot at stake. He is not with me; I can't see him. He says he wants to die. Tone, pitch, and pacing of my words are as important as what I say; I need to regulate him. Slowly, deliberately, softly, and calmly, but with energy, I say, "I love you; I care about you. My life is considerably better for having you in it. I would miss you if you were gone." This is a pivotal moment. In the next session we metaprocess what it was like to have me tell him how much I care about him, how he has impacted my life, that I love him. He reports that his mood changed dramatically after our phone call. He woke up the next morning feeling buoyant and exuberant. Knowing that I love him and that he impacts on my life changes how he feels about himself. He says that he did not realize how much he wanted to feel loved. In the metaprocessing I tell him specifically the things I love about him ("saying all of it," Greenberg & Watson, 2005). It is in these details that I make explicit that my love is not erotic or sexual; it is a caring kind of love that has grown out of his letting me get to know him. It is because I really know him that my loving him matters to him.

I notice that I am leaving love to the very end of the chapter, and using a very extreme example as the context for writing about saying "I love you" to a patient. We are almost at the end. I want to avoid doorknob therapy. So let me say that if I feel loving feelings for a patient (and I think I feel loving as often as I feel, say, sad or angry) then why would I hide those feelings? Well, historically there are plenty of reasons to do so. But if I let mothers and infants inform me, why would I? So how does one decide? There is a feel to people in the room with me: if it feels sexual or noticeably asexual, I generally avoid saying, "I love you." And I know there are patients male and female that I would not say "I love you" to for a variety of reasons. So how did I decide? I think it often has to do with feel and one's sense of the patient's developmental age or stage. Jay felt so young in treatment: he felt like a little boy needing to know he was valuable and lovable. This is what guided my feeling free to tell him how I felt. He needed me to teach him about feelings, feel his feelings, and reflect back to him who he was, and more than anything else he needed to feel loved. The late-night call was a turning point and was the first round of many cycles that revolved around his needing to know I loved him. And I did. And I do.

Final words

As I come to the end of this chapter, I find my Freudian superego kicking up. I hear whispered accusations of narcissism and gratification and my unmet needs. I hear you all, but what about detachment and silence and the withholding of affect? I find more often than not if I am unsettled at the end of the day, it is because I wasn't brave with my feelings when a patient needed something emotional from me. I want to end by advocating that self-disclosure take its place as an essential, integral, teachable part of the fabric of every treatment and that we question why we didn't disclose as much as we have traditionally examined why we did! The goal is not to be perfect, but as Karen Maroda says, echoing Winnicott, let's strive to be "good enough" and learn to self-disclose as effectively as possible.

References

Bowlby, J. (1980). *Attachment and loss: Vol. 3. Loss, sadness, and depression.* New York: Basic Books.

Brazelton, T. B., & Cramer, B. G. (1990). *The earliest relationship: Parents, infants and the drama of early attachment.* Reading, MA: Addison-Wesley.

Bromberg, P. M. (2006). *Awakening the dreamer: Clinical journeys.* Mahwah, NJ: The Analytic Press.

Ehrenberg, D. (1992). *The intimate edge.* New York: Norton.

Farber, B. A. (2006). *Self-disclosure in psychotherapy.* New York: Guilford.

Fosha, D. (2000). *The transforming power of affect: A model for accelerated change.* New York: Basic Books.

Fosha, D. (2002). The activation of affective change processes in Accelerated Experiential-Dynamic Psychotherapy (AEDP). In J. J. Magnavita (Ed.), *Comprehensive handbook of psychotherapy. Vol. 1: Psychodynamic and object relations psychotherapies* (pp. 309–344). New York: John Wiley & Sons.

Fosha, D. (2003). Dyadic regulation and experiential work with emotion and relatedness in trauma and disorganized attachment. In M. F. Solomon & D. J. Siegel (Eds.), *Healing trauma: Attachment, mind, body, and brain* (pp. 221–281). New York: Norton.

Fosha, D. (2006). Quantum transformation in trauma and treatment: Traversing the crisis of healing change. *Journal of Clinical Psychology/In Session, 62*(5), 569–583.

Greenberg, L. S., & Paivio, S. C. (1997). *Working with emotions in psychotherapy.* New York: Guilford.

Greenberg, L. S., & Watson, J. C. (2005). *Emotion-focused therapy for depression.* Washington, DC: American Psychological Association.

Hughes, D. (2007). *Attachment-focused family therapy.* New York: Norton.

Maroda, K. J. (1999). *Seduction, surrender, and transformation: Emotional engagement in the analytic process.* Hillsdale, NJ: The Analytic Press.

Maroda, K. J. (2004). *The power of countertransference: Innovations in analytic technique* (2nd ed.). Hillsdale, NJ: The Analytic Press.

Russell, E., & Fosha, D. (2008). Transformational affects and core state in AEDP: The emergence and consolidation of joy, hope, gratitude and confidence in the (solid goodness of the) self. *Journal of Psychotherapy Integration, 18*(2), 167–190.

Schore, A. N. (1994). *Affect regulation and the origin of the self: The neurobiology of emotional development.* Hillsdale, NJ: Lawrence Erlbaum.

Tronick, E. Z., Als, H., Adamson, L., Wise, S., & Brazelton, T. B. (1978). The infant's response to entrapment between contradictory messages in face-to-face interaction. *Journal of the American Academy of Child Psychiatry, 17,* 1–13.

Yalom, I. D. (1995). *The theory and practice of group psychotherapy* (4th ed.). New York: Basic Books.

Yalom, I. D. (2002). *The gift of therapy: An open letter to a new generation of therapists and their patients.* New York: HarperCollins.

chapter seven

Lessons learned from adolescent girls*

Andrea Bloomgarden and Rosemary B. Mennuti

Introduction

Three years out of graduate school, I became the director of outpatient services at a well-known eating disorder facility. This was a very visible position, and for the shy person that I was, it was also unnerving for me to suddenly be so seen. I was a bit self-conscious, wondering what everyone thought of me, wondering if I could live up to this amazing opportunity. Pretty soon I would be asked to partake in TV and radio spots, do keynote addresses at the annual conference, and the like. I said yes to everything and wanted to impress and succeed.

Now that I was in the limelight, I felt pressure to excel at everything that came my way. So when a therapist who had been running our adolescent eating disorder group was leaving town, the group needed a new leader. "Andrea, you should do it. You are great with teenagers!" people told me. Perhaps this was yet another opportunity to show that I was up to each and every challenge. Plus, I loved teenagers, and it was something that I was drawn to do, but at the same time I had this gut feeling that it was going to create a dilemma. What none of my colleagues or supervisors knew was that I could really relate to these kids. Back in the 1970s when I was a teenager, I too had an eating disorder. Less was known and I missed out on the kind of help available now—I recovered, but it was a much harder process than it might have been. I yearned to give those teenagers something I had missed: a therapy relationship with an adult that offered experience as well as connection, empathy, and wisdom.

My gnawing feeling was about this question: What should I do if these kids ask about my personal past with eating disorders? A therapist self-disclosing about having had an eating disorder is fairly taboo. Still

---

* Bloomgarden, A. (2000). Therapist's self-disclosure and genuine caring: Where do they belong in the therapeutic relationship? *Eating Disorders, 8,* 347–352. (Some of the material in this chapter was previously published in this article.)

striving to prove myself in my new role, I wondered this: What would my supervisors, colleagues, and supervisees think of me if they found out that I disclosed to a group of teenagers that I also had an eating disorder at their age?

Eating disorders vs. addictions—different cultures, different biases

The eating disorder treatment community and the addiction treatment community have two very different cultures and biases about recovered clinicians. In the eating disorder treatment community there seems to be a negative bias against recovered clinicians: Whereas some people believe that therapists who've experienced eating disorders may be uniquely qualified to treat this population, others are suspicious of them. What if the therapist isn't really recovered or suffers a relapse? At the very least, it's controversial. In addictions treatment, the bias is exactly the opposite: Having a history of addictions is considered, by some, the *best* way to have credibility. There, therapists *without* a history may find themselves on the defense, having to demonstrate their expertise regardless of *not* having experienced an addiction.

There is a reason for the difference, as I understand it. Addictions treatment began when two men, Bill W and Dr. Bob, helped each other with their drinking problems and went on to share their stories and encourage each other. They built the Alcoholics Anonymous self-help movement, based on recovering people helping each other, which became the foundation of all addictions treatment. Later, professionals researched alcoholism and developed treatment protocols. Eating disorder treatment began in the opposite way, first with professionals writing and understanding it in psychodynamic terms and eventually through other frameworks (e.g., feminist, cognitive-behavioral). The difficulty in treating it successfully made it quite mysterious. So whereas one disorder was normalized by its history, the other was pathologized. This difference led to more ambivalence in the eating disorder treatment community among recovered clinicians, regarding disclosure of their own past experiences (Bloomgarden, Gerstein, & Moss, 2003).

Teenagers ask questions

So I had not yet told any colleagues about my past, and now I was panicked. What did I get myself into? How would I answer these kids? Teenagers ask therapists questions, more so than adults. This is normal and age-appropriate—it helps build trust and safety in the unfamiliar culture of psychotherapy. They tend to not quite understand the role, and so, innocently, they ask questions not realizing the typical rules of therapy that most adults understand. Adults often preface politely, "Am I allowed to ask you..." or "I know I'm not supposed to ask you this, but..." showing their awareness of the commonly held belief that therapists are not supposed to reveal much about themselves. Most teenagers and young adults are less aware of these expectations and treat the relationship more like a normal one with any doctor, teacher, or adult they know. More so, few if any teenagers are comfortable walking into a room and disclosing personal information to some unfamiliar adult. Their questions are not motivated to inappropriately probe the therapist; quite the opposite—to engage in a little bit of mutual dialogue of sorts so that some rapport is evident before they open up about themselves (Gaines, 2003).

For all of these reasons, I believed it might really help these teenagers to know that even as an adult, I really "get it"; I had been in their shoes at one time. Clients often believe that eating disorders have to be for life, and based on my own life experience and that of plenty of other people I know, I truly believe that full recovery is possible for many people. "Do you think that I'll always think about every calorie I eat every day for the rest of my life?" or "Do you think I could ever eat a hamburger and not feel guilty and disgusting?" are fairly normal questions that teenagers with eating disorders might ask a therapist. If I could answer those questions authentically I might be able to inspire hope that they too, someday, would not think or feel as they do now.

CBT and self-disclosure

My belief about the acceptability of self-disclosure was shaped by a particular incident in a graduate school class, in the cognitive-behaviorally oriented program in which I was trained. A fellow student raised his hand and asked this question: "How do you decide whether to self-disclose, how much or how little?" Without missing a beat, the professor bluntly answered, "You don't," with a tone that said "end of discussion," and in fact, that thread of conversation was dropped. Because I was still fairly young and impressionable, that one professor's curt dismissal led me to believe that this topic was closed from a CBT perspective. Although I secretly disagreed, I lacked the courage to press the question. I never heard it raised again in any graduate class in my training years. Thus, I was left with the impression that even in CBT, a treatment that diverged significantly from Freudian theory, therapist self-disclosure was simply wrong.

Beliefs about self-disclosure from a CBT perspective have evolved enormously since the 1980s—many authors now tout its acceptability and usefulness. Goldfried, Burckell, & Eubanks-Carter (2003) in their article on therapist self-disclosure from a cognitive-behavioral perspective, for example, assert that it may be valuable for such effects as strengthening the therapeutic bond, normalizing client reactions, reducing client's fears, enhancing positive expectations and motivations, and modeling an effective way of functioning (p. 555). It makes sense that self-disclosure could be positive from a cognitive-behavioral perspective, because according to its theory, it is essential to create a strong "therapeutic alliance" which includes a "bond" with the client. Aaron T. Beck (1979), the founder of CBT stressed the importance of an active interaction with clients and noted that a common error in CBT treatment is "slighting the therapeutic relationship" (p. 27).

How is that good alliance created? Sometimes appropriate degrees of self-disclosure can be helpful. Although my training was strong in research and theory, less emphasis was placed on learning how to build this alliance, particularly with regard to navigating the complicated terrain involving self-disclosure. What if disclosing a little of my past could help? How am I to balance sharing something that might help build an alliance with my own need for privacy? I needed guidance but had nowhere to turn.

My personal challenge and moment of truth

I hoped I was getting ahead of myself, creating worries about something that wouldn't even happen. On the first day of group, in the normal course of setting treatment agendas, I inquired about their treatment goals and what they wished for from me, as their group leader. The response was a resounding: "Be real with us." "Answer us honestly when we ask things." "Really 'get it.'" Sidestepping the issue probably wasn't realistic. Should I disclose, I might as well grab a megaphone and announce my history to everyone. The information would go viral since many of the members in my group were also involved in other services and it was likely they would bring up my disclosure in their other therapies as a matter of course. I couldn't disclose but say, "And don't tell anyone I told you." Obviously, that would be completely inappropriate. Clearly, if I was going to do it, I'd have to work up my courage to face whatever the fallout might be. I'd have to face my fear.

One day, it happened. The unofficial leader of the group, a tough, street-smart 16-year-old, in great need of an authentic adult as a role model, baited me directly in accusatory tones: "Why do you run this group? Is this just a job for you? Do you personally even *get* what we are *going through*?" This came from the sense that I didn't understand them, and she was speaking for the group. My preoccupation with the question of disclosure had made me remote, and they were feeling disconnected in response to my distance. Perspiration forming upon my face and confused about what to do, I grew even more distant and quiet, while the real answers screamed loudly in my head: "I totally do understand, and that is why I want to run this group! Can't you sense it?" My heart cried out to tell them. I kept thinking about my colleagues knowing about my eating disordered past and I would not let myself give them what I believed they needed. As much as I thought the disclosure might have built a bridge of connection between us, I could not bring myself to answer. I chose instead to follow the "good therapist" rules, which protected my reputation. Truly, I put my own needs first.

After that group session I tried to think of another approach. "Self-disclosure cannot be the only way. There must be something else to do." Maybe I could share a little information, enough for them to feel understood, without being specific and making a real disclosure. I knew if I opened the door at all, they'd ask questions and I wouldn't know how to answer them. There was no middle ground that was authentic. I was aware that my behaviors were increasingly giving them the impression that I was unfamiliar with and puzzled by their eating disorders. When I would say something that I meant to be hopeful such as, "You can get better from this if you work at it" I was treated as a therapist who was just reading from a textbook—I had no credibility because they could sense I was not all the way there. I was just one more adult who didn't get it. I know they would have heard it differently from someone who had been there. I ached to connect with them and share of myself and I knew it would be helpful. So long as I was withholding, I was creating a layer around myself that was not genuine. It was that disingenuous therapist who was leading their group—not me.

I asked myself this: "Why was I *so* worried about what my colleagues would think?" I was worried, first, that my colleagues would not approve of my use of self-disclosure, and second, that perhaps some would be judgmental about the information itself. Although personally I do not believe that anyone should be ashamed of whatever experiences they have been through that result in growth and wisdom, I feared others would judge me negatively. If so, I feared this would undermine my leadership role at work. Eventually, I sought outside consultation, and it only validated that my fears were realistic—it could undermine my role at work, it could harm my reputation, and many people still believed that good therapists don't self-disclose, especially about their eating disordered past. I was defeated and I realized I had to quit running the group. I adored the kids and it broke my heart to do it. But I had to. At the time I was truly not strong enough to take the risk and face the potential consequences.

What do adolescents need from therapists?

Treating teenage girls is not for everyone. First, they usually start off feeling wary of adults and therapy (Gaines, 2003), and so developing a trusting relationship takes quite a bit of effort. Second, they are facing a developmental task of forging their own identities, learning to use their voice authentically while in connection and to be valued for who they really are (Steiner-Adair, 1991; Pipher, 1994). The girls in my group were in conflict in almost the same way that I was—they wanted to voice their truths, but they feared judgment and rejection. Adolescent girls typically suppress their true identities to reduce conflict, fit in, conform, and be accepted rather than face rejection and isolation, thus losing touch with their authentic selves. This is especially the case with eating disordered adolescent girls—their eating disorder itself is often borne of their conflict between who they feel themselves to be authentically and who they think they should or must be to be accepted by someone whose view of them matters: boyfriends, girlfriends, parents, society at large.

They might have core negative beliefs (i.e., distortions) about them-selves—such as "I am no good," "I am different," "I am unlovable," "I don't belong"—and these beliefs cannot be tested or overturned if they are too afraid to be authentic and talk openly about them. At the heart of their conflict and reason for therapy was their own struggle to be truly honest first with themselves and then with others, to develop the cour-age to relate authentically with one another, to risk telling their truth and discover that they will not necessarily be rejected but can remain in con-nection with others, even if different, or even if what they say is not wel-comed by the other. As I see it now, I was in a parallel process with them: How could I be a role model if I could not accomplish the very task that they too were struggling with? Clearly, I too was not willing to risk say-ing my truth, albeit for different reasons and on a whole different level. Nonetheless, if I couldn't face my own fears, how could I really help them face theirs?

Relational-cultural theory and CBT: A natural synergy

Aside from my different perspective on self-disclosure at this point in time, I also now know something I did not know: Adolescent groups can be facilitated with the treatment goal of clients and therapists relating authentically while remaining in connection with each other, using rela-tional cultural theory (RCT), based on the work of the Jean Baker Miller Training Institute. And, in that context of that trusting, good relationship, CBT strategies and techniques can be employed to build skills and coping with particular symptoms (Bloomgarden, Mennuti, Conti, & Weller, 2007;

Fidele, 2004). According to RCT, it is within the context of a mutual and empathic relationship with "growth-promoting" qualities that a healing connection is formed and promotes therapeutic growth and change (Jordan & Dooley, 2001; Miller & Stiver, 1997).

Mutual and empathic does not mean that therapists reveal anything and everything about themselves or that they are in a process of mutual therapy. That is a misunderstanding based on the conventional use of the word *mutuality* in nontherapeutic contexts. Rather, when used as a term describing a therapy relationship from an RCT perspective, Surrey (1991) explains that "mutuality describes a creative process, in which openness to change allows something new to happen, building on the different contributions of each person" (Surrey, 1991, p. 12). It is not a matter of simple reciprocity, as though two people are equally sharing and disclosing. To the contrary, the therapist is still ultimately responsible for awareness of power dynamics and for keeping the process geared toward helping the client. Mutuality describes the quality of presence and a dynamic between people that facilitates a creative growth process for all involved. The therapist may get something out of it too, but it is likely to be more along the lines of learning to understand or feel more deeply, making her a better therapist, not necessarily healing personal wounds. What teenage girls need is a role model and facilitator of this way of relating, where learning may occur from the respectful, authentic way they are treating each other in the course of their therapy. And so, being in a real relationship where the therapist chooses to self-disclose appropriately, in response to the client's needs, he or she teaches and models for them how to make the choice to be open, share an appropriate amount of information, and forge a therapeutic bond based on authenticity and mutuality.

Self-disclosure with teenagers who have eating disorders

In the case of a therapist who has had relevant experience in the past as an adolescent, life experience, disclosed thoughtfully and without too much detail attuned with client need, has the potential to not only model and facilitate more self-disclosure between the adolescents, but also to give them the benefit of adult life experience, without forcing it on them, allowing them to take what they need to build their own identities. In fact, I am aware of a study where adolescents with eating disorders were interviewed about their views on therapist self-disclosure, and the findings support the idea that some types of self-disclosure may be helpful with this population (Gabriel, 2005). Gabriel found that these clients reported that they benefited from therapist self-disclosures that were personal and about past experience, so that the therapist may be viewed as a real person with a past, but one who is not currently in need of help. Gabriel reports the distinct reasons the subjects indicated for wanting that sort of self-disclosure:

> Promotion of feelings of universality; "normaliz-
> ing"; increasing the perception that the therapist was
> more "real"; introduction of a positive role model;
> and giving hope and inspiration.... Three examples
> of helpful disclosure included: past experiences as
> an adolescent, past coping with familial relationship
> and recovery from an eating disorder .... Three types
> of self-disclosure that were negatively received by
> adolescents were comments about therapist's cur-
> rent body image, current struggles with another
> psychiatric illness and personal views of family and
> religion. (Gabriel, 2005, p. 81)

Regrets, with acceptance

The experience of the group encounter changed me. Although I was left with some regret about my lack of courage and true leadership, I also truly believe that I did the best I could at the time, and I do not, as a result of that experience, believe that therapists should force themselves beyond their own comfort zone to self-disclose even if they think it is the right thing to do for the client's needs. To be authentic means also be true to oneself—being who I was at that time, I was not ready or able to share that information. Had I answered their question authentically I would not have been able to share the information in a confident, comfortable, and constructive way. They would have sensed my anxiety in sharing it (just as they sensed my inauthenticity) and that too would have been discon-necting and problematic.

In recognizing the unique developmental needs of adolescent girls with eating disorders, it is clearer to me now that a therapist who works with this population needs to be aware that it is clinically appropriate if the girls seek some information from the therapist. It is the responsibility of the therapist to answer honestly, even if by admitting that she is not ready to answer that question. Perhaps if the therapist has strong and clear limita-tions about such disclosure, supervision could be helpful in either allow-ing the therapist to evolve or in reaching the conclusion that working with adolescents is not a good fit. Thus, therapists must know who they are, what they can and cannot share comfortably and should not work in iso-lation on the issue of self-disclosure decisions. Getting help from trusted colleagues and supervisors is crucial, as is proceeding with decisions in a thoughtful and self-aware manner. My missed opportunity with those wonderful kids highlighted the value of authenticity and real presence as a healing ingredient in therapy, and it motivated me to be more courageous in the future, in taking some reasonable, thought-out risks around self-disclosure with my clients when appropriate moments arose.

Moving on

An opportunity arrived shortly after I quit running the group; it was in the form of a client I will call Allie. She had a difficult and traumatic history involving abuse, neglect, and other trust-violating experiences. She often needed reassurance that I truly cared about her as a person and that therapy was not just a façade, where the therapist is being paid to act like she cares. Our problem began when she chose to read a book about therapy relationships. Allie was distressed by her evolving belief that "the therapist means so much more to the client than the client does to the therapist." Of course, Allie experienced the inherent power imbalance in therapy but tried to reassure herself that I could really care too. However, she could not internalize this thinking.

I did care about her quite a bit and had been working with her for a few years. Therapists grow to love some of their clients, but traditionally it has been taboo to admit it even to other therapists, as though it is inappropriate and unprofessional to feel such love. Perhaps this goes back to the Freudian admonition to practice "like a surgeon...devoid of human sympathy," as though our parental, tender feelings for clients might get in the way. Unconditional love, akin to the Rogerian concept of unconditional positive regard, is about giving: giving to our clients a feeling of safety, acceptance, and feeling cared for. This kind of love is not to be confused with other types of love, those connected with taking. For example, falling in love includes idealizing, wanting something back, needing something, and yearning for sexual expression. Clearly, this is a completely different kind of love, quite the opposite of unconditional love. It is romantic love, love that is about getting something for ourselves, that is associated with the unethical behaviors of having sex with a client. After reading the chapter on transference in this book, Allie got fired up. "Fine, maybe I do have a mother transference towards you," she said, "but some of my feelings are really about you. Therapists aren't willing to admit that there is a real relationship, and that it's not all transference. I want to know if there is anything in this that is real for you, too!"

Risking connection

Over the months that Allie had been reading the book, she had become more and more symptomatic. She began cutting her arms with a razor, regressing to a behavior she had barely exhibited in the past year, but had done in previous times. Dissociative states increased. At one point she fired me as her therapist, but within a few days, in a different mind frame, asked me to please stay on as her therapist. Finally, when she decompensated to the verge of needing a hospitalization because her suicidal feelings were so strong and her dissociative states were becoming so unpredictable and severe, I pleadingly asked what was really going on. "If you want to understand me, read the book," she exclaimed. Although I had wanted to, I had not yet gotten around to reading the book. Never could I have imagined the extent to which it had impacted our therapy. Once I had read the book (which I did that next weekend) I understood her better. Her interpretation had eroded her belief that I was a real person in her life. Before reading it, she implicitly believed I cared about her and that our relationship was real and valuable to the both of us and that had been a stabilizing force in her life. Reading of the book cast doubt on the whole therapy relationship making her feel that it was false, and she felt abandoned thinking that perhaps she meant nothing to me after all, that she was simply a paycheck to me. She really needed more reassurance than I had been giving. Perhaps I had been too focused on trying to rationally talk her out of her feelings, or problem solve with her around her symptoms, and I was not truly addressing the real problem, which was truly about what was happening between us. "I need someone to reach out and help me, and I need it to be you," she pleaded. I really didn't know what to do, and again my textbooks and classroom discussions had been devoid of these scenarios. Instinctively I knew she needed to know that I was a real person who cared for her. Yet, I did not know how best to convey this to her. I hoped I was doing the right thing when I stepped into the relationship in a new way, and began to speak from the heart. I was full of feeling, truly passionate, as I said this: "Allie, I really do care about you. I want so much to help you. What do you need from me?" In a shaking little voice, barely able to get herself to say what she wanted, she forced out the answer. "Sometimes I need you to hug me, and I need reassurance from you that you really care, but I feel *guilty* asking that of you. I know you are my therapist, and I think it's wrong for me to ask. I feel like it makes you hate me, and it makes me a bad patient for asking too much of you. That's what it said in the book." The traditional therapeutic response would probably have been not to gratify her but to allow her to struggle with and accept the reality of my limited role in her life. But, by now, I was finally realizing that part of her problem was that my professional distance and "healthy" boundaries were being experienced as a reenactment of the traumatic experience of her parents' emotional absence at times of great need. My clinical instincts told me that continuing the traditional boundaries approach would have been destructive to her now. She had hardly gotten out of bed for days and had been crying nonstop. It would have been easiest for me to play it safe, stay boundaried, take no risks, and follow the standard, traditional formula: no disclosure and keep challenging her negative distortions. I was finally questioning that perspective: "If the traditional formula worked so well, why does it feel so wrong right now?" Sometimes you have to try something different. I decided to continue to speak with a presence that showed that my words were heartfelt:

> Allie, I want you to stop being afraid of being inappropriate and ask me for what you feel you want. I will hold the boundaries. You don't need to worry about that for me. If you want a hug, ask for a hug. If you want to know something about me, then ask me. It's not inappropriate for you to ask. Let me handle it. If there are times I don't want to answer or can't give, I'll let you know. I want to tell you something, you are noticing some flaws in me, as your therapist and as a person. As a therapist, sometimes I worry too much about what other therapists might think of me, and I might act more rigid about my boundaries than I really want to. And, as a person, I'm not a "touchy-feely" type. I feel uncomfortable, and sometimes I'm not the best person at being nurturing and soft. I'm sorry I haven't been there for you in ways you've needed sometimes. But it's something I am willing to work on, and I'm really glad you are telling me—it helps me grow too, and that's a good thing! I really do care about you. Can you believe me? Will you work through this with me?

Finally, something new was happening. We were talking about what had gone underground: our real relationship which included my emotional responsiveness and presence, which would allow her to feel a genuine connection with me. As this conflict had been underground and was not getting talked about, her symptoms has worsened to express the words she could not say, the request she did not feel entitled to ask of me. Her near relapse was not because her medication was not working (as the psychiatrist had suggested), nor due to her own psychopathology. It was about the dynamic between us, which included my fears of being more emotionally available to her and her sense that she had no right to ask more of me even though she needed it.

Not all clients need this kind of "real" presence and connection to the extent that Allie did. Often these issues just don't come up, and that is much easier for me. Many clients had felt satisfied with my level of presence and I had thought that I had been doing well enough in building successful therapeutic alliances. But Allie needed a little more, and my reluctance to give it to her had been harming her. The next session she thanked me for being so open with her and said that she had needed that kind of contact. Now she was feeling much better.

That session made a world of difference to her. She had renewed interest in her therapy. Her self-abusive symptoms came to an immediate halt. She explained that her parents had never apologized for hurtful things they had done, so that my apology was profoundly meaningful. It had taught her about working through an impasse where both people do their part. Instead of blaming her for wanting too much, I had essentially validated her need and helped her feel less crazy and bad for wanting something from me. Where textbooks and classroom talk had been absent, I did something right this time because I used the totality of my clinical wisdom, instead of holding the old party line for fear of taking any risks for change. After monitoring its effects over the next six months, I observed that my choice had really improved the therapeutic alliance and we moved on to do better and better work together.

Reflections on self-disclosure, CBT, and RCT

In the adolescent group, my lack of genuineness and presence created a vacuum and a void that ultimately ruptured the relationships with the girls, ruining the healing opportunities before me. The error of "slighting the relationship" that Beck warns about is exactly the one that I made, and true to his warning, treatment suffered. There had not been enough emphasis in my training on how to navigate that aspect of treatment, particularly with self-disclosure dilemmas, so I defaulted to the traditional guidelines, which did not work for this situation. Although the lost opportunity remains a sad memory, thankfully, I was able to learn from the experience and move on to future exchanges in a more mutual and authentic way. Clearly, Allie was validated by my self-disclosure and also sensed my real presence and caring, which changed our relationship, and we both grew from it. After that rupture was repaired, we were able to reconfigure the quality of the relationship to better suit her needs, and from there, she was able to continue to evolve in her therapy. I learned from Allie how to really listen and attune myself to my clients' needs, to become more willing to be flexible in my treatment style, and more willing to give emotionally when called upon to do so. I am grateful for being challenged in that way, as I am certain it has made me a much better therapist.

In looking to understand what I had stumbled upon in treating Allie, relational cultural theory, which is a perspective on therapy relationships, provided the needed theory and guidance about building a really strong therapeutic alliance. I learned that there is theoretically sound reason for being more present and mutual than I had believed was appropriate in a therapeutic encounter. And while having a great alliance is crucial to good therapy, it is not sufficient to constitute good therapy. As a CBT (and now DBT) oriented therapist, I take an active role in helping to teach change and acceptance strategies for better coping, but without a good relationship, no one will stick around very long to get the help. Combining CBT and RCT, as I had unwittingly done with Allie, is how I conceptualize good treatment now—the relational component facilitates healing ingredients in the relationship, and the cognitive-behavioral strategies provide tools for change and acceptance for clients to practice in their coping (Bloomgarden, Mennuti, Conti & Weller, 2007). Weaving together RCT concepts about mutual growth, empowerment, and connection with the techniques and strategies of CBT creates a powerful, compatible synergy.

As I reflect upon my understanding of what makes for a therapeutic self-disclosure, I believe that because I was open and willing to be attuned to Allie's clear need for it, the disclosure was the right choice. My affect was balanced—very present and alive, but not over the top. For example, I was not crying, but I was feeling very strongly and intently that I wanted her to know truly, I cared and was all there and she could see it in my face; she read it in my body language. I was comfortable enough to own up to my mistake, and able to correct it in the moment without feeling ashamed. In doing so, I modeled that adults can be wrong and can take responsibility for their actions. Had I not felt clear-minded and centered about doing that, I don't believe it would have been as effective. Why was it different with the adolescent group? With the group, part of the problem was too current for me—the eating disorder itself was in the past, but my fear of my colleagues' judgments was current and I was not ready to resolve it. I was not ready to be out about my past to my colleagues; I was not psychologically strong enough to confidently move ahead whatever the consequences might be. With Allie, there was also a way that I was being challenged to grow, but it was something I was ready and willing to change and so I could do it without ambivalence. As I stepped up and participated with her in mutual growth, this is an example of mutuality in the RCT theory; when client and therapist alike are both impacted by the relationship, and invited to change, mutual growth occurs even though what Allie and I each had to change were different things. Allie was not giving me therapy—I was still providing it for her, but because I was open, something new happened for me. That pivotal time in my career is something for which I will be forever grateful because it made me not only a better therapist, but a more present and vibrant person, and in all of my significant relationships more able to be vulnerable and willing to grow.

References

Beck, A. T., Rush, A. J., Shaw, B. F., & Emery, G. (1979). *Cognitive therapy of depression*. New York: Guilford Press.

Bloomgarden, A., Gerstein, F., & Moss, C. (2003). The last word: A "recovered enough" therapist. *Eating Disorders, 11*, 163–167.

Bloomgarden, A., Mennuti, R., Conti, A., & Weller, A. (2007). A relational-cultural cognitive-behavioral approach to treating female adolescent eating disorders. In R. Christner, J. Stewart, & A. Freeman (Eds.), *Cognitive-behavior group therapy with children and adolescents* (pp. 447–464). New York: Routledge.

Fidele, N. (2004). Relationships in groups. In J. V. Jordan, M. Walker, & L. Hartling (Eds.), *The complexity of connection* (pp. 194–219). New York: Guilford Press.

Gabriel, N. (2005). *A qualitative analysis of female adolescents' perceptions of therapists' self-disclosure within the therapeutic process.* Unpublished doctoral dissertation, Philadelphia College of Osteopathic Medicine, Philadelphia.

Gaines, R. (2003). Therapist self-disclosure with children, adolescents, and their parents. *Journal of Clinical Psychology, 59*, 569–580.

Goldfried, M. R., Burckell, L. A., & Eubanks-Carter, C. (2003). Therapist self-disclosure in cognitive-behavior therapy. *JCLP/In Session, 59*(5), 555–568.

Jordan, J., & Dooley, C. (2001). *Relational group practice*. Wellesley, MA: Stone Center Publications.

Mennuti, R., Bloomgarden, A., & Gabriel, N. (2005). Female adolescents with eating disorders: A cognitive-behavioral approach. In R. B. Mennuti, A. Freeman, & R. W. Christner (Eds.), *Cognitive-behavioral interventions in educational settings: A handbook for practice* (pp. 271–287). New York: Routledge.

Miller, J. B., & Stiver, I. P. (1997). *The healing connection*. Boston: Beacon Press.

Pipher, M. (1994). *Reviving Ophelia: Saving the selves of adolescent girls*. New York: Putnam.

Steiner-Adair, C. (1991). When the body speaks: Girls, eating disorders and psychotherapy. In C. Gilligan, A. G. Rogers, & D. L. Tolman (Eds.), *Women, girls and psychotherapy* (pp. 253–266). New York: Harrington Park.

Surrey, J. (1991). "What do you mean by mutuality in therapy?" In J. B. Miller, J. V. Jordan, A. G. Kaplan, I. P. Stiver, & J. L. Surrey (Eds.), *Some misconceptions and reconceptions of a relational approach*. Works in Progress, No. 49, Wellesley, MA: Stone Center Working Paper Series.

chapter eight

Behavioral treatment of a case involving obsessive-compulsive hoarding

Case formulation, the therapeutic relationship, and in vivo therapy

Victor J. Malatesta

In vivo treatment

The use of in vivo treatment procedures requires special planning and meticulous attention to issues regarding professional boundaries and ethical decision making. In the course of conducting in vivo treatment, the behavior therapist is faced with a multitude of questions and considerations involving boundary crossings and therapist self-disclosure. The seasoned therapist negotiates this complex therapeutic process by first possessing a thorough understanding of the clinical research literature, developing an effective therapeutic alliance with the patient, utilizing peer consultation and supervision when necessary, and relying on an individualized case formulation. The case formulation, which helps to determine the focus and pace of treatment, also provides guidelines with respect to managing the therapeutic relationship and timing the introduction of various therapeutic techniques, including in vivo procedures. Finally, the case formulation offers the therapist direction regarding when and how best to utilize self-disclosure and to effectively manage therapeutic boundary crossings.

The purpose of this chapter is to discuss therapist self-disclosure and planned boundary crossings as they pertain to the behavioral treatment of an anxiety disorder case involving compulsive hoarding. An initial introduction addresses compulsive hoarding, OCD treatment, and case formulation, followed by a discussion regarding the therapeutic relationship, therapist self-disclosure, boundary crossings, and in vivo treatment. Using the case as a vehicle while providing therapist commentary, attention will then focus on behavioral case formulation, the therapeutic relationship, and treatment. Emphasis includes clinical decision making in planning and executing in vivo treatment.

Compulsive hoarding, OCD treatment, and behavioral case formulation

Behavioral and cognitive approaches have made great strides in conceptualizing and treating the range of anxiety disorders (Barlow, 2002). Cognitive behavior therapy, in the form of exposure and response prevention, is also regarded as the psychological treatment of choice for obsessive-compulsive disorder (OCD: See March, Frances, Carpenter & Kahn, 1997). For purposes of this presentation, however, I selected a type of anxiety disorder that is often classified within the OCD category, but is less well understood and less responsive to psychological as well as pharmacological treatments (Keeley, Storch, & Merlo, 2008). It is also a disorder for which in vivo assessment and treatment are typically regarded as an essential component of treatment (Steketee & Frost, 2007a).

There are no formal diagnostic criteria for compulsive hoarding based on the Diagnostic and Statistical Manual of Mental Disorders (DSM-IV-TR: American Psychiatric Association, 2000). Clinical researchers, however, have identified four major characteristics that define compulsive hoarding: (1) acquisition of a large number of possessions that are accumulated through excessive saving, buying, and/or collecting; (2) marked difficulty in discarding possessions that may have limited value; (3) clutter that interferes with or prevents activities for which living spaces were designed; and (4) significant distress in the individual and/or significant others, and/or impairment in functioning caused by the hoarding (Neziroglu, Bubrick, & Yaryura-Tobias, 2004; Steketee & Frost, 2007a).

In my own practice with treating anxiety disorders, I had the good fortune while in graduate school to be trained both in the behavioral case formulation method and in the treatment of OCD disorders by two pioneers in behavior therapy (Henry Adams, Ira Turkat). They had worked and/or trained with Victor Meyer, an early proponent of case formulation and the originator of response prevention and in vivo exposure therapy for OCD (Meyer, 1966). This work emphasized the close relationship between science and practice. Additional training in single case design provided an excellent format to integrate these two areas, while also allowing us to identify unique case formulations (e.g., Adams, Malatesta, Brantley, & Turkat, 1981; Malatesta, 1985, 1990; Turkat, 1985).

Behavioral case formulation has been defined as an explanatory hypothesis that "1) relates all of the patient's complaints to one another,

2) explains why the individual developed these difficulties, and 3) provides predictions regarding the patient's behavior given any stimulus conditions" (Meyer & Turkat, 1979, p. 261). For example, it is not uncommon to encounter young adult patients with OCD who display additional problems including social anxiety/avoidance, excessive dependence upon parents, depression, and difficulty with college work and/or employment. In many of these cases, the case formulation model might hypothesize that anxiety about independent (or imperfect) functioning, in conjunction with a biological predisposition toward OCD, represents the primary mechanism determining the patient's problems. The formulation might relate to the patient's childhood history of parents who were inclined or forced to be overinvolved (e.g., because of illness or perceived weakness in the child), and who were thus more likely to reinforce dependency and discourage autonomous functioning. Using this formulation, to focus initially upon the patient's OCD symptoms with exposure/response prevention (ERP) therapy would likely result in increased anxiety, "resistance," relapse, and/or early treatment termination because decrease in these OCD symptoms would then result in expectations for greater independent functioning. Instead, the case formulation would indicate that initial therapeutic emphasis would be on decreasing fears, avoidances, and misbeliefs about autonomous functioning and on basic skill building. The therapist would also need to adjust the pace of treatment to accommodate the patient's level of comfort and confidence with change. In this way, the case formulation helps guide the treatment process. Stated differently, two patients may have the same OCD diagnosis, but differing case formulations and treatment plans. While most patients with OCD will eventually receive trials of ERP (often in conjunction with medication), one patient may tolerate rapid implementation of these procedures, while another patient because of mistrust or control issues, for example, will require more initial attention to the therapeutic relationship and a more gradual introduction of specific treatment procedures.

By definition, therefore, the case formulation incorporates biological, developmental, personality, and environmental influences. It is typically part of a comprehensive plan that is divided into discrete phases, including initial interview, assessment tailored to the specific case, case formulation and proposed treatment plan, patient feedback on the formulation and plan, treatment implementation, periodic monitoring, patient feedback, and adjustment of the plan where necessary. Behavioral case formulation has been shown to be effective with a range of disorders (e.g., Bruch & Bond, 1998; Malatesta & AuBuchon, 1992), although controlled group studies are lacking. Case formulation has also been regarded as a core psychotherapy skill that traditionally was emphasized more by psychoanalytic and psychodynamic approaches (See Eells, 1997; Perry,

Cooper, & Michels, 1987). Cognitive and schema-based formulation models have also shown development (Persons, 1989; Young, Klosko, & Weishaar, 2003), and studies have examined the psychotherapy case formulations of expert versus experienced or novice cognitive-behavioral and psychodynamic therapists (Eells, Lombart, Kendjelic, Turner, & Lucas, 2005). Finally, it should be noted that case formulation is not without its critics. In this regard, it has been argued that evidence for the reliability of cognitive case formulation is modest at best and that there is a paucity of research examining validity or its impact on therapy outcome (see Bieling & Kuyken, 2003).

The therapeutic relationship, therapist self-disclosure, and boundary crossings

In developing an individualized case formulation, I conduct one or more clinical interviews that include attention to developmental, family of origin, and interpersonal history. I begin to develop hypotheses about many aspects of the patient's presentation, including appearance, interpersonal style, and behavior toward the therapist and therapy situation (e.g., lateness). The case formulation helps me to understand how certain behaviors were learned and how the patient is likely to respond to potential ways of relating (e.g., nondirective style or lack of feedback)—which in turn guides my interactions with the client. For instance, in working with a middle-aged executive woman who had received extensive previous treatment, her OCD and four additional problem areas (e.g., explosive anger, difficulty with nondirective therapy) were conceptualized as a fear of not being in control of interpersonal situations, particularly those situations where information is withheld (see AuBuchon & Malatesta, 1998). In utilizing the formulation, my initial interactions with the patient included a complete sharing of information, including provision of handouts and reading about her case formulation and treatment—in order to engage her effectively in treatment, and to accommodate, at least initially, her fear. My provision of printed and verbal information may be regarded as a therapeutic boundary crossing. As treatment progressed, however, my degree of information disclosure changed to reflect more real-world expectations.

How a therapist interacts with a particular patient has been labeled as *therapist style*, and has been defined as "a collection of purposeful interpersonal behaviors exhibited by the therapist when in contact with the patient. Although these behaviors are genuine for the therapist, they are also primarily determined by the therapist's formulation of the patient's difficulties" (AuBuchon & Malatesta, 1998, p. 144). While psychotherapists from all orientations share certain commonalities in interacting with their patients (e.g., interest, trust, genuineness), behavioral and cognitive therapists rely less on transference as a therapeutic tool and thus do not need to behave in a "technically neutral" manner (see Papajohn, 1982, for a discussion). In contrast to the cognitive-behavior therapist, the technically neutral style displayed by classical psychoanalysts is less directive, provides less feedback, conducts sessions only in an office for a specified period of time, and rarely uses self-disclosure.

Table 8.1 provides a listing of two sets of therapist behaviors. Those items under the heading *Constant* are regarded as necessary for establishing a productive therapeutic relationship and will be displayed with all patients. Those items listed under the heading *Systematically varied* will be employed on a case-by-case basis, according to the case formulation. These therapist behaviors are hypothesized to be valuable in strengthening the therapeutic alliance, improving the likelihood that the patient will benefit from implementation of specific treatment techniques, and modifying interpersonal anxieties and skill deficits displayed in interactions with the therapist. Inspection of Table 8.1 also reveals that the behavior therapist will need to be sensitive to a number of potential boundary crossings and therapeutic self-disclosures— the latter of which may occur either on a verbal level and/or nonverbal

Table 8.1 Two Sets of Therapist Behaviors

Therapist behaviors			
Constant		Systematically varied	
Will be displayed with nearly all patients		Will be varied according to the case formulation and clinical experimentation. These behaviors will vary in *amount* and *type*.	
Respect	Trustworthiness	Agenda	Structure
Interest	Caring	Self-disclosure	Directiveness
Understanding	Acceptance	Criticism	Praise/social
Accurate empathy	Competent	Encouragement	Homework
Expected change	Genuineness	Humor	Control
		Availability	Session length/locale
		Session frequency	Modeling/ shortcomings
		Sharing notes	Limit setting
		Confronting	Validating feelings

Source: Adapted from AuBuchon & Malatesta (1998). (Reprinted with permission from *Beyond Diagnosis: Case Formulation Approaches in CBT*. Edited by Michael Bruch & Frank Bond, Copyright 1998. John Wiley & Sons, Ltd.)

level (e.g., personal characteristics of the therapist). This challenge is particularly acute when conducting in vivo work.

In vivo behavioral assessment and therapy

In vivo assessment and therapy procedures have enjoyed a long history in the behavioral and cognitive-behavioral treatment of a range of conditions, including panic and agoraphobia, post-traumatic stress disorder, phobias and social phobia, schizophrenia, and childhood/developmental disorders (e.g., see Adams et al., 1981; Craske & Barlow, 2001; Craske, Antony, & Barlow, 2006; Hickling & Blanchard, 2006). In vivo procedures are based on the simple learning principle that behavior that is observed directly provides the most accurate indication or measure of performance (Arnoult, 1976). Clinically speaking, in vivo procedures also utilize the principle of generalization that positive behavior change is facilitated and made more durable by practice that occurs outside of the therapist's office and in the natural environment. In vivo practice may also occur within the therapist's office, depending upon the condition under treatment.

More practically, some conditions are difficult to treat effectively without planned in vivo exposure and mastery of situations previously avoided by the patient (e.g., phobias, PTSD, skill training in schizophrenia). Steketee and Frost's (2007a, 2007b) work on compulsive hoarding includes systematic strategies for in vivo assessment and treatment. Patients who deal with hoarding problems have always expressed appreciation for my willingness to travel to their homes and witness firsthand the difficulties, challenges, and emotional pain associated with clutter and their inability to gain control over their possessions. Finally, the ultimate goal of in vivo treatment is to gradually facilitate the patient's ability and skill in conducting in vivo procedures on their own and without the direct guidance of the therapist.

In conducting in vivo treatment outside of my office, my experience has been that it occurs only after a thorough and complete in-office assessment, and only after the patient fully understands the rationale, gives full consent, and agrees to the plan and procedures of in vivo assessment and treatment. In vivo work typically begins first within the office setting. Depending upon the patient's comfort with and outcome of office-based in vivo treatment, I will then develop a plan for at-home in vivo treatment when appropriate. For the majority of patients with whom I have worked, in vivo work outside of the office does not occur until at least 2–4 months of in-office session work. For a sizeable minority of patients who hoard and who come into my practice (25%), I will never have the opportunity to conduct at-home in vivo assessment or treatment for any number of reasons. From a risk management perspective, I also try to make sure that a colleague is aware of, understands the plan, and has been available for peer consultation during at-home in vivo treatment for a given case.

Commentary

It should be noted that I rarely conduct an at-home in vivo procedure without the presence of a third party (e.g., spouse, sibling)—especially when working with individuals who exhibit complex psychopathology (e.g., personality disorders) and/or issues involving potential romantic or sexual attraction to the therapist. In these situations, I am concerned about transference issues and am attuned to any conflictual feelings or fantasies that the patient may experience either before, during, or after an in vivo treatment experience. Typically, the in vivo treatment experience is monitored, reviewed, and "processed" periodically—from the outset through the end of the session. Sometimes, a subsequent in-office session is utilized for this processing before considering additional in vivo work. The presence of a third party also addresses concerns about the "appearance" of any impropriety. (I thank my colleague and former boss, Michael Kowitt, for helping me to understand these concerns from his psychoanalytic risk management perspective.) Despite these precautions, there are situations where even the presence of a third party is insufficient to allow me to conduct in vivo treatment in a professional manner while also maintaining effective therapeutic boundaries. In these situations, I will attempt to develop an alternative method. Taken together, adherence to these risk management procedures helps to anticipate, minimize, and hopefully eliminate the possibility of perceived or real boundary violations.

Related to conducting in vivo treatment outside of the therapist's office, I also want to address the important challenge that the therapist faces in both maintaining the "frame of therapy," while also exercising reasonable flexibility and social skill. In this regard, there is often a natural tendency in many types of in vivo therapy for there to be certain boundary crossings that may occur. For instance, there may be a degree of normal social discourse while doing in vivo therapy with individuals, for example, who are suffering from certain anxiety disorders (e.g., social phobia, driving phobia). As noted earlier, because there is less reliance upon transference as a therapeutic tool, the behavior therapist has greater flexibility and is less concerned about therapeutic neutrality. These situations also provide the therapist with valuable assessment data regarding the patient's interpersonal style and social skill, as well as regarding targeted symptoms and actual coping skill. Similarly, when doing in vivo therapy at a patient's home, it is not uncommon to be offered a beverage, such as coffee or a soda. While keeping the case formulation in mind, I will sometimes accept this offer. In many cases, participating in this common social exchange may actually help the patient to feel more relaxed and more in control. Throughout the process of in vivo therapy at the patient's home, however, I am constantly (a) observing the nonverbal behavior of the patient, (b) assessing, "checking in," and intervening when necessary, (c) referring to and discussing the treatment plan, (d) describing to the patient what the clinical research shows about her or his given problem, and (e) discussing expectations and outcome regarding the in vivo intervention. These interventions help to maintain the "frame of therapy," while also allowing me to catch potential problems early and to reinforce professional boundaries.

Referral and case description

At the time of the initial referral, Frank Campbell (a pseudonym) was a 64-year-old, married, Irish-American attorney who was in good health and who was the father of two adult children. Mr. Campbell presented with a 40-year history of obsessive-compulsive disorder (OCD) involving excessive saving and "hoarding" of professional materials and family "mementos." He also presented with a 20-year history of episodic depressive feelings. He had been referred to me for behavior therapy by his psychiatrist who had been treating him on an intermittent basis over the past 12 years. Current medications included Prozac 40 mg daily. Previous treatment included several medication trials, two trials of psychoanalytically oriented psychotherapy, a course of cognitive-behavior therapy, and periodic marital therapy.

Commentary

In working with any patient, I feel it is an incredible privilege to be allowed into another individual's world to share in their struggles, challenges, and triumphs through our work in psychotherapy. I feel that we play many therapeutic roles that change over the course of therapy. Some of these roles include that of detective and clinical scientist during the assessment phase (e.g., through expertise in psychopathology, diagnosis, and functional analysis), teacher and guide during the treatment phase, and witness during the patient's growth and change during the treatment process.

The fact that Mr. Campbell presented with a 40-year history of obsessive-compulsive hoarding and multiple treatments is not unusual. Compulsive hoarding typically begins in childhood or early adolescence, follows a chronic course, and appears to increase with age (Steketee & Frost, 2003; Steketee & Frost, 2007). Many compulsive hoarders may view their behavior as reasonable and may report minimal distress. Their hoarding activity is regarded as more egosyntonic when compared to OCD in general. Not surprisingly, compulsive hoarding has been more resistant to treatment when compared to other types of OCD (Keeley et al., 2008). Hoarding is also associated with depression, social anxiety, and compulsive personality traits (including perfectionism), and may have a high comorbidity with other disorders (Steketee & Frost, 2003, 2007). Armed with this information, the scientifically oriented clinician is already at an advantage in formulating hypotheses about the patient and his difficulties.

The initial telephone call

In receiving the referral, I received an initial telephone call from his psychiatrist who provided a brief history. He noted that a primary difficulty involved Mr. Campbell's lack of treatment success and "resistance" around efforts to change his pattern of compulsive saving and hoarding. An accompanying problem was chronic marital distress. The next day Mr. Campbell called me about setting up an appointment. After noting that he had been referred by his psychiatrist Dr. Bennett (a pseudonym), he then quickly asked if he could call me by my first name. While mentally noting his request, I welcomed him to use my first name and then I offered him information about setting up an initial appointment. During this brief call, he presented himself as a friendly individual who spoke in a solid, confident voice.

Commentary

At least three aspects of my telephone calls with Dr. Bennett and Mr. Campbell are notable. First, Dr. Bennett's portrayal that the client has "resistance" with respect to compulsive hoarding is consistent with the literature. In many cases, attempting to treat hoarding without behavioral intervention may look like resistance, but in fact, traditional psychotherapy has not been particularly helpful with OCD and hoarding in particular. Second, it is not uncommon to receive referrals for behavior and cognitive therapy regarding patients who have experienced a plateau in other therapies in overcoming their maladaptive behaviors, especially OCD. Often, these patients are already frustrated about therapy and have been regarded as "resistant" to change. As a consequence, there is often more of an urgency to engage the patient quickly in treatment, while also an acute need to increase the patient's hope that change is possible. The issue of resistance or noncompliance, as discussed earlier, is important to understand via the case formulation. In other words, is there truly resistance to change or has the previous treatment just not been a good fit? If there is resistance, what is the cause? For example, if it is fear of change, perhaps the behavioral formulation will help target and reduce that fear, and thus improve the ability of the patient to engage in treatment. Third, I readily allowed Mr. Campbell to call me by my first name, which may be regarded as a minor boundary crossing. Although his request may have been a function of his comfort level achieved through years of previous treatment or simply his desire to speak as one professional to another, the immediacy of his request also suggested possible hypotheses about anxiety, control, or wanting to "level the playing field" with respect to our roles. Rather than postpone, challenge, or question his request, it made more sense to me to agree—with the initial goal of hopefully enhancing the prospect of our working together.

The initial interview

Mr. Campbell arrived 15 minutes late for the first appointment. He apologized briefly, noting that he had been at his office and was running late. Mr. Campbell was well dressed in a dark suit, white shirt, and tie. He presented as a friendly and personable individual who displayed good basic social skills. When asked to described his concerns, he focused on his history of excessive acquiring, saving, and hoarding of legal papers, financial periodicals, sentimental papers, and other materials (e.g., newspapers, magazines). Over the years, he noted that these materials had accumulated to such an extent that clutter was everywhere. He described having 17 full-sized file cabinets at home that were filled with his papers. In certain rooms of his home, he described 3- to 4-foot piles of books, papers, and magazines that made walking nearly impossible. Not surprisingly, Mr. Campbell indicated that the clutter was having a negative effect on his marriage and his wife was very angry and embarrassed by the state of things. At the same time, he expressed great enjoyment in reading and "burying" himself in his papers.

Mr. Campbell was unable to date clearly the onset of these difficulties, but he reportedly sought help at about age 40 when his wife remarked that, "You need to get some help or I'll leave you." Mr. Campbell also noted that like his father, he was always a collector (e.g., stamps, coins) and a "saver." Of important note, Mr. Campbell also reported that his father had "loved books" and that he worked as a printer who regarded "the printed word as sacred."

The remainder of the session focused on developing a problem list, tracing the onset and course of his symptoms, and understanding some of the reinforcing aspects or "functions" of the symptoms. I learned that his saving of school, professional, and legal papers, and what he described as "over-over-preparation" for tests, various meetings, and court proceedings, started in law school and had increased significantly after he started to practice law during his late 20s. In particular, he cited several episodes of feeling embarrassed and making mistakes in front of his peers, and in particular, having to say "I don't know" to a judge. Mr. Campbell noted that his law practice had evolved to where he avoided trial work, and was regarded by his peers as a "settlement specialist."

At the same time, Mr. Campbell noted that he had had some success in "playing" the stock market, and he attributed his success to "being up" on many of the market and financial trends. He reportedly subscribed to several financial periodicals and three daily newspapers. He also expressed a love, pride, and sentimentality regarding his family, including his wife and her business, his three grandchildren, and his daughter and son, one of whom was an attorney and the other a stockbroker. In this regard, he described saving a multitude of items about his family, dating back to the years when he and his wife dated, and back to his children's kindergarten years (e.g., drawings, report cards, assignments, papers).

With respect to therapist self-disclosure, I shared with Mr. Campbell that my father had also been a printer by trade and that he enjoyed collecting coins. I also shared with him that I too had attended Catholic school and related to some of the anxiety of being asked to answer questions in front of the class. The purpose of these self-disclosures was to normalize his experience and to increase his confidence that I very much understood him and the genesis of his difficulties. In so doing, I also hoped to "de-pathologize" to some extent his view of his problems and to decrease his level of embarrassment. He responded to these self-disclosures in a positive way by smiling, by appearing to relax more, by asking me questions in an animated manner about which Catholic school I attended and what kind of coins my father collected, and by sharing more about his developmental experiences. He related that his father, while a loving and supportive man, "could" also be a perfectionist who "could" be critical of him and his two younger brothers. Not surprisingly, the developmental role of evaluative anxiety made sense to Mr. Campbell. Finally, before the session ended, Mr. Campbell spoke briefly about some of his previous therapists and complained that "I didn't know where we were going."

Commentary

From the first contact, the behaviorally oriented therapist is concerned with accomplishing four major interrelated therapeutic tasks: (a) developing a therapeutic alliance; (b) making a diagnosis (when necessary); (c) beginning to share his/her conceptual model with the patient (e.g., the role of learning, anxiety, and avoidance as a way of coping, the close relationship between the person and his/her environment, and the contributing role of developmental history); and (d) generating and testing clinical hypotheses, and developing an initial case formulation.

In the case of Mr. Campbell, his 15-minute lateness for the initial appointment could have been an oversight. I learned later, however, that his lateness was a chronic pattern that was specific to his therapy appointments and to a lesser extent with social engagements involving his spouse. He was never late for legal-related activities and for those involving his children and grandchildren. This pattern again raised questions about control—namely, that his lateness was not a matter of pure disorganization, but that it was selective to some degree, and responsive to reinforcing contingencies (e.g., negative response by a judge for his being late or the positive consequences of being on time to be with his children and grandchildren). His lateness for therapy appointments also raised questions regarding ambivalence about treatment and also as a way of possibly expressing anger toward his wife. Her remark that "you need to get some help or I'll leave you" was consistent with this hypothesis and that involving control issues.

Through my self-disclosure about my father's work as a printer, I acknowledged the special importance of the printed word and the special meaning that his father attached to printed materials. His enjoyment of reading, his experience with the stock market, and his excessive (although some would say, comprehensive) reliance upon financial periodicals and newspapers were viewed as powerful positive reinforcers that obviously would be egosyntonic with respect to "hoarding" behavior. In other words, many of these behaviors were associated with positive consequences (e.g., greater success in the stock market). Being very knowledgeable about financial matters, Mr. Campbell shared with me later that his expertise in this area allowed him to connect and interact in a special way with his son who worked as a stockbroker. In this regard, Mr. Campbell pointed out that he enjoyed talking with his son about the stock market, and sharing his financial and investment knowledge.

My self-disclosures, especially those involving Catholic school and evaluative anxiety in speaking before the class, were used to help build the therapeutic alliance and help normalize his experiences. Mr. Campbell related that he believed that his problem originated there and knowing that I understood that environment, having experienced it myself, made him feel better. The fact that he stated several times, "You know what I went through," provided self-report data that this self-disclosure was effective.

Mr. Campbell's evaluative anxiety became more acute in law school and was worsened by occasionally having an episode of feeling embarrassed and making mistakes in front of his peers. Thus, he coped with the anxiety by overpreparing and avoiding trial work. It can be argued, however, that overpreparation in the legal realm is an adaptive behavior that is more likely to be associated with career success. Similarly, his degree of avoidance of trial work could also be viewed as adaptive and reflective of his specialization in case settlement. In ending the session, his final remark about his previous therapy that "I didn't know where we were going" was regarded by me as a request for direction (or need for control), and an opportunity to share with him eventually my thinking about his problem and the proposed treatment plan.

Sessions 2 through 10

Mr. Campbell continued to display a pattern of lateness for sessions. While he was typically gracious and apologetic, attempts to change session times did not improve compliance. Although I viewed this lateness as a treatment-interfering behavior, we did not discuss its meaning and purpose until the third session. By that time, I had developed an initial formulation which I shared with him on a blackboard that I keep in my office.

Commentary

Sharing the formulation with the patient is a boundary difference when compared to some other therapeutic approaches. In so doing, I am engaging in a collaborative process to an extent, by discussing my own "interpretations" about what the patient has told me thus far about himself. Also, I am giving him the opportunity to have input and also to help prioritize his treatment, thus reducing the perceived power differential created by, what some would say, the more "mysterious" nondisclosing therapist who does not share as much about the treatment process up front in such an explicit way.

What follows is what I began to share with Mr. Campbell during the third session and in the two subsequent sessions, which included his feedback, as well as our discussion about how treatment might be organized and prioritized. To start the process, I listed five problem areas on the blackboard:

1. Ambivalence about working on the symptoms of acquiring, saving, and "hoarding."
2. Multiple reinforcing qualities associated with the hoarding behavior, including self-nurturing, success at law and at financial decisions, maintaining positive memories of the family, a way of avoiding mistakes, and a way of retreating from marital conflict.
3. Marital stress, conflict, and difficulty in negotiating differences and problems. It became clear that much of the impetus for Mr. Campbell's treatment was based on his wife's frustration with the condition of

the home caused by his excessive saving. I raised the question as to whether or not his clutter and lateness for social engagements with his wife were ways of expressing anger toward his wife. He was reluctant to accept this possibility.
4. Chronic but selective lateness.
5. Depressive feelings (which I hypothesized were more a function of problem area 3 and, to a lesser extent, a function of his pattern of overpreparation).

Although evaluative anxiety/avoidance associated with work situations represented a primary maintaining mechanism, Mr. Campbell expressed minimal interest in working directly in this area. In this regard, he cited his advanced age and the late phase of his career. I also addressed the issue of control and how he may be attempting inadvertently to control aspects of the therapy. Looking at the problem list, however, he agreed that perhaps the best use of our therapy time would be to focus on problems 3–5.

Although some therapists might argue that I "let him off the hook" with respect to problems 1 and 2, I did not expect to be successful if I decided instead to emphasize problem areas 1 and 2. I would most likely instead encounter "resistance." Rather, the case formulation suggested that control issues, aspects of the marital relationship, and his wife's response to his clutter were pivotal. Although resistance might be challenged in another case, I believed that I could better engage Mr. Campbell in treatment—and be more helpful by allowing him to choose to work on what he was ready for, as well as to choose not to focus on another problem area, or some would say to choose not to accept an "interpretation." In many respects, therefore, this approach is truly client centered because there is a great empowerment of the client. Similarly, by presenting the formulation openly to the patient, it helps to prevent the therapist from having a hidden agenda or his or her own secret interpretations guiding the therapy.

During this time, intervention also included education and bibliotherapy (see Norcross, 2006). So as not to contribute significantly to his degree of clutter, I provided him with a single folder that included handouts and readings regarding compulsive hoarding and its treatment, along with the Web site for the Obsessive Compulsive Foundation (http://www.ocfoundation.org). I also included a few handouts regarding John Gottman's excellent work involving effective marriages (Gottman & Silver, 1999). These materials were assigned as therapeutic homework that would be discussed during a later session in planning our treatment. Although this represented a therapeutic boundary crossing, I viewed this intervention as a way to share control and responsibility for the treatment.

Using a modified treatment protocol developed by Steketee and Frost (2007a, 2007b), sessions 6–10 included skills training (organization, problem solving), motivational strategies to address ambivalence, and in-session exposure and response prevention (ERP) involving three boxes of material that Mr. Campbell was willing to bring into session and to "go through" with me. In this regard, a hierarchy of anxiety/difficulty associated with discarding items was developed, again using my blackboard. Initial ERP focused on low-hierarchy items that were easier to discard and included newspapers, old magazines, and some older journals. He also agreed to stop subscriptions for one of the three newspapers and one of several magazines. It should be noted that his lateness with appointments did not reflect notable improvement. This problem was effectively "bypassed" (see Papajohn, 1982) with the introduction of in vivo ERP home visits.

Sessions 11 through 26

After reading about and discussing how in vivo treatment would proceed, Mr. Campbell agreed to discuss the matter with his spouse. She readily agreed to and was very supportive of the plan. Together, they reviewed a copy of Steketee and Frost's (2007b) workbook and discussed some of the relevant information. It should be noted that the accompanying "Therapist Guide" (Steketee & Frost, 2007a) provides some very good guidelines for therapists interested in learning about in vivo treatment of compulsive hoarding. The guidelines include explicit detailed information and are listed by category in Figure 8.1.

For the first home visit, I arrived in the Campbell's driveway in my black Ford pickup truck, but also wearing a customary dress shirt and tie. Mr. Campbell greeted me at the door and remarked that with my vehicle "I was ready to get down to business." I am unsure how this nonverbal self-disclosure was interpreted by Mr. Campbell, but some patients have reported that they are "pleasantly surprised" to see me driving a pickup truck, rather than an upscale imported sedan. Such patient responses may strengthen the therapeutic alliance through enhancing their perception of me as a "common man." On the other hand, some may argue that such self-disclosure may lower one's perceived professionalism. This is a relevant concern.

Commentary

Therapists who have not had the opportunity to carry out in vivo therapy outside of their office or in a patient's home may have several questions and concerns. First, I view it as another incredible privilege—that is, to be allowed to enter the home of a patient to conduct therapy—being fully aware of the degree of trust and confidence that has been placed with

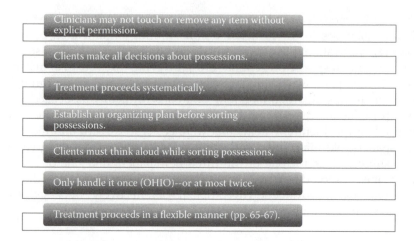

Figure 8.1 General guidelines for in vivo treatment of compulsive hoarding. Adapted from *Compulsive Hoarding and Acquiring: workbook* by Steketee, Gail & Frost, Randy O. (2007). Reprinted with permission of Oxford University Press, Inc.

me. Second, while I am always looking for any signs that the patient is uncomfortable or anxious with this intervention, it is not uncommon for the therapist to have her or his own initial anxiety. In my own case, I had the opportunity during my graduate school training and internship year to gain supervised practice and experience conducting in vivo therapy. After I started my own practice, I continued to receive supervision in in vivo therapy and collaborated with dear colleagues and friends, including Harvey Doppelt and Peter AuBuchon.

In many respects, comfort in conducting in vivo therapy is developed the same way one would overcome any fear or challenge—that is, by initial education and observation, followed by supervised practice, and then gradual exposure and mastery. Finally, while I have not encountered some of the extreme kinds of hoarding cases described by Steketee and Frost (2007a), there is always some degree of the unknown when entering a patient's home. In this regard, I can recall entering the basement of an older widowed gentleman who saved empty coffee cans and other containers—to the point where they were piled 6 to 7 feet high, literally filling the basement. On the other hand, I usually have a pretty good idea about what to expect, based on my initial assessment. Similarly, I have often been provided previously by the patient with photographs of the cluttered rooms during the in-office assessment and treatment phase. In any case, the therapist must be ready to handle any situation in a sensitive and professional manner.

Upon entering a client's home, it is also not uncommon to hear one say, "I'm embarrassed for you to see how messy it is." My response is usually affirming or reassuring in some way (e.g., "I think it takes courage to let me see what you've been dealing with." Or, "You've been working very hard on this problem. This is another big step. Give yourself credit." Or, "this part of your living room looks pretty good."). I am also usually able to comment on something positive about the home and their particular possessions. Similarly, I refer often to the fact that much of hoarding and other types of OCD are a matter of degree—that is, it is very normal to a degree to save or collect certain items. I also share with them that there is always "meaning" and/or a "story" behind each saved item or possession. These comments appear to help normalize the patient's experience, while also help to decrease his or her level of anxiety and feelings of embarrassment. These comments also emphasize the role of learning (and avoidance of anxiety) in the development and maintenance of maladaptive hoarding behavior.

Upon entering the house, Mr. Campbell introduced me to Mrs. Campbell, who was gracious and welcoming. She expressed embarrassment about the condition of several of the rooms, but also expressed some hope that we could make a difference. It had been decided previously, through development of a second hierarchy, that the best place to start our work would be in the family room where large stacks and piles of newspapers, magazines, papers, and mail had accumulated. The family room also represented a shared area that was particularly important to Mrs. Campbell. As planned, Mr. Campbell began by discarding low-anxiety items (old newspapers) into a large recyclable trash bag that I held while he monitored his anxiety level, verbalized his thoughts, and resisted the urge to "check" for content and particular news stories in these periodicals. By the end of this session, we had filled two large bags, which were placed in the bed of my truck and were discarded later at a local recycling center. This format was used initially to prevent and block urges to go back and "check" the discarded items for potentially useful information. Therapeutic homework included self-directed ERP that would be completed at least twice during the week. During a subsequent at-home in vivo session, Mr. Campbell was able to discard more than four large trash bags of newspapers and magazines, which again were placed in the bed of my truck for disposal. By the third in vivo session, Mr. Campbell was ready to utilize his own trash receptacles and was generally successful in resisting the urge to "check."

Following the fifth in vivo session, I conducted two couple's sessions in my office with the goal of reviewing progress thus far, addressing marital issues of relevance, and beginning to plan for the couple to start working together in sorting and discarding various items. In the past, attempts to work together in this way resulted in conflict and abandoning the plan. I encouraged the couple to practice some of the marital principles offered by Gottman's work noted above (e.g., working on the marital "friendship," building positives, emphasizing praise and appreciation, conflict resolution). Some of my training and experience in working with older adults was helpful in this domain (Malatesta, 2007). During the next two in vivo sessions at their home, Mr. and Mrs. Campbell participated in joint sessions that focused on discarding items in their dining room. After the second session, they agreed to plan a 1-hour time on Saturday when they would conduct a "throw away" session on their own and then reward themselves by going out to lunch together. The couple was successful in this arrangement and these "dates" were scheduled periodically.

Subsequent therapy sessions included a blend of individual and couple in vivo sessions, interspersed with individual and joint office-based sessions. These sessions focused on problem solving, troubleshooting, and relapse prevention. An ongoing focus was also on decreasing and moderating urges that Mr. Campbell experienced to acquire additional materials. In total, there was about a 60% improvement as measured by degree of clutter. Although excellent success was achieved in their living room, family room, dining room, and bedroom (with Mrs. Campbell remarking that these rooms were "almost normal"), Mr. Campbell was reluctant to focus on the basement, garage, and storeroom. In this regard, he was able to advance up to about two thirds of the hierarchy. What remained in these rooms was a range of materials related to his law practice, college and law school days, and mementos related to his family. In many respects, a reasonable compromise was achieved: Mrs. Campbell felt that she "had a good part of [her] house back," while Mr. Campbell maintained possession of items that were most important and had special meaning to him. Mr. Campbell indicated that he "had gone far enough—for now," and he indicated, "I know what to do and how to do it now." He was also pleased with the status of their marital relationship, although they continued to "have [our] moments." A "break" in therapy was requested by Mr. Campbell, to which both Mrs. Campbell and I agreed. Therapeutic gains were maintained at 3- and 6-month follow-up, and the couple gradually included their adult children in some of the "throw away" sessions.

Concluding comments

In vivo therapy can be extremely helpful for patients who are dealing with various psychological problems that have not responded to more traditional psychotherapy approaches. For some conditions, such as compulsive hoarding, the use of in vivo assessment and treatment procedures is regarded as an essential component of effective intervention. At the same time, conducting in vivo therapy poses significant challenges for the therapist. With full awareness that boundary crossings and self-disclosure could be misused and potentially damaging, the therapist who uses these interventions in a planned and thoughtful manner has greater ability to target and treat difficult problems, and human suffering is reduced. In using self-disclosure judiciously and therapeutically in these types of scenarios, I attempt to build rapport by normalizing and validating and by sharing in some way that I may relate to their fear or problem, in order to help them feel less embarrassed, more in control, and more hopeful about change. Also, in so doing I convey that I am not judging them, which can help to reduce the level of shame in this process. My case formulation will guide how much or how little I would self-disclose to this end. The case formulation also helps me to make decisions about the boundary crossing itself—for example, who should be there with me, how and where I go to the location, and evaluating whether or not the intervention is leading to the expected symptom relief. The therapist must always keep in mind that there is a level of vulnerability and exposure for the patient to allow someone into his or her home, to reveal their most embarrassing clutter, and hope to not be judged while receiving needed help. It is a great privilege to be trusted in this way by another human being. By being thoughtful and careful in utilizing this treatment approach, there is great power to create needed change, and a person's quality of life can be restored.

References

Adams, H. E., Malatesta, V. J., Brantley, P. J., & Turkat, I. D. (1981). Modification of cognitive processes: A case study of schizophrenia. *Journal of Consulting and Clinical Psychology, 49*, 460–464.

American Psychiatric Association. (2000). *DSM-IV-TR: Diagnostic and statistical manual of mental disorders* (4th ed., text rev.). Washington, DC: American Psychiatric Association.

Arnoult, M. D. (1976). *Fundamentals of scientific method in psychology* (2nd ed.). Dubuque: IA: William C. Brown.

AuBuchon, P. G., & Malatesta, V. J. (1998). Managing the therapeutic relationship in behavior therapy: The need for a case formulation. In M. Bruch & F. W. Bond (Eds.), *Beyond diagnosis: Case formulation approaches in CBT* (pp. 141–165). Chichester, UK: John Wiley & Sons.

Barlow, D. H. (2002). *Anxiety and its disorders* (2nd ed.). New York: Guilford Press.

Bieling, P. J., & Kuyken, W. (2003). Is cognitive case formulation science or science fiction? *Clinical Psychology: Science and Practice, 10*, 52–69.

Bruch, M., & Bond, F. W. (Eds.). (1998). *Beyond diagnosis: Case formulation approaches in CBT*. Chichester, UK: John Wiley & Sons.

Craske, M. G., Antony, M. M., & Barlow, D. H. (2006). *Mastering your fears and phobias* (2nd ed.). New York: Oxford University Press.

Craske, M. G., & Barlow, D. H. (2001). Panic disorder and agoraphobia. In D. H. Barlow (Ed.), *Clinical handbook of psychological disorders* (3rd ed., pp. 1–59). New York: Guilford Press.

Eells, T. D. (Ed.). (1997). *Handbook of psychotherapy case formulation.* New York: Guilford Press.

Eells, T. D., Lombart, K. G., Kendjelic, E. M., Turner, L. C., & Lucas, C. P. (2005). The quality of psychotherapy case formulations: A comparison of expert, experienced, and novice cognitive-behavioral and psychodynamic therapists. *Journal of Consulting and Clinical Psychology, 73,* 579–589.

Gottman, J. M., & Silver, N. (1999). *The seven principles for making marriage work.* New York: Crown/Three Rivers.

Hickling, E. J., & Blanchard, E. B. (2006). *Overcoming the trauma of your motor vehicle accident: A cognitive-behavioral treatment program.* New York: Oxford University Press.

Keeley, M. L., Storch, E. A., Merlo, L. J., & Geffken, G. R. (2008). Clinical predictors of response to cognitive-behavior therapy for obsessive compulsive disorder. *Clinical Psychology Review, 28,* 118–130.

Malatesta, V. J. (1985). Formulation of geriatric organic syndromes. In I. D. Turkat (Ed.), *Behavioral case formulation* (pp. 259–307). New York: Plenum Press.

Malatesta, V. J. (1990). Behavioral case formulation: An experimental assessment study of transient tic disorder. *Journal of Psychopathology and Behavioral Assessment, 12,* 219–232.

Malatesta, V. J. (Ed.). (2007). *Mental health issues of older women: A comprehensive review for health care professionals.* Binghamton, NY: Haworth Press.

Malatesta, V. J., & AuBuchon, P. G. (1992). Behavior therapy in the private psychiatric hospital: Our experiences and a model of inpatient consultation. *The Behavior Therapist, 15,* 43–46.

March, J. S., Frances, A., Kahn, D. A., & Carpenter, D. (1997). Expert consensus guideline series: Treatment of obsessive-compulsive disorder. *Journal of Clinical Psychiatry, 58*(Suppl. 4), 3–72.

Meyer, V. (1966). Modification of expectancies in cases with obsessional rituals. *Behaviour Research and Therapy, 4,* 273–280.

Meyer, V., & Turkat, I. D. (1979). Behavioral analysis of clinical cases. *Journal of Behavioral Assessment, 1,* 259–270.

Neziroglu, F., Bubrick, J., & Yaryura-Tobias, J. A. (2004). *Overcoming compulsive hoarding.* Oakland, CA: New Harbinger.

Norcross, J. C. (2006). Integrating self-help into psychotherapy: 16 practical suggestions. *Professional Psychology: Research and Practice, 37,* 683–693.

Papajohn, J. C. (1982). *Intensive behavior therapy: The behavioral treatment of complex emotional disorders.* New York: Pergamon.

Persons, J. (1989). *Cognitive therapy in practice: A case formulation approach.* New York: Norton.

Steketee, G., & Frost, R. O. (2003). Compulsive hoarding: Current status of the research. *Clinical Psychology Review, 23,* 905–927.

Steketee, G., & Frost, R. O. (2007a). *Compulsive hoarding and acquiring: Therapist guide.* New York: Oxford University Press.

Steketee, G., & Frost, R. O. (2007b). *Compulsive hoarding and acquiring: Workbook.* New York: Oxford University Press.

Turkat, I. D. (Ed.). (1985). *Behavioral case formulation.* New York: Plenum.

Young, J. E., Klosko, J. S., & Weishaar, M. E. (2003). *Schema therapy: A practitioner's guide.* New York: Guilford Press.

chapter nine

Treating addictions
A balanced approach to boundaries and therapist self-disclosure

Alyson Nerenberg

Introduction

Would you disclose your own history of addictive behaviors when treating a recovering addict? Would you disclose whether there was addiction in your family? What about if you do not have a history of addiction? Can you still have credibility? How much personal information do you disclose about yourself when you are a therapist treating a recovering addict? How does what you share or don't share impact the therapeutic relationship? This chapter explores many of these questions and offers my own perspective on them, to give the reader an example of how one psychologist specializing in addictions handles these issues. The topic of therapist boundaries in addiction treatment is addressed, and a clinical example of being invited to a recovering client's wedding is provided as an illustration.

Psychodynamic vs. addiction model

Generally, there have been two extremely divergent schools of thought regarding self-disclosure and boundaries in the treatment of addicts: psychodynamic psychotherapy and the addiction treatment model in the field. Psychodynamic theory favors more rigid boundaries in order to not contaminate the transference, because working through the transference is viewed as an important mechanism of change, not to be diluted by too much gratification. In contrast, the addiction community of Alcoholics Anonymous (AA) is built upon the concept of "leading by example." This framework views the mechanism of change as teaching/role modeling and endorses recovering people helping each other through support and encouragement, thus self-disclosure is essential and valued as inherently helpful and positive.

In this chapter, I consider aspects of both the psychodynamic and AA approaches, therefore advocating for a moderate approach to boundaries and self-disclosure. Following Mallow's (1998) recommendation for "a delicate balance" between the two worldviews of AA and psychodynamic thinking, I believe that good therapy means thoughtful and sensitive evaluation of boundaries, and careful reflection about whether or not it is advantageous for the client and therapist to consider crossing a boundary. Similarly, when it comes to deciding about what, when, and how much to disclose to a client about myself, I think about the pros and cons of the various options and will provide examples of my decision-making process.

A personal perspective on self-disclosure with addictions

I was trained psychodynamically in a doctoral program where they discouraged a therapist from sharing personal information. In this model, self-disclosure is viewed as potentially violating the unique dynamic that is inherent in the therapeutic relationship and contaminating the transference (Wells, 1994). Freud condemned therapist self-disclosure in his writings of psychoanalytic technique. He explained that "the physician should be impenetrable to the patient, and like a mirror reflect nothing but what is shown to him" (Freud, 1912/1963, p. 121). In the past few decades, relational psychodynamic writers have challenged that viewpoint, and have developed psychoanalysis as a "two-person" dynamic, describing an "intersubjective" environment, where the person of the therapist can never be, nor should it be, eradicated (e.g., Orange, Atwood, & Stolorow, 1997). It is beyond the scope of this chapter to elaborate upon relational psychodynamic therapy theory and technique, but suffice it to say, I was trained in the more classical psychodynamic worldview, where self-disclosure and boundary crossings of any kind were frowned upon.

By contrast, humanistic theorists such as Rogers (1989) and Jourard (1964) regard therapist authenticity and genuineness as essential to promoting client self-acceptance and personality change. "No patient can be expected to drop all his defenses and reveal himself except in the presence of someone whom he believes is *for him*, and not for a theory, a dogma, or a technique. I believe that the therapist who abandons all attempts to shape his patients' behavior according to some predetermined scheme, and instead strives to know and respond honestly to what he has learned, the therapist who aims at the establishment of a relationship of I and Thou, is doing his job as well as it can be done" (Jourard, 1964, p. 65). My true clinical orientation is more aligned with this humanistic worldview, whereby genuine therapist self-disclosure can be a relationship-building tool. When working with clients who struggled with addictions, in my opinion, a humanistic stance is very helpful for reasons I will explain in the paragraphs to come. Nonetheless, sometimes I feel like a rebel when I deviate from the model in which I was originally trained.

I treat addicts: all types of addicts, drug addicts, sex and love addicts, and food addicts. They are generally turned off by people who are not authentic. I truly love working with this population because it allows me to be human and genuine; they really appreciate that quality and it typically helps build rapport. My addicted clients have great "radar" for falseness and can immediately tell if someone is being sincere and really likes them or is "putting on a front" to achieve some end. This is probably because they are often "street smart," readily detecting hidden agendas. Portraying oneself as a detached, neutral therapist is likely to be received negatively by this clientele for being "not real," not vulnerable or human, and therefore, someone not to be trusted. Their attunement to falseness is ultimately self-protective, as addicts are generally hypervigilant to the possibility of being judged or shamed.

Given my own experiences with addiction in my family, I relate to my clients both from a personal and a professional perspective. I too developed many of the perfectionistic "trying to please" qualities that are common among adult children of alcoholics. I also definitely understand numbing yourself to pain and have had the desire to overindulge, whether it is through excessive shopping, eating, or people pleasing. In sum, an addict is a person not so different from me. Early on in my career, while I was a graduate student, I did an internship at an inpatient rehabilitation program with an inner-city population. Some of the clinicians there distanced themselves from the clients, acting superior and creating a dynamic of "us" versus "them." What a disappointment! We are all human beings who have suffered life's hurts and dealt with them the best way we knew how.

Shame and addiction

Shame is a core problem among addicted clients. Bradshaw (1998) describes shame as the experience of having a core sense of badness and being unworthy of having good things come into your life. He explains that shame is the "all pervasive sense that you are flawed and defective as a human being" (p. 16). For addicts, shame often begins in childhood as a result of abuse: physically, sexually, and emotionally. Additionally, they too often participate in addictive behaviors which may get them into humiliating and shameful situations. Whether they have been binging and purging with food, masturbating to pornography on the Internet, or prostituting for drugs, their addictive behaviors increase their sense of shame and isolation. In essence they are living "double lives" and often believe that if anyone found out, they would be rejected. Carnes (1991) describes the phenomenon of double lives in his description of the core beliefs of sex addicts. He states that addicts feel unlovable, believing that if anyone really knew the truth about them, they would be abandoned. Due to this core sense of feeling unlovable, a person feels intense shame and acts out to relieve the pain. Carnes (1991) explains how the "inherent shamefulness of the addict brings on the self-destructive shame cycles, in which the addict's efforts to stop seem only to intensify the failures" (p. 95).

Self-disclosure decisions

The "blank screen" approach with clients with addictions is too anxiety producing to be productive in many cases because of their deep sense of shame and fear of rejection. Listening to my client's history, I may choose to share some of my feeling reactions (i.e., known as self-involving disclosures or disclosure of countertransference) as a way of showing my compassion for their story. The intent of this would be both to decrease shame and to reduce the fear that I am judgmental. For example, when interviewing a new client who shared with me a history of sexual abuse underlying his drinking problem, I responded by saying, "It makes me feel sad for you that you went through all of that, and no one was there for you. Of course it makes sense that you needed some kind of comfort and you turned to drinking." I looked him straight in the eye and said, "Listening to you, I felt sad for you—this abuse was not your fault." He later told me that was the most powerful moment in therapy. No one had ever told him, with deep compassion, that it wasn't his fault.

Along with disclosing my feelings, I may also reveal a part of my own history, which is a more personal self-disclosure meant to be a "reciprocal" one; its purpose is to encourage more self-disclosure on their part, normalize their experience, and provide hope. For example, I might tell a new client, during the intake process, that I too come from a family with a significant history of addictions. I have seen the recovery process, work and have a close family member with over 20 years of recovery. I do not generally tell that piece of my history unless I am asked, or if I see a client desperately struggling with a sense of hopelessness. A "reciprocal" self-disclosure is one that either answers a client's question or is directly relevant to the issue at hand. Hill and Knox (2002), in their empirically based guidelines for self-disclosure, support the use of reciprocal self-disclosures. If a therapist simply decides on his own to self-disclose without being in some way queried, it may be that the therapist is revealing more than the client wants or needs to know or is doing it in an unattuned manner, which is rarely helpful and possibly destructive.

On a cautionary note, I recognize that when I disclose information to one of my clients, I am essentially potentially disclosing information to any number of my clients. As many of my clients know each other, any piece of information I share with one client can be communicated with others in my practice. Many are either in one of my psychotherapy groups together or attend the same 12-step fellowship. It is not uncommon for clients to run into each other in the waiting room and greet each other enthusiastically. I believe this is an important element of recovery and I encourage clients to build a sense of community in their lives and use recovering people instead of addictive behaviors in order to fill their sense of emptiness. Also, I would not expect a client to maintain confidentiality about something I disclose. Putting a client in a position of holding a secret mirrors the earlier abuse that a trauma-surviving addict has experienced in childhood. Thus, whenever I disclose something, I am fully prepared for it to be shared with others and would not self-disclose something that couldn't be made public.

"Are you in recovery?"

When a recovering addict asks a therapist, "Are you in recovery?" some clinicians who are not recovering addicts feel uncomfortable by this question. Trained to not self-disclose or answer genuinely, just as I was trained, they might feel that the question is inappropriate or that it would be unprofessional to answer it. Another reason for discomfort is a fear that the addict's question is meant as a challenge, inherently accusing them of being incapable of helping them. Some therapists distance themselves from the client by answering no, or explaining why they are skilled to do this work regardless of not having been through the same thing. I believe that the addicted client is not actually asking "Are you good enough?" but rather, "'Will you accept me and not judge me?' or "Am I too different from you to understand?'" I usually ask the client where he is coming from when he asks the question and by exploring it with him, without making him feel judged for asking. It becomes an opportunity to discuss the fears involved in trusting a therapeutic relationship. Although I am not a recovering sex addict or drug addict, I do describe myself as a "recovering therapist," since I, like we all are, am recovering from life's pain.

Another reason that addicted clients ask that question is perhaps steeped in the Alcoholics Anonymous treatment philosophy. Mallow (1998) gives an excellent analysis of how AA leads clients to expect their therapists to also be disclosing and may need some education on the difference between an AA sponsor and a therapist. The 12-step model was founded upon addicts helping each other. Given the history, there are still some people who believe that addicted people in recovery are more qualified helpers. While there is a huge benefit from having someone who has been there, that too can have its downside.

Many clinicians who are recovering addicts themselves disclose that information to their clients. That can be a very powerful tool of connecting with clients, providing hope and gaining their respect quickly. The negative side is that if a clinician reveals too many details of his story it may not feel safe for the client, or the client may worry that the therapist overly identifies with him or is weak. Also, the client could be worried that too much stress on the therapist could lead the recovering therapist to relapse. In fact, I have treated clients whose therapists have relapsed and it has been devastating for the clients. They experience their therapists' unreliability, poor boundaries, and lack of accountability. This event is not only counter-therapeutic for the client, but it also may rob the client of the hope of the recovery process working for them. Additionally, it may mirror an earlier experience of having an addicted parent who could not be counted on and failed them at an earlier time in their life.

Overall, there is value to a therapist sharing that he is in recovery given that it can reduce the client's shame and isolation. In my psychotherapy groups for recovering addicts, I often co-facilitate my groups with a male therapist who is a recovering addict. He does not provide all of the details of his addiction, but shares that he has been through hell and has survived. Clients really appreciate hearing his personal experience.

When recovering therapists and clients both need 12-step meetings

Another difficult boundary dilemma that occurs with recovering therapists is the need for both the therapist and the client to attend 12-step meetings. This is not a problem for therapists living in large cities where there are enough 12-step meetings available so that the client and therapist can go to different meetings for their own support. However, in small towns where there is a limited amount of meetings, a client and therapist attending the same meeting frequently occurs. It can be awkward for both of them. If possible, it is best for the recovering therapist to attend different meetings, so that the therapist has a safe place to be vulnerable too. Another option for recovering therapists is that they can attend 12-step meetings online, or begin a "therapist only—closed 12-step meeting" in order to protect their own boundaries. If a recovering therapist is attending a meeting and a client walks in, the therapist must proceed with caution and think carefully about what he reveals in the meeting. Once again, the therapist has an opportunity to be a wonderful role model by working his program and using good self-care. It can be a healthy learning experience as long as the therapist proceeds with caution, dignity, and respect for both his client and himself.

Boundary concerns with addicted clients

Many addicts who come for treatment display poor boundaries, therefore I use moderation in self-disclosure and keep clear boundaries. Clients may know some general information about me but nothing too specific. For example, my clients know that I am married and have two daughters; however, I do not have pictures of my husband and children in my office since some of my clients have infertility issues and others have attractions to children. I do disclose some information about my relationship with my husband and children. For example, I have disclosed that although my husband and I are happily married, there are times we have disagreements and my feelings get hurt. I will also share that one of my character defects is that I am a "sulker." I believe that acknowledging our own shortcomings makes us seem more human, complete with some flaws of our own; that realness can foster a sense of safety, increasing our clients' willingness to disclose their shameful secrets to us.

Dressing professionally

I put thought into how I dress as a psychologist working with addicts. Portraying a professional appearance is important when working with addicts. As many of my clients are compulsively sexual, I do not wear any tight-fitting/seductive clothing. I also believe that many of our clients look to us as a model of how to present themselves to others. Body-image issues are crucial for my clients who are food addicts or sex addicts. Many of the sexually compulsive women have considered their value to be mainly as sexual objects. I strive to help them develop a sense of self-worth beyond appearance. We may discuss clothing as a part of their setting boundaries or self-care. Other clients may have turned off their sexuality and view themselves as "sexually anorexic." For these women it is most helpful if the therapist can role model her own comfort with her sexuality and body image, dressing neither too conservatively nor provocatively, while demonstrating her own sense of style.

The office: A safe place

The color in my office and warm surroundings are a way of trying to help my clients feel comfortable and more vibrant and awake in their lives. Entering therapy, many addicted clients have been so obsessive with their addictions that they feel mentally, physically, and spiritually empty.

They have lost all hope for the future. A major goal of treatment is to help them rediscover hope and passion for life. They need to learn to develop excitement about activities to replace their obsession with finding the next drug of choice. I may ask a client to write a list of 10 things in his life he is passionate about other than heroin. He may look at me like I'm crazy because *passion* is a word he has not thought of for a very long time. Many clinicians in private practice work from home offices but I would not do that with my particular clientele. Because of the obsessive nature of many addictions, I feel that having a separate home and office makes it easier for both my clients and me. For example, I have worked with clients who have stalked ex-girlfriends, or crossed boundaries in their search for their drug. Although my clients have generally been respectful of my boundaries, addictions can drive people to desperate measures such as obsessively calling or driving by a desired person's home. I like the fact that I can leave my work behind and live in a different place. It has the twofold effect of providing good self-care for me and also conveying that my office is a place designated solely for my clients' well-being.

The therapeutic relationship

Aside from wanting to reduce addictive patterns, clients also come to therapy to increase intimacy in their lives. Our therapy relationship becomes a place to work on building a safe yet intimate connection. I try to model a sense of genuineness and authenticity, but with boundaries. There is a balancing act between being gentle and firm. Due to the tremendous shame addicted clients carry, a therapist needs to be accepting and compassionate. However, the addict often lives in a sense of denial about how devastating his behavior is to himself and others. Sometimes it is necessary for a therapist to be honest and direct as she confronts the unhealthy behaviors. A crucial part of this work is helping our clients set boundaries in order to cope with urges and prevent relapses. Along with helping clients set healthy boundaries, it is essential that we model solid yet flexible boundaries for ourselves.

Case illustration

The clinical example illustrates my relationship with my client as well as my decision to challenge strict psychoanalytic boundaries. Although I have stated that many of my clients have poor boundaries, that does not mean I have a rule that I would never cross a boundary, such as go to a wedding. It only means that I am fully aware that my clients have experienced true boundary violations in their lives and may have committed them in some cases. I need to carefully decide in each situation whether it would be safe, therapeutic, and wise to engage in any sort of boundary crossing. As you will see, when it came to deciding about going to Jerry's wedding, I felt very sure that it would not have a negative effect in any way or cause him to be confused about my role in his life.

Jerry's story

"I am unlovable. I don't deserve to live. No one will ever love me again."

Jerry had committed a sexual offense as a result of his sexual addiction. He had just lost everything that mattered to him: his marriage, his children, his professional career, and many of his friends. At the lowest point in his life, Jerry contacted me for help.

I am about to tell you the story of Jerry. To protect his confidentiality, his name and many details of his case have been changed, but the essence of his story remains.

My journey with Jerry began when a well-respected therapist friend of mine called to refer Jerry to me. "Please take care of him. He's a good man who has made some terrible mistakes." Shortly after, Jerry called me. "My world is crashing down and I can't believe what I've done." Jerry was talking to me on the phone, reaching out for help at the worst moment of his life. "I'm so glad you called. We will get a plan together for you." I wanted in that moment to commend Jerry for reaching out and also immediately begin to help him have hope that he could survive this and that I would help him.

I had to tell Jerry some difficult news. He was going to have to immerse himself into residential treatment, which would be 10 hours of therapy daily for 2 months and 12-step meetings in the evenings; in order to work with me in outpatient treatment, he was going to need to show this level of commitment. I knew that if he engaged in treatment in this way, he would reap the benefits of that environment and really begin to understand the cycle of his offending behavior. If he did follow through with this, I had hope for him, and would work intensely with him to rebuild his life.

Compared with other addictions, sexual addiction has a higher stigma than drug, alcohol, or food addiction: There is little compassion for people who have committed sexual crimes. Although not all sex addicts have committed sexual crimes, those who have are more shunned by those even within the addictions community. Jerry had his work cut out for him.

I was pleased to find out that Jerry completed the residential treatment with courage, and put the maximum effort into his recovery. And, unlike many other clients who hoped to be done with it and feel that they paid their dues by going to residential treatment, Jerry, who was accustomed to a comfortable upper-middle-class home, humbly moved into a halfway house for sex addicts to stay immersed in a treatment environment, per treatment team's recommendations. It was from this new abode that he would commute to his outpatient appointments.

Jerry had learned that his commitment to recovery needs to be life-long. When under stress, he may have the urges that got him into the trouble, for the rest of his life, and he will have to be 100% responsible for recognizing that and preventing himself from ever acting on it. Like all addictions, even in recovery, there is always relapse potential, and the person must remain vigilant for the course of his or her life to offset that possibility.

Jerry had an admirable attitude about his situation. Although he wished that someday he could have a relationship again, he also knew that he could not begin dating until he had reached a significant level of insight about his symptoms and potential triggers. Twelve-step treatment recommends a 1-year celibacy commitment. Unlike many clients who try to bargain with that boundary, Jerry went the other direction and was even more strict, imposing a 2-year or longer commitment upon himself, so that he would truly be able to make needed changes before he ever engaged in another relationship. He also knew that when he did start dating, he would be completely honest about his past, with full awareness that a potential partner might reject him once she knew his history.

After several years of working hard in treatment, we decided that he was ready for the dating process, which would need to include telling any woman about his past before engaging in sexual activity. Unlike sexual offending, which is simply about gratification of needs and abuse of power, he was clear that he did not want to have sexual intimacy without emotional intimacy first, and that would entail having his partner really know him. He also recognized that not telling his partner would amount to manipulation by withholding relevant information with which she could make an informed decision. Choosing to be honest was not easy, but it was the only way: There would be women who would reject him once they knew. And even though he expected it, it was a huge disappointment when he was rejected by women after disclosing about himself, although he completely understood their perspective. The experience, however, left him wondering if he would ever find someone who could truly love and accept him.

And then Megan arrived. They met volunteering in church and developed a friendship. She too was in the recovery community for a different addiction, and had a physical disability that had taught her to not judge people at the outset. No stranger to emotional pain and rejection, her own struggle had shaped her to become a person of great perseverance and strength. She and Jerry built a foundation of friendship and he was able to open up to her about his past—she listened quietly and asked appropriate questions. To his complete surprise, it seemed unbelievable and beyond his greatest hope: She was accepting and supportive even knowing all of this about him. In his next appointment he told me about Megan. Shaking his head in utter disbelief, he said "I never experienced such love."

Sexuality merged with acceptance and safety. It was not a traditional love story—it was uniquely beautiful, in a class of its own.

"Is this healthy?" "Is this not healthy?" Jerry meticulously worked at being a good partner in relationship with Megan. He leaned on his group for support and feedback—he sought guidance, advice, and a sounding board for the building of the first healthy intimate relationship in his life. He was determined to maintain and utilize his support network for pioneering this relational new ground. In so doing, he relied on all of his supports: Sex and Love Addicts Anonymous (SLAA), his therapy group, and me, his therapist. In sum, we all were rooting for him every step of the way. It wasn't a surprise, then, that he wanted us all there at his wedding.

The decision to attend Jerry and Megan's wedding

As discussing boundaries was such a large part of our work together, Jerry was sensitive enough to say to me: "I would love for you to be at my wedding, but I understand if you feel that it would be breaking your boundaries to see me in a social setting." Before considering my invitation, first, I wanted to help the group members decide for themselves about their attendance. I brought up the decision to go to Jerry's wedding to the group for discussion. Everyone seemed enthusiastic about going and no one reported discomfort with any aspect of it. In fact, they often see each other at 12-step meetings, so no one seemed to have any concerns. I later learned, however, when one group member did not go, she had made an excuse because in truth, she had shared about intimacy issues with her husband and felt worried about having the other group members meet him. Upon reflection, I could have spent more time as a group leader, challenging and exploring the group members' fears about seeing each other at a social engagement.

When it came to my own decision whether or not to attend, on the one hand, my psychodynamic training would admonish that going to the wedding is a boundary violation; on the other, the AA addictions worldview would suggest that of course you should go, you are part of his support team. So, there was an argument for either position. A humanistic perspective teaches that being genuinely caring and authentically involved is a healing component of therapy, but it doesn't specifically advise about whether a therapist should attend a client's wedding. But this latter perspective guided my thinking.

Here is how I thought about it: I had known Jerry for almost a decade and felt that I really wanted to honor the work he had done on developing honesty and intimacy by being there to share in a really positive and special moment in his life.

Upon further thought, although I was honored to have been asked, I knew that it could be potentially awkward if, for example, someone asked me how I knew the couple. I knew too that I did not feel comfortable staying for the reception. Many of my clients would be there and I agree with the psychodynamic perspective that socializing with clients is not appropriate. I also knew I did not want to bring my husband and be in an awkward position of introducing him to clients. What would I say if someone asked me how I knew Jerry? Jerry and I discussed it and came up with an answer that he was comfortable with—I would answer "through his recovery community." Jerry was a vocal participant in his recovery community and was comfortable with his guests knowing that much about himself.

So in the end, I decided that I did want to go, but would attend with another therapist who was also part of their team, and would go to the ceremony but not stay for the party afterwards. The other therapist was a trusted friend of mine, and together, we discussed the pros and cons of our decision before we chose to attend.

Zur (2007) describes the decision to attend a client's wedding as a boundary crossing in psychotherapy. He defines a boundary crossing as any deviation from traditional, strict "only in the office," emotionally distant forms of therapy. It is a departure from the traditional psychoanalytic process. He also states that sometimes a boundary crossing can be an effective treatment intervention. In this situation, my decision to attend Jerry and Megan's wedding was to honor their union. I discussed my decision to attend with a trusted colleague first and felt comfortable with my decision. I wanted to show my client that he mattered to me, and I believed that would be therapeutic.

Being there was a wonderful experience for me too. It gave me great joy to see so many of the clients I am fortunate enough to treat celebrating the union of two people who genuinely love each other. Typically, therapists are immersed in the sadness and losses of our clients, and rarely do we get to really share in their happier moments. Being there at Jerry's wedding, looking at all the people who had grown and changed their lives, most of all Jerry, I felt hopeful about recovery and love's capacity to help people heal. I thought of possibilities and redemption, something that has great meaning for me as I choose to work with wounded addicts. I am an optimist who believes in healing and love.

Consequences of my decision

In my situation, my motive for attending Jerry's wedding was fairly simple. I wanted to honor the work he had done over many years of therapy.

I would not have been so inclined to attend the wedding of a client I had just started counseling. My free time is valuable and I would only want to spend it celebrating with a client for whom I really have a truly special feeling. It also would be less appropriate had I just recently started working with him, as there needs to be a strong enough reason to cross the traditional boundary. The downside of my decision to go is that I inadvertently set an expectation that I would do that for all of my clients. In fact, I have another client in my psychotherapy group who is getting married in several months and wants to invite me and the rest of the group to her wedding. Again, a careful deliberation of the best course of action will be necessary. However, now that I've attended one client's wedding, I need to be sensitive to others' feelings in the group.

Although I am pleased with my choice to have attended his wedding and feel that it was positive experience for Jerry, what I will do differently is spend more time discussing with group members their feelings and fears about seeing members and their significant others outside of group. To avoid blurring the line between client and therapist, professionalism needs to be maintained during the event, and the client's thoughts and feelings ought to be discussed both before and afterward in therapy. In Jerry's case, I did spend plenty of time discussing all of these things.

A decision like this must be considered carefully on a case-by-case basis. For some clients with very poor boundaries, the therapist might conclude it is not wise to attend events outside of therapy. For example, perhaps a severely personality-disordered client might interpret the attending of an outside event as meaning that the therapist is changing from therapist into friend, misconstruing the therapist's intent completely. If the client cannot understand that the therapy relationship will still be the same afterwards, and explore fully the pros and cons together, it is likely not a good idea to do it.

In Jerry's situation we had talked about what it would mean to him if I attended; he completely understood that my role in his life would not change regardless, and he also respected my decision if I did not feel comfortable going.

Summary

In closing, upon exploring the topics of boundaries and self-disclosure in treating addicts, several important points have emerged. Maintaining solid boundaries in conducting psychotherapy with addicts is essential. It is crucial for the therapist to model healthy boundaries. These boundaries do not need to be rigid; they can be flexible but need to be in place to keep both the client and the therapist feeling safe. When a boundary is altered, it should be done in the best interest of the client and not simply to satisfy the needs of the therapist. Also, before deciding whether to cross a boundary or not, it is important to consult with a trusted colleague or supervisor. Understanding the rationale and some of the consequences that may result from altering a boundary is important before making a decision.

After the ceremony, Jerry brought me over to meet Megan and she warmly hugged me. She thanked me several times for my work with Jerry. Both she and Jerry stated that they appreciated all that I had done for them and that I had come to celebrate their marriage. Could I have honored their relationship without attending their wedding? Probably, yes, but you rarely have the opportunity to show clients that they matter to you, and that your work with them has not only changed them as patients, but also you as a therapist.

References

Bradshaw, J. (1988). *Healing the shame the binds you.* Deerfield Beach, FL: Health Communications.

Carnes, P. (1991). *Don't call it love: Recovery from sexual addiction.* New York: Bantam Books.

Freud, S. (1963). Recommendations for physicians on the psychoanalytic method of treatment. In S. Freud, *Therapy & technique.* New York: Collier. (Original work published 1912)

Hill, C. E., & Knox, S. (2002). Self-disclosure. In J. C. Norcross (Ed.), *Psychotherapy relationships that work* (pp. 255–266). New York: Oxford University Press.

Jourard, S. (1964). *The transparent self.* Princeton, NJ: D. Van Nostrand Company.

Mallow, A. J. (1998). Self-disclosure: Reconciling psychoanalytic psychotherapy and Alcoholics Anonymous philosophy. *Journal of Substance Abuse Treatment, 15,* 493–498.

Orange, D. M., Atwood, G. E., & Stolorow, R. D. (1997). *Working intersubjectively: Contextualism in psychoanalytic practice.* Hillsdale, NJ: The Analytic Press.

Rogers, C. (1989). The therapeutic relationship. In H. Kirschenbaum & V. L. Henderson (Eds.), *The Carl Rogers reader.* Boston: Houghton Mifflin.

Wells, T. L. (1994). Therapist self-disclosure: Its effects on clients and the treatment relationship. *Smith College Studies in Social Work, 65,* 23–41.

Zur, O. (2007). *Boundaries in psychotherapy.* Washington, DC: APA Press.

Interface of therapist and client ethnic/racial/cultural factors

chapter ten

Healing the wounds of attachment
An EMDR relational approach

Deany Laliotis

Introduction

I never saw it coming. She was young, beautiful, smart, and matter-of-fact. She had done well in her professional life and by anyone's standards would be considered a high-functioning adult. What I didn't notice was beneath that exterior was a very young girl who desperately needed a mother and didn't know it.

Melina was in her late 30s when she first came to see me. She was twice divorced, had no children, and was in a relationship with yet another "bad boy" with whom she had been on and off for the last 5 years. She couldn't live with him, yet she couldn't stand the loneliness that overcame her when she was without him. It was a desolate place that she was all too familiar with from her earliest years as a little girl.

Early attachment issues

As the youngest of four children with three older brothers in a Greek-American family, one would have expected Melina to be coveted by her family as the precious little girl to be protected and adored, as is typical of these immigrant families. Instead, her mother was narcissistic and controlling, critical and neglectful. Her father was passive, dependent, and emotionally unavailable. Her brothers were self-absorbed with their own interests, and when they paid attention to her, it was only to tease and bully her. Having come from the same cultural background myself, it was stunning to me that her mother resented taking care of her and her brothers treated her with the same contempt her mother had for her. The only person in her life who adored her was her maternal grandfather, who, tragically for Melina, died when she was 6 years old.

As an EMDR therapist with a psychodynamic, object relations background, I began to explore with her how her early experiences as a child informed how she felt about herself as a person and how she relates to family and friends as well as her intimates. She moves through the world with a sense of self that is inadequate, insecure, and "not good enough" to be loved or accepted by others. By her own admission, her sense of self was organized around pleasing others and being accepted by them as a means of feeling worthy of being loved and having an identity as a person. She is strongly identified with her mother's negative and neglectful treatment of her and has internalized her mother's inadequacy as a parent as her own inadequacy as a person.

In addition to her poor sense of self, Melina has a real fear of being abandoned, as she was often left alone, frequently coming home to an empty house from a young age. After her grandfather died, Melina was getting herself up in the mornings and getting dressed to go to school from the first grade. She was so ill-prepared that the school called her parents to see if they needed financial assistance, as she was going to school wearing the same clothes every day and they were inappropriate for the weather. Her mother was often late on the days she was to pick her up from school. She describes remembering being dropped off at school on a day that school was closed with nowhere to go and no way to contact her parents.

The story that best describes Melina's insecure/avoidant attachment style and inferior sense of self is a memory of being an 8-year-old at the playground with her family and getting stung by a bee. Despite the pain of being stung, Melina did not make a sound and did not tell anyone. She decided at that moment that "it didn't hurt," and from that point on, her emotional life went underground. She has had limited access to her feelings, so when people treat her badly, she often doesn't notice it, and when she does, she is numb to her feelings and does nothing about it. Consequently, her inferior sense of self has been reinforced by subsequent life experiences and bad object choices, especially with intimates.

EMDR: A brief overview

When Melina first came to see me, she already had an expectation from the person who referred her that working with me would be different than the other psychotherapists she had seen because I did this "special kind of therapy" called eye movement desensitization and reprocessing (EMDR). EMDR is a methodology that was originally developed by Dr. Francine Shapiro in 1987 to process traumatic experiences using eye movements or other forms of bilateral stimulation (Shapiro, 1995). These traumatic experiences are stuck in the brain in their original form, causing the client to have symptoms because the brain cannot successfully process these events and integrate them with other, more adaptive experiences. The bilateral stimulation that is applied in EMDR therapy is used to activate the information-processing system in the brain that is designed to process and integrate experiences with all the other information we have about ourselves and the world. When disturbing events are not adequately processed by this information-processing system, these memories do not successfully integrate with other experiences. Instead, they are stored with the perceptions of the person at the time of the event, along with all the components of experience—that is, images, thoughts and sounds, feelings and sensations. These components of past memories get "triggered" by current events in which the person is experiencing themselves in a similar situation or with a similar kind of person or feeling which then activates these other past associations in the brain. This causes the person to react "as if" they're in the same situation in the past, rather than responding to what is going on in the present. Therefore, any time the person is having a reaction that is out of proportion to what is going on, or the current event is having a lingering effect that seems beyond the scope of what is happening now, the person's experience in the present is informed more by the past. When those past associations, either consciously or unconsciously, inform the person about their present situation, they react in a way that is usually maladaptive to their current context.

Neglect is traumatic

Today, EMDR is not limited to the treatment of PTSD but is widely used to treat everyday problems and self-esteem issues that are informed by earlier experiences that similarly have not been adequately processed and integrated by the brain (e.g., Cvetek, 2008; Shapiro, 2007). In Melina's case, her many memories of neglect and abandonment in her early childhood were still actively shaping her adult emotional life, thus, driving decisions that were not best for her. EMDR psychotherapy, then, is about identifying and processing these earlier experiences that are informing the current difficulties, thereby allowing the client to respond more adaptively to their current situation and to similar situations in the future. The client is then better able to respond to the current demands from the perspective of an adult as they have all their adult options available to them. Sometimes, however, the client has developmental deficits that need to be addressed before they can fully incorporate the necessary skills, feelings, and behaviors that correspond to the current demands and to future challenges. EMDR's three-pronged approach of past, present, and future is designed to address the client's current difficulties by reprocessing past events, targeting present triggers that may remain, and developing future templates of action that are adaptive for the client given what is ecologically appropriate for them within the current context of their lives.

When Melina and I first discussed her relationship problems with men, it became clear that her belief about herself as "not good enough" was the pervasive issue in her life that cut across all contexts, both at home and at work. This meta-perception of herself as a worthless person became the organizing theme of our work together. From an EMDR perspective, she was developmentally stuck at the "responsibility" level; that is, she is over-identified with the perpetrator of her neglect and abuse and it is because of her that she was mistreated. The added component for Melina is that children of Greek immigrant parents are often placed in positions of actual responsibility to help them assimilate into the culture by translating for them when they don't understand or interpreting for them what the cultural norms are. To this day, Melina continues to take care of her parents in ways that her brothers are not expected to.

Shared ethnicity

The other not-so-hidden ingredient to this therapeutic recipe is that I, too, am a first-generation Greek-American who was born to parents that emigrated from Greece as adults. I am all too familiar with that sense of responsibility to care for one's elders and the demands to maintain and carry on the traditions of the Greek culture, not unlike Dina in *My Big Fat Greek Wedding*. Melina's struggles for acceptance, identity, and differentiation are issues I understand well from my own experiences, although our familial stories are very different. In addition to becoming a well-educated, professional woman who has a life and identity of her own, I, too, was expected to marry a Greek man and have a Greek family. I tried this conventional route and divorced my Greek husband 3 years into the relationship. I am now happily married to my American husband of Scotch-Irish-Jewish descent for 15 years with two stepsons that I have raised as my own. We also share a home-based private practice together where his office is across the waiting room from mine. Melina, of course, is very interested to understand how I have succeeded in my lifestyle choices and managed to navigate these cultural demands at the same time. She is aware of the choices I have made, both from me in the form of self-disclosures as well as from other sources. So, from the beginning of our work together, the stage was set for me to be more transparent to her than I was accustomed to being.

The "promise" of EMDR for Melina is that she would ultimately feel good about herself as a person, especially as a Greek-American woman, and make better choices in her relationships, particularly with a life partner. In order for these changes to occur, the early memories of being alone and feeling lonely and worthless that are informing her current life experiences have to be reprocessed with EMDR. Meanwhile, she comes for therapy at a time when she is still in this relationship of five years knowing there is no future with this person, but is unable to sever her ties with him because every time she attempts to do so, she plunges into that familiar place of despair and desolation. Although she is able to acknowledge on an intellectual level that the relationship isn't working for her, she believes that if she keeps trying to make it right that "just maybe" it will work out. In addition, her mother is pressuring her to marry him even though she knows Melina isn't happy in the relationship. By Melina's own report, it was her mother that insisted she marry both of her former husbands in order to join the ranks of Greek women who are married with children. Before she was married the first time, Melina had approached her mother with serious misgivings about marrying her fiancé. Her mother's response was to hit her head against the wall and scream, "How can you do this to me?" From these kinds of past experiences, it is understandable that Melina also feels trapped in her current situation because the boyfriend meets the mother's criteria for a husband and she can't see her way out of it. She presents as depressed, feeling hopeless that she will ever "get it right" with anyone and that she should settle for this relationship. She also attributes her feelings of despair and loneliness to her current situation, not recognizing that it is much more about the past that is driving her experiences as well as her choices.

The first stage of therapy was to help her understand the connection between how she's experiencing herself and her circumstances in the present and how it's being informed by the past. This recognition helped her appreciate why she is unable to act on the intellectual understandings she has about herself but is behaving in response to her emotional reactions. She speaks of feeling numb much of the time, just going through the motions, assuming that it doesn't matter how she feels because other people's feelings and needs are more important. As we explore this early territory in greater depth, it becomes painfully clear that her mother was absent and disinterested in being a mother to her, unlike how she was with her brothers. As we commenced with EMDR processing, these early experiences of neglect started to thaw and what became available to her was the emotional desolation that would get triggered every time she attempted to separate from her boyfriend. Working through these pervasive experiences in her childhood were painful, intense, and rewarding all at the same time. The therapeutic challenge was for Melina to actually feel the emotional desolation of being alone in the past while maintaining a dual awareness that she is not alone with these feelings in the present, and that she is actually an adult going through this experience. This awareness allows her to process and successfully integrate these early states where she was without the necessary resources to integrate them at the time they first occurred.

Invoking the "mother function"

Week after week, we continued to work through networks of memories that were all about the same meta-conclusion: that she's not worthy of being loved. Despite the fact that we would get a complete reprocessing of these early experiences, it was a challenge for her to step into a more adult self that understood her value as a person. Her core identity of worthlessness was a constant competitor. She often looked to me to validate her and reassure her that she is good enough and that her needs are important when attempting to navigate transactions with her family or her boyfriend. While she was making progress with them, her internal sense of entitlement was tentative, and she would have trouble holding onto her resolve when faced with their disapprovals. She used me and our relationship as an anchor to help her hold onto her sense of self as "good enough." I, of course, became her greatest support and biggest fan. She would send me e-mails of transactions with her boyfriend and her family, asking for advice, which I of course responded to. At the time I had some concerns about allowing her to send me e-mails, as it was outside the structure and boundaries of our relationship. On the other hand, she was judicious in her use of e-mail and it seemed more important to integrate e-mail as a more "normal" boundary crossing, as it is such a common form of communication, especially for her. It also gave her a forum to actively examine what she was doing in her life in a way that added structure to our sessions. We would then examine her choices, her experiences, how and when she got "triggered" into those old places, giving us a platform to pursue the old memories that were informing her difficulties in her current life.

Melina would also ask me questions about my own experiences with my family, with the community, about being different from other women in the community. Inherent in these queries, I believe, is Melina looking for permission to differentiate, to be okay with who she is as well as identifying with me as a woman. Of course, I was happy to validate her, as I am very fond of her and increasingly incredulous with her mother for being so self-centered and neglectful. As a psychotherapist, I am aware of the importance of the positive transference that she is developing toward me as a self-object to identify herself with. I also recognize that the biggest challenge of all was for her to internalize my genuine support and affection for her as her own. The "mother function" that I was invoking was giving her the opportunity to deconstruct this negative core belief of defectiveness and to reconstruct a sense of self that was inherently good. As we were systematically working through these negative experiences from childhood, there was a parallel process going on in the room; that I, as her therapist, was emotionally holding her and available to her. So, not only were we changing the way these early memories were informing her current experience of self, but we were also cocreating "new" memories of being held and validated as a worthwhile person. What was happening on a number of levels is that, not only was she getting the mother she always needed, but I was getting a daughter, too.

Therapeutic relationship: Reparative or dependency fostering?

As our relationship deepened, I was aware that she was depending on me more and more, not just on our therapeutic relationship and the connection we have, but in me as the agent of change and the source of wisdom for navigating her life. I was especially concerned given her history of seeking out authority figures with whom she would deposit her faith and trust, not unlike a child who idealizes a parent. At the same time, however, I understood the importance of shifting her identification of self from a negative self-object to a positive one. What was less clear to me was the therapeutic line between the healing of a developmental wound and the enabling of an unmet childhood need. What was clear enough, however, was that her identification with me and the holding she was experiencing in our connection made it possible for her to assert herself in the world more as an adult. To what extent, then, is my role in her life and my genuine affection for her actually helping her come into her own sense of self? Is my being known to her as a person compromising the integrity of our work or is it actually potentiating it? Is it enough that I am aware that my affection for her also invokes the therapeutic function of being seen and felt by the other? "How else does it happen?" I am asking myself. How does someone with this degree of insecurity in her attachment history develop the capacity for true intimacy unless she has the experience of actually being held by the other in order to come more fully into herself as a person?

After much contemplation and consultation with colleagues, I decided that as long as Melina is able to continue to develop as an adult in her world that my role and function in her life was beneficial to her. What continued to be a question for me was when was the shift going to take place from me as the person whom she depends on and trusts to herself? Was she happy just being taken care of, or is it going to take more time because the neglect was so pervasive in her earliest years that, even with EMDR, it was the nature of the territory we were in? I decided to explore this with her directly, speaking to the importance of navigating her own direction, using her own felt sense of what was right for her versus using my support and validation as her source of guidance. I also shared with her that I was concerned about her making choices for herself that she thought I would want her to make, either because that's how she's always done it with her mother or because she wanted to mimic some of the choices I have made in my own life. This conversation opened up another level of work that she was willing to explore: her looking to others to tell her what to do (looking for a mother), despite her own intuitions about what was right for her. What she was aware of was that she sought the advice of others because she didn't trust herself to make good choices on her own behalf. She has a long history of enlisting a number of authority figures in her life to guide her in her decisions, from professional mentors to fortune tellers and psychics "predicting" what would happen in her life and what she should do about it. The other aspect of this issue, which was out of her awareness until we explored it together, was the satisfaction of actually being taken care of by these authority figures. I was glad when this dynamic became explicit, as her unmet childhood dependency needs were on the table for both of us to hold and to work with. While I, too, enjoy caring for her, it was out in the open that, while the need to be taken care of is a legitimate need of hers, getting it met by a person who is an equal to her is more satisfying and more appropriate to her stage in life and to her therapeutic goals. I also took the opportunity at this juncture in our work together to share with her how I have made some bad decisions for myself, and how those choices have helped me learn more about myself and others, encouraging her to do the same. It was at this point that the relationship dynamic shifted again; this time from mother-daughter to two adult Greek-American women; one is the therapist and the other is the client.

Despite her continued struggle to hold onto her sense of self as "good enough" and her lifelong challenge of making her own choices, Melina finally broke up with her boyfriend once and for all 9 months into therapy. Although she was sad, she wasn't devastated. She had developed sufficient ego strength in the months of our work together to tolerate her feelings without shutting down or acting on them inappropriately. I was elated! I saw this as an existential decision for her, that for the first time in her adult life, she was choosing herself over everyone else.

Developmental plateaus

The next therapeutic challenge in Melina's life was going to be about continuing to make better choices, particularly in relationship to choosing a potential life partner. Saying "no" became a joke between us as it became a necessity for Melina to learn how to turn down the multitudes of men that were pursuing her. The global challenge, however, was to learn how to embody her sense of self as a vibrant and vital being and to actively navigate her direction in life. Our EMDR work during this period focused on working through her passivity in relationships, which brought us to another developmental plateau. In EMDR, this plateau is about working with one's sense of "control of choices," because the reaction in the present is as if there is no choice in the matter and other people or circumstances make the decision for you. As an example in Melina's case, she would go out on a date with a guy she's not interested in to avoid telling him she's not interested. The developmental challenge, then, is for her to develop a more internalized locus of control so that she has a greater sense of agency about herself as an adult and can assert her needs and preferences in any given situation. Her ex-boyfriend provided Melina with a great opportunity to assert herself as she had to say "no" to his repeated attempts to get back together, which had been an ongoing pattern throughout the course of their relationship. This time she was able to struggle with her feelings of guilt and responsibility, rather than act on those feelings and collapse back into the relationship at her own expense.

After a whirlwind tour of the dating scene, Melina starts going out exclusively with a man that she has been friends with for many years, but up until now had no romantic interest in. As they spent more time together, Melina is remembering what it felt like to be "adored," in the same way she was adored by her grandfather. She is experiencing for the first time in her adult life being loved and cared for by a man who wants to be with her because he likes her. He enjoys cooking for her, takes care of her dogs, helps her around her house, and plans weekend getaways. They have always liked each other and there is clearly a friendship at the foundation of this growing partnership. As the relationship is moving beyond the honeymoon phase, however, Melina is challenged to speak up for herself when she needs something from him that she experiences in herself as a demand, such as asking him to clean up after himself at her house. This time, she is clear that she is entitled to ask for what she wants; her avoidance behavior is informed more by her fear that he will punish her or abandon her for making such demands. Fortunately, he has not responded to her in this way, so we know that her current situation is triggering earlier fears of abandonment. Our EMDR sessions at this juncture in the therapy focused on her fears that were based on the earlier experiences with her previous spouses, as well as her mother. From an EMDR perspective, this developmental plateau is a "safety" issue; that is, she doesn't feel safe enough to ask for what she wants because it wasn't safe in the past. The fear is that she will be cut out of the herd—an annihilation anxiety, in the same way she was actually left alone as a child and was afraid she wouldn't survive. In addition, she had subsequent experiences as an adult being left both emotionally and physically in both of her marriages, as well as the emotional abandonment by both her parents.

At the time of this writing, Melina continues to work on developing her sense of self as a worthwhile person and is continuing to learn how to negotiate her relationships with family, friends, coworkers, and, of course, her current partner. Although the future of this relationship is uncertain, what is clear is that it's the best relationship she's ever had, and the best choice for herself she's ever made. She's experiencing joy and pleasure in his company, and she likes who she is when she is with him. She is no longer on antidepressants, which she had been taking for almost 20 years, and is experiencing a broader range of affect due to the reprocessing effects of EMDR as well as being off the medication. Although on occasion she will complain that it's harder now that she experiences her feelings more fully, she is happy to have the capacity to experience her self and her life on its own terms.

Mutual growth in relationship

As for our relationship, we continue to meet on a regular basis, as her continued personal development is an important part of her life. While she continues to struggle to hold onto her sense of self as a person of value, she is functioning as an adult more now than ever. She is more self-aware (versus being aware of others and not herself), and has come to know herself and appreciate who she is as a person, rather than accepting others' projections of her as her definition of self. As she has differentiated more into who she is now in her life, she has also differentiated from me. She rarely sends me e-mails anymore, and when she does, her request is that I review a particular transaction in advance of our session together. Our schedule has shifted from a once-weekly appointment to sessions every other week, another indication that she has developed more autonomy in the context of our relationship. In our sessions, I am much less active about the focus or direction of our time together, and I encourage her to decide what is most important to her. Our sessions now are more about consolidating the gains she has already made and to facilitate a stronger identification with a self as an integrated whole. For Melina, being a whole person is about holding onto her sense of self as a lovable person in the context of being in relationship without sacrificing herself or her connection to the other person.

As for me, Melina has been a gift, as I have learned so much from working with her. The existential struggle that my relationship with her presented for me was nothing I would have asked for, but am grateful for the opportunity that it has afforded me. I recognized early on that Melina wanted and needed a mother; I also knew that I could be that mother for her. What I learned about was the difference in being a mother to someone versus invoking the "mother function" that is inherent in the nature of our existence. When I, as her therapist, carried out the function of mothering her into real time, place, and person, it brought forth the possibility of my own limitations and liabilities that come out of my own experiences of mothering. I was acutely aware of the danger of acting out of my own story, my own internalizations, and the potential harm it could do to her. At the same time, however, I was also in a position to share with her the strengths that come out of my own mothering experiences: providing a solid holding environment and validating her right to exist in the world as a lovable person. She also needed a role model that she could identify with so that she could define for herself what it means to be a woman of Greek descent who is also part of a Greek-American family and community. As I reflect on the transparency of my role, it was there from the beginning as a function of the larger social context of being part of the same community. It would have been artificial not to acknowledge it; it made more sense to use it as a resource for the work as the opportunity presented itself. I was also aware that I was responding to her need for me to be a real person. Given her long history of bad choices, betrayals, and losses of attachment, it was important for her to experience my devotion to her as something that was about her, not about me or my function as a therapist.

Final reflections

The benefits to me in this process are both measurable and immeasurable. I continue to reflect on my learnings, both about myself as well as the process of psychotherapy and the intersubjectivity of the relationship between therapist and client. Helping Melina define herself as a Greek woman has helped me more fully embrace my own identity as a Greek woman. It has been a rapprochement of sorts for me as a first-born, first-generation Greek who has found other communities to be a part of. In assuming the function of mother to Melina for that time period, it became an opportunity for me to deepen my awareness and my understanding of my own experiences with mothering, and as a result, I was able to transform those experiences for myself and move beyond those internalizations. I now have a deeper appreciation of those experiences, especially what was positive about them, allowing me to take more complete ownership of the archetypical mother in me.

As a psychotherapist, my experience with Melina has challenged my thinking about transference and countertransference as a regressive phenomenon where the client or therapist are feeling and acting out of their own internalizations. Although this phenomenon is clearly an occupational hazard not to be ignored or minimized, I learned to appreciate that what is happening between the therapist and the client is a coemergent process; that is, it is configured organically through the attunement between both parties (Bauer, 2008). To the extent that the psychotherapist is able to hold in awareness what is happening in the moment determines to what extent the therapist can meet the client in their experience. While we all strive to maintain a professional posture of neutrality as therapists, it seems that even the very notion of that stance is an objective that is questionable, if not unrealistic. Perhaps the best we can strive for is that we, as psychotherapists, bring a level of awareness about our own selves into the therapeutic dance. I learned that the integrity of the work we do is not only about our good intentions and keeping our skills up to date; it's about our capacity to be present and provide a holding environment where possibilities for healing can emerge. The self of the therapist is a necessary part of that healing equation.

References

Bauer, R. (2008). Personal communication.

Cvetek, R. (2008). EMDR treatment of distressful experiences that fail to meet the criteria for PTSD. *Journal of EMDR Practice and Research, 2*(1), 2–14.

Shapiro, F. (1995). *Eye-movement desensitization and reprocessing.* New York: The Guilford Press.

Shapiro, F. (2007). EMDR, adaptive information processing, and case conceptualization. *Journal of EMDR Practice and Research, 1*(2), 68–87.

chapter eleven

Learning to be authentic with clients

The untold journey of a relational practitioner

Elizabeth Sparks

Introduction

I am a middle-aged, African American psychologist who was trained during the 1980s as a psychodynamic psychotherapist at a traditional, APA-approved doctoral program in counseling psychology in the Northeast. I received both my predoctoral and postdoctoral training at a private psychiatric hospital in a wealthy New England suburban town. There I became very skilled at listening to my client's narratives, making few, if any, comments except when it was clinically appropriate to provide feedback or, better yet, interpretations that would facilitate my client gaining much-needed insight into her inner feelings and psychic conflicts. As a psychologist of color, I was acutely aware of multicultural issues, and often felt the need to adapt my traditional psychodynamic approach to meet the culture-specific needs of my clients of color. But my understanding of myself as a therapist, and the "appropriate" therapeutic role to maintain with my clients at all times, remained the same. As a psychodynamic therapist, self-disclosure was to generally be avoided unless it could be strategically used to facilitate the development of insight for my client. This was the only way to conduct psychotherapy, and for the first few years of clinical practice I never really questioned the legitimacy of the "blank slate" demeanor that was expected of a well-trained, clinically sophisticated psychotherapist.

Later in my clinical training, I was exposed to feminist theories in general, and to the Stone Center Relational Cultural Theory (RCT) in particular. As a result of these experiences, it was apparent that there were other ways for a therapist to be "present" with her clients. Concepts such as *authenticity*, *mutuality*, and the importance of therapists engaging with clients in such a way that the client can experience a *growth-fostering relationship* were introduced. I began to change my understanding of the "frame" that an effective therapist maintains with clients, and to begin a journey that would ever so gradually move me toward becoming a relational therapist.

This chapter is about that journey. My goal is to share with you the questions, thoughts, fears, anxieties, frustrations, and joys that I experienced as I moved from being a traditional, psychodynamic psychotherapist, to a relational therapist who is comfortable being "known" and "seen" by my clients. I will explore with you the terrain that was crossed to gain this comfort level, and the clinical expertise that I developed from sharing myself with clients in a way that I believe (and they often confirm) has been beneficial to their process of recovery and healing. This journey was taken without a road map or a guide. I talked with fellow travelers along the way, and received directions and guidance from many wise and gifted relational therapists. Mistakes were made, and at times I felt lost in the wilderness. But, these experiences were eventually overshadowed by the many times that I felt courageous and brave as I (and my clients) took steps that led us into caring, mutually empathic, and authentic relationships.

The first steps in the journey

I entered a doctoral program in counseling psychology after practicing for 5 years as a master's level mental health practitioner. As a young woman of 25 my first job was in a child welfare agency in an inner-city community where the residents were predominantly African American and Latino. It was in my first position at Aggasiz Children's Services* that I began to learn what it means to be "authentic" and real enough for my clients to feel comfortable talking with me. Most of the clientele were low-income African American women whose children were involved with either the Department of Social Services or the juvenile justice system. Engaging with my clients and working to establish a therapeutic alliance, I was reminded of all of the poor, African American women I had known throughout my life growing up in legal segregation in Kansas. I remembered the feelings of respect that I held for these women because of their hard work and valiant efforts to provide for their families. I tried to have this same feeling of respect for my clients, recognizing their strengths, as well as their challenges, as we departed on a journey toward healing.

* All names of facilities have been changed.

At that time, as a single young woman who was well educated, my clients openly questioned whether I would be able to truly understand their lives because of my educational and social privilege. Dealing with the cultural and socioeconomic differences that existed between us led to my initial encounters with the issues surrounding therapist self-disclosure. If my clients were going to be able to trust me enough to open up about their concerns and problems, I would need to somehow let them know that I could understand their experiences of racism, discrimination, and poverty. It is within this context that I realized the need to make the journey from being "unseen" and "unknown" by my clients to becoming a clinician who is real, authentic, and able to be personally affected by my clients' struggles. Some measure of self-disclosure and transparency would be essential in order to be a helpful and ultimately healing presence in their lives. This realization became clearer over the years while working at Aggasiz Children's Services. I often had to contend with my own doubts and fears as I gradually learned to manage the uncomfortable feelings of vulnerability that typically accompany this process.

Moving forward and making progress

For the next 4 years I worked with clients in a psychiatric hospital where the majority of psychologists embraced a psychodynamic theoretical perspective. I felt "at home" in this clinical environment, and the supervision and collegial support that I received during these years endorsed the perspective that therapist self-disclosure was not to be totally avoided but that it should be used with extreme care and sound clinical judgment so that the therapeutic alliance would not be "damaged" in any way. It was during this period, however, that I was first exposed to the writings of the Jean Baker Miller Training Institute and had the opportunity to work directly with Dr. Miller. The hospital where I did my predoctoral internship, and later worked as a staff psychologist for 3 years, was the site of one of the first women's units within a private psychiatric hospital. The unit was a collaborative effort between the JBMTI and the hospital, and Dr. Miller served as the consultant to the unit staff for a number of years following its implementation. On this unit as a predoctoral intern for one year, my knowledge about RCT increased and I became convinced that it was not necessary, or even desirable, to maintain a blank slate demeanor with clients. It was clinically more effective to develop a therapeutic relationship where the therapist is authentic and real with clients, which would further the therapeutic alliance and the effectiveness of the psychotherapy process. The clinical supervision process included a relational perspective and was helpful in my becoming more comfortable with therapist self-disclosure.

In an effort to learn more about therapist self-disclosure and how to handle it appropriately in psychotherapy, I turned to the clinical literature that was available at the time. The findings in the existing literature represented two very different perspectives. There was one group of studies that found that therapist self-disclosure was harmful to the therapeutic relationship and psychotherapy outcome (Basescu, 1990; Kaslow, Cooper, & Linsenberg, 1979; Mathews, 1989). These researchers were representative of those who viewed therapist self-disclosure through the lens of psychodynamic theory, and believed that such self-disclosures would dilute transference and interfere with the therapeutic process. Other researchers believed just the opposite—that therapist self-disclosure was beneficial and enhanced the therapeutic relationship because it equated therapist realness with a more open, honest, genuine, and personally involved stance toward the client and the therapy process (Knox, Hess, Petersen, & Hill, 1997; Knox & Hill, 2003; Watkins, 1990). My previous training had not acquainted me with this later group of studies. The studies conducted by researchers who were more supportive of therapist self-disclosure typically found that therapist self-disclosure was perceived by clients to be helpful and it had a positive effect on the development of a genuine and authentic therapeutic relationship (Knox et al., 1997). They also found that therapist self-disclosures seemed to contribute to a more balanced distribution of power in the therapeutic relationship, suggesting that clients come to view their therapists as more human (Knox et al., 1997; Chelune, 1979; Kaslow et al., 1979; Lander & Nahon, 1992; and Robitschek & McCarthy, 1991). This research was encouraging, and I started to explore, albeit tentatively at first, becoming more "real" in my relationships with clients.

Basic tenets of relational cultural theory

At this point it is important to review the basic tenets of Relational Cultural Theory (RCT). The theory was built on the early work of Dr. Jean Baker Miller (Miller, 1976) and proposes that women's psychological development differs in fundamental ways from the traditional model of development derived from men's experiences (Covington & Surrey, 2000). Miller (1976) suggested that for women the primary motivation throughout life is the need to establish a basic sense of connection to others. The theory posits that women feel a sense of self and self-worth that arises out of their connections to others, which leads them into increasing the number of significant connections in their lives. RCT describes the attributes and qualities of relationships that foster growth and healthy development. Psychological well-being is the result of healthy connections with other human beings that are mutual, creative, energy releasing, and empowering for all participants. Psychological problems (or pathologies) arise as a result of disconnections or violations within relationships at personal/familial levels as well as at the sociocultural level (Covington & Surrey, 2000). It is beyond the scope of this chapter to provide a full, detailed description of the theory. But to help the reader understand the theoretical perspective that I used with my clients, I will address three of the basic tenets of RCT: *mutuality, authenticity,* and *mutual empowerment.* These factors are thought to be critical to the development of an optimal therapeutic relationship and to be the framework surrounding an effective psychotherapy process.

The tenet of *mutuality* refers to the interaction between two individuals where each is both affecting and being affected by the other. Quoting from Judith Jordan's paper entitled *The Meaning of Mutuality*, a mutual exchange occurs when there is "openness to influence, emotional availability, and a constantly changing pattern of responding to and affecting the other's state" (Jordan, 1986, p. 2). A mutual relationship allows one to feel heard, seen, understood, and known. Both parties are equally invested in developing a level of intimacy and trust within the relationship, where each can be known fully. Within a therapeutic relationship, mutuality does not mean that therapists must constantly self-disclose. It does mean that therapists are actively present and engaged with clients during sessions. It also means that therapists strive to be authentic in their interactions with clients, and to convey respect and caring. The relational therapist is focused on establishing this type of a therapeutic bond with his/her client from the very beginning of therapy, and pays careful attention to the relationship as she and her client move through the therapy process.

The RCT tenet of *authenticity* is defined as an individual representing his or her true experience within the relationship and responding authentically to the thoughts and feelings of the other. This is a key element in developing and maintaining an optimal therapeutic relationship, and RCT therapists strive to be authentic in their interactions with clients at all times. The accurate assessment and communication of feelings and reactions are key to developing a relationship where trust and intimacy develop and flourish. Therapists are also expected to reach an agreement with clients on the goals and methods of therapy in order to develop a strong therapeutic alliance. In this process there are many opportunities for sharing ideas and perspectives, and for negotiating differences—all of which contribute to the development of intimacy and trust within the relationship.

Researchers have found that clients' outcome expectancy is related to therapeutic alliance, such that when there is congruence between client outcome expectancy and therapeutic goals and methods, there is a more positive therapeutic alliance that develops. This in turn contributes to a more positive therapy outcome (Joyce et al., 2003). In order for this agreement to develop, there needs to be open and honest communication (which is another way of describing authenticity) between the therapist and the client. RCT therapists are communicating authentically with clients to bring about mutual understanding and a shared commitment to treatment goals and methods in order to maximize the possibility that there will be a positive treatment outcome.

The RCT tenet of *mutual empowerment* contains five components: zest (feeling a real sense of connection); action (immediate relational interplay); knowledge (an enlarged and accurate picture of self and other); worth (feeling worthy of another's recognition and attention); and a desire for more connection (Miller, 1986). As therapists and clients work toward establishing mutually agreed-upon goals, clients are encouraged to set the pace and the direction of therapy. This leads to them feeling a sense of empowerment within the therapeutic relationship, which will hopefully be generalized to the external world. As the alliance deepens over time, clients increase their commitment to the treatment process, and expect a positive outcome at the end of therapy. Thus, it seems reasonable that clients who are involved in the development of such therapeutic relationships would feel a sense of zest, knowledge, and worth, and would desire to have these relationships continue to deepen.

As can be seen from the description of the basic tenets of RCT, therapist self-disclosure is a component of the relationship-building process. These self-disclosures are most often in the form of a therapist's demographics and practice orientation, but they also can be used to provide feedback to clients when narratives evoke reactions and feelings within the therapist. The goal of this self-disclosure is to facilitate clients' self-understanding and to further clarify the therapeutic process.

The second phase of the journey: What it means to be "seen"

I left the women's unit after my internship year, and became a staff psychologist at the same hospital on the locked unit that housed both male and female clients. Most, if not all, of the clients on the unit were acutely psychotic, or had long-standing mental disorders that severely limited their ability to function in the world. In this setting, diagnoses were determined using a medical-model perspective, and finding the appropriate medication to stabilize the patient (as they were now called) and/or identifying community-based supports that might help to prevent a relapse became the highly desirable goals of effective treatment. Knowing that RCT had a lot to offer, it remained difficult to figure out how these relational skills and techniques could be applied to my work with patients on the locked unit. The following case vignette illustrates how I gradually became more committed to working from the perspective of RCT even with my most psychologically challenged patients.

Case vignette #1

James* was a 28-year-old young white male who was diagnosed with chronic schizophrenia and had been in and out of psychiatric facilities (including hospitals, group homes, and day treatment programs) for most of his adult life. When I first met James, he was a very friendly and affable young man who had been hospitalized after becoming highly agitated and somewhat regressed while living in a community group home. He reported to me that the reason it had become difficult for him to manage in the group home was because of his sadness and frustration over his "relationship" with one of the milieu workers there. According to James, the director of the group home interfered with the relationship and made it impossible for him to make plans for the future.

The information that had been sent to the hospital indicated that James was delusional—that there was no relationship since the young woman in question did not return his affection and only behaved in a friendly, professional manner with him. The group home had made every effort to help James realize that this was a psychotic experience; however, to no avail. All of these efforts were unsuccessful, and he had been sent to the hospital so that we could help him face the situation from a more realistic perspective.

As I worked to develop a therapeutic relationship with James, I kept asking myself, "How can I be authentic and mutual with a young man who has developed a delusional system that is affecting his perceptions of relationships?" Despite my reservations, it was clear to me that James was in dire need of a therapeutic relationship where he could feel that the therapist cared about him and his experiences. So I set out to develop just such a relationship with him. James and I met for coffee in my office three times a week. This was the way that he characterized our sessions. It became a time for him to share his thoughts and feelings about life and his illness, and the toll that it had taken on his life.

As I worked with James over the next couple of months, I realized that there was no way to dislodge his delusion. The treatment team decided that the most supportive and therapeutic intervention we could do was to transfer him to a longer-term facility where he could continue to work toward returning to a new community-based setting in a different location. James and I continued to meet on a regular basis to discuss

---

* James is a fictitious name for a composite representation for a number of chronically ill patients that I worked with on the locked unit.

plans for his life and for the next step in his journey toward stabilization and community-based living. We had a strong and positive therapeutic relationship and we both worked hard to prepare him for the transfer to a longer-term facility. On the day before James was to be transferred to a state facility, he left the grounds without permission and was listed as AWOL by the hospital. A group of staff getting lunch in the local town center saw him in a flower store, and when they inquired, he told them that he had left the hospital grounds without permission to purchase a goodbye gift. The staff remained with James while he purchased a plant, and they escorted him back to the hospital where he was put on a security watch for the remainder of the evening.

When I arrived on the unit the next morning to pick up James for our final session, the nursing staff informed me about the previous evening's incident and showed me the plant that he had purchased. To my surprise, the card attached to the plant had my name on it. James had written a note to thank me for helping him during his hospitalization. In our session that afternoon, I talked with James as openly and authentically as I could about his decision to leave the hospital without permission to purchase a plant for me. I shared both my positive feelings at receiving the gift, as well as my concern about his decision and behavior. I don't think that I will ever forget James's response to me. He said, "Well, Liz, you have to admit that this is a better way for me to say goodbye to someone that I care about than the way I did it the last time. That time, I lay on the railroad tracks and tried to kill myself. This time, I bought you a plant!" I smiled and openly admitted that he was correct—purchasing a plant for me was a much better way to say goodbye.

This experience with James has stayed with me for more than 20 years. He taught me so much about the importance of authenticity, mutuality, and growth-fostering relationships for clients, regardless of their diagnosis or ability to function in the outside world. As I continued to work with clients and to learn about relational psychotherapy, I became more and more committed to the principles of RCT and the importance of developing a growth-fostering relationship with each and every client. At that point in my clinical practice, my intellectual and emotional commitment to RCT was clear, but it still took me a few more years to thoroughly understand the challenge that is inherent in this way of working with clients. Intellectually I knew that being mutual and authentic with clients would involve self-awareness and the management of my own feelings of vulnerability. What I wasn't prepared for was how uncomfortable at times this would feel, or the confusion that I sometimes experienced as I tried to chart my way through a relationship process that I had little formal training or preparation to navigate.

The next case will illustrate my journey through uncharted relational territory as I moved with clients toward establishing and maintaining authentic and mutual therapeutic relationships.

Case vignette #2

Sarah was a 40-year-old white woman who was admitted to the hospital following a nonlethal suicide gesture. She had a history of severe sexual abuse during her childhood, and had been the victim of rape as an adult. At this time in my clinical practice, I treated a number of women who had been physically, emotionally, and sexually abused as children. For many of these women, it was critical that their therapist be able to join with them in their pain and "feel" with and for them. In working with Sarah, I learned to openly express my reactions of distress and profound sadness as she shared with me the episodes of ritualistic sexual abuse that she had suffered from the time she was 5 years old until she finally left home at age 17. I learned not to be ashamed of the tear that fell unbidden from my eye when she talked of her confusion and sense of betrayal when remembering incidents where her beloved older brother had repeatedly told her of his love and devotion while sexually molesting her. At times during the sessions, the pain and sadness was palpable and I learned to be comfortable sharing with Sarah how hard it was for me (and I would venture to say for her as well) to breathe.

One incident in particular helped me to gain a level of comfort at being "seen" by my clients. My father died during my second year at the hospital, and because I had to leave unexpectedly, the director of psychology shared with my clients (with my permission) that I had experienced a family loss. Upon resuming work with my clients I had to share my grief to some degree as I responded to their condolences and inquiries. Sarah was one of my patients during this period, and in sessions the depth of my loss and my coping with this loss was acknowledged. Sarah was as concerned about my well-being as I had always been about hers. Sharing the coping strategies I used to deal with loss and sadness seemed to deepen our connection and she began to believe that she too might be able to learn how to cope with dysphoric affect without becoming overwhelmed with feelings.

This experience with Sarah contributed to my growing awareness of the meaning of *authenticity, mutuality,* and *mutual empowerment* within a therapeutic relationship. It was becoming easier for me to be comfortable with the level of vulnerability inherent in self-disclosure and mutuality. I could see the benefit of working from a relational perspective on the quality of the therapeutic relationship that was developed with clients, as well as the positive outcomes that they experienced from our work together. I knew at this point that I could never go back to being the "blank slate" type of therapist, and was even more determined to practice from a relational perspective in my work with *all* of my present and future clients.

Understanding the role of culture

I left the psychiatric hospital to become the clinical director of a mental health department in a community health center. At the Warren Center, my clients were primarily African American and Caribbean families and children who were on welfare, and many were survivors of long-term abusive relationships. They were often embattled with the Department of Social Services (DSS) over custody of their children, and many were involuntary clients that made issues of trust paramount in the establishment of a therapeutic relationship. This work also took place within a cultural context that required that a therapist had to be both "known" and "accepted" by clients in order to be effective.

The clinical literature on treatment issues with clients of color suggests that there are complex dynamics involved in the establishment and maintenance of a productive therapeutic relationship (Jackson, 1983; Boyd-Franklin, 1989; Cauce et al., 2002; Ridley, 1984; Sue & Sue, 2003; Terrell & Terrell, 1984; Thompson, Worthington, & Atkinson, 1994). One of the key issues involved in developing a therapeutic alliance is trust. The attainment of trust is often complicated with clients who have experienced racism and discrimination, and are therefore uncomfortable with authority figures who are representative of the majority culture, or who are agents of institutional systems. In order for therapists to establish a sense of trust with clients of color, it is necessary to communicate an understanding of the clients' cultural experiences, particularly those related to racism. According to Jackson (1983) interactions in therapy with African American clients are influenced along the dimension of trust, where cultural knowledge and evidence of the therapist's loyalty may be tested. It is also likely that the client will be more comfortable with the therapist taking a less authoritarian stance within the relationship.

Burkard, Knox, Groen, Perez, and Hess (2006) reviewed the literature on therapist self-disclosure in cross-cultural counseling and identified three themes that are useful in the establishment and maintenance of a productive therapeutic relationship with clients of color. The first theme involves the concept of *cultural mistrust*, where the experiences of racism and discrimination that clients of color have experienced in their interactions with institutional systems make them distrustful of contact with whites and other representatives of these systems. The authors suggest that therapist self-disclosure can be critical to demonstrate to the client that the therapist is culturally sensitive, and can acknowledge the validity of the discrimination and racism that the client has experienced in his/her life (Helms & Cook, 1999; Sue & Sue, 2003). The second theme focuses on the *importance of therapists being seen by clients of color as sensitive to and skillful in working with cultural and racial issues in therapy*. Research suggests that when a client of color encounters a therapist who does not appear to be comfortable or responsive to discussions of racial issues, they tend to withdraw from these interactions (Thompson et al., 1994). In these situations, self-disclosures may be an important way for therapists to demonstrate an understanding of the clients' frustration with oppression and racism (Constantine & Kwan, 2003).

The third theme is related to the way in which therapist self-disclosures can be helpful for clients of color as *modeling the role that disclosures play within the psychotherapy process* (Berg & Wright-Buckley, 1988; Wetzel & Wright-Buckley, 1988). It seems to help clients of color feel more comfortable disclosing when the therapist is willing to be vulnerable and to disclose personal information in the session as well. In their empirical study on the effect of therapist self-disclosure in therapy with African American clients, Berg and Wright-Buckley (1988) found that high-self-disclosing African American therapists elicited more self-disclosure from African American participants than did low-self-disclosing African American therapists or high- or low-self-disclosing white therapists. This finding is consistent with my experiences working with clients of color at the Warren Center and in my private practice.

As I began to engage with clients, it was critical to find a way to establish and maintain a level of trust within the therapeutic relationship that would facilitate our work together. Many times, this was a challenging endeavor. Although we often shared the same racial identity and cultural background, there were obvious class and hierarchical differences that were barriers to establishing a positive therapeutic alliance. My clients often questioned me to determine if I had sufficient knowledge and sensitivity about their life circumstances to be trustworthy. They would ask me such personal questions as my marital status, whether I had children, where I had grown up, and if I lived in the neighborhood. They knew that I was an African American psychologist working at the Warren Center, but they needed to know more to determine if I was the type of person who could understand their feelings and life experiences. They were searching for a way to connect, and therefore to trust me. They suspected that I might be like other professional black women they encountered in the institutional systems that intersected their lives who blamed them for their misfortunes.

It was critical to disclose various facts about my life in response to their inquiries. I often shared my familiarity with the struggles and challenges faced by families living in poverty, both from my personal and prior professional experiences. I also talked about the class differences that existed between my clients and myself, and how I would be careful to try to recognize both the similarities and differences in our experiences so that we could process any misunderstandings that might arise in our work together. From my perspective, these self-disclosures were helpful as the client and I worked toward developing a deeper, more trusting and authentic relationship.

Through the years it seems that clients have needed to ask me fewer personal questions. What I have found, however, is that I now more often engage in self-disclosure that shares my values and perspectives on the issues that are raised in sessions. This self-disclosure seems to be important to not only my clients of color, but also to white clients. This form of self-disclosure becomes a matter of informed consent, in the sense that having this information about me will help clients determine whether or not I am suited to be of help to them. Feminist theorists and practitioners argue that clients should have information about therapists that will help them to make an informed decision about working with a particular therapist (Brown & Walker, 1990; Mahalik, Van Ormer, & Simi, 2000). There is also an expectation that feminist therapists will serve as role models for clients; therefore, knowing about the therapists' values, biases, and class background can help clients determine if a particular therapist is a suitable role model (Brown & Walker, 1990).

Currently, I tend to engage in self-disclosures that are consistent with the literature on the typical content of therapist self-disclosure (Bridges, 2001; Hill et al., 1989; Peterson, 2002; Wells, 1994). I more often use self-disclosures to share my reactions and thoughts about a client's behavior or response to a situation that is being discussed in the session. I also tend to use self-disclosures to share my observations when a client is unable to accept her own affect or to understand why others react to her in a particular way that causes distress and/or confusion. My intentions for using self-disclosures in these situations are to help the client connect to her feelings and gain more insight into the nature of her relational style. Self-disclosure is also used when attempting to repair an empathic failure that has occurred during a session and as a way of making conscious affective and relational patterns that are out of the client's awareness. Over time, I have learned to be more comfortable with these types of self-disclosures in therapy, and clients have reported that they find this type of communication helpful.

Encountering new challenges

Whether or not to disclose my religious and spiritual beliefs is currently a new area of challenge for me. During the last 7 years or so, I have provided pro bono psychotherapy for members of the congregation through my church's counseling team. I am now receiving referrals from non–church members who are looking for a Christian counselor, but I find myself less comfortable disclosing my religious orientation to these new clients. A case that served to heighten my awareness of this issue was my work with Samantha.

Case vignette #3

Samantha was a 27-year-old African American young woman who was single at the time that we began therapy. She later married and had a child before we terminated due to her relocating out of state. Samantha was a graduate student who was struggling with feelings of depression and suicidal ideation. She had a history of severe and chronic neglect, physi-cal, and sexual abuse. Her mother was the perpetrator of the neglect and the physical abuse, and her uncle and a male acquaintance of the fam-ily perpetrated the sexual abuse. The therapy with Samantha was a long and complex process. In the initial phase of treatment, Samantha used a number of different strategies of disconnection in order to keep me at an emotional distance. I worked hard to establish the type of therapeutic relationship where there was mutuality, authenticity, and mutual empow-erment. This required that I was highly responsive to Samantha, which at times meant disclosing my feelings and reactions to her narrative so that she would experience being "heard" and "understood" by me. I encour-aged her to let me know if she felt rejected, abandoned, or misunderstood so that we could address her feelings and perceptions in the moment.

Within the first 2 years of our relationship, Samantha and I managed to establish a solid therapeutic alliance where she felt heard, accepted, respected, and cared for. She occasionally wrote notes to me, and the fol-lowing passage was taken from one of her notes and illustrates the way she felt about our work together:

> I want you to know how much I appreciate the sup-port you have given me over the last couple of years. The extra time you have spent with me will not be forgotten or the many times you have spoken with me on the phone. I know I have been difficult at times. I thank you for not giving up on me.

Given her history of neglect and abuse, it was critical that I verbally acknowledge the way that her narratives affected me. It was important that Samantha receive authentic and accurate feedback from me, since she often believed and expected negative and punitive reactions from others. When disconnections occurred during sessions, I tried to directly address the interaction that was occurring between us in an effort to find a way to reconnect. Although Samantha often asked personal questions about my life, and frequently challenged me to tell her how I was reacting to her difficulties in communicating with me, the aspect of the therapy process that I found most challenging involved her requests for my beliefs, opinions, and experiences surrounding religion. For Samantha one of her enduring strengths and sources of support had been her relationship with God and her church. She had strong spiritual and religious beliefs, and attended church services regularly. Samantha often relied on her church family for the support and assistance that she had never received from her biological family. Yet, she continued to have difficulty feeling worthy of others' help and support, and often would not ask members of her church community for assistance with her emotional and psychological difficulties. Samantha had a strong desire to get better and to find a way to overcome her past. At times she felt that God had led her to work with me, and was sustaining her during times when she longed to run away from the relationship and leave therapy. At other times, she was angry with God for not rescuing her from the abuse and neglect of her childhood, and she wondered whether she was being punished for some unknown sin.

We spent many hours in therapy discussing Samantha's definition of spiritual well-being, and what her relationship with God had taught her about love, forgiveness, and caring. Initially, it was very uncomfortable to authentically respond to Samantha's direct questions about my spiritual beliefs. Gradually, however, I became more comfortable with disclosing my own spiritual beliefs and sharing some of my personal spiritual experiences with her. These self-disclosures seemed to give Samantha "permission" to share her spiritual struggles and challenges with me, and we worked through many of these during her therapy. We used Biblical stories and scriptures at times in our discussions, and Samantha was encouraged to more actively use her church network as a support during times of intense stress or depressive symptoms. Over time, Samantha seemed to embrace more of the positive, loving aspects of her relationship with God, and to gain a sense of hopefulness about her life and future.

Working with Samantha taught me a great deal about integrating spirituality and religion into the psychotherapy process, and about managing my feelings of vulnerability that arise when I engage in self-disclosures about this very private aspect of my life. Although working with Samantha did help me become more comfortable with this type of self-disclosure, I still have questions about integrating religion/spirituality into the psychotherapy process, and plan to continue to explore this issue through continued study and clinical supervision.

Concluding thoughts

I have traveled a long and winding road to become a relational therapist. The path has not always been clear or direct, but I have learned a great deal along the way. The most was gained from the challenges and detours that I encountered and from the interactions with, and feedback from, my clients. Some roads traveled were familiar, while others were uncharted territory. I started this journey as a traditionally trained psychologist who conducted therapy from a psychodynamic perspective. Therapist self-disclosure was something that was seldom done, and if it did occur in a session, you spent a significant amount of time in supervision to make sure that your intentions were clinically sound and that nothing you said could interfere with the transference. My journey ended as a feminist therapist who works from a relational perspective and who has learned to be comfortable with being "seen" and authentically experienced by clients.

Self-disclosures are appropriate and can be critically important in the development of a mutual and authentic relationship with a client. I am comfortable with certain types of therapist self-disclosures, and plan to continue to journey toward gaining a better understanding of how to integrate religion/spirituality into psychotherapy for those clients where it seems to be beneficial. I have also learned the importance of being flexible as a relational therapist, and take my "cues" from the client in terms of depth of the connection that he/she desires (or can tolerate). I have learned to be comfortable with being a "blank slate" if maintaining a good therapeutic relationship with the client requires this approach. I am just as comfortable NOT disclosing my beliefs and values, especially when a client has expressed no interest in knowing this information about me. During the course of any given day, I often have these two types of sessions back-to-back, without any change in my being "authentic" or "mutual" with my client. RCT has been the guiding light throughout my journey, and I am certain that it will continue to serve as my navigator as I move through the next uncharted territory that has arisen in my clinical practice.

References

Basescu, S. (1990). Tools of the trade: The use of self in psychotherapy. *Group, 14*, 157–165.

Berg, J. H., & Wright-Buckley, C. (1988). Effects of racial similarity and interviewer intimacy in a peer counseling analogue. *Journal of Counseling Psychology, 35*, 377–384.

Boyd-Franklin, N. (1989). *Black families in therapy: A multi-systems approach*. New York: Guilford Press.

Brown, L. S., & Walker, L. E. (1990). Feminist therapy perspectives on self-disclosure. In G. Stricker & M. Fisher (Eds.), *Self-disclosure in the therapeutic relationship* (pp. 135–156). New York: Plenum.

Bridges, N. A. (2001). Therapist's self-disclosure: Expanding the comfort zone. *Psychotherapy: Theory, Research, Practice, and Training, 38*(1), 21–30.

Burkard, A. W., Knox, S., Groen, M., Perez, M., & Hess, S. A. (2006). European American therapist self-disclosure in cross-cultural counseling. *Journal of Counseling Psychology, 53*(1), 15–25.

Cauce, A. M., Domenech-Rodriguez, M., Paradise, M., Cochran, B. N., Shea, J. M., Srebnik, D., et al. (2002). Cultural and contextual influences in mental health help seeking: A focus on ethnic minority youth. *Journal of Consulting and Clinical Psychology, 70*, 44–55.

Chelune, G. J. (1979). *Self-disclosure: Origins, patterns, and implications of openness in interpersonal relationships.* San Francisco: Jossey-Bass.

Constantine, M. G., & Kwan, K. K. (2003). Cross-cultural considerations of therapist self-disclosure. *Journal of Clinical Psychology, 59*, 581–588.

Covington, S. S., & Surrey, J. L. (2000). The relational model of women's psychological development: Implications for substance abuse. *Work in Progress, No. 91.* Wellesley, MA: Stone Center, Working Paper Series.

Edwards, C. E., & Murdock, N. L. (1994). Characteristics of therapist self-disclosure in the counseling process. *Journal of Counseling and Development, 72*, 384–389.

Epstein, R. S. (1994). *Keeping boundaries: Maintaining safety and integrity in the psychotherapeutic process.* Washington, DC: American Psychiatric Press.

Helms, J. E., & Cook, D. (1999). *Using race and culture in counseling and psychotherapy: Theory and process.* Boston: Allyn & Bacon.

Hill, C., & Knox, S. (2001). Self-disclosure. *Psychotherapy: Theory, Research, Practice, and Training, 38*(4), 413–417.

Hill, C. E., Mahalik, J. R., & Thompson, B. J. (1989). Therapist self-disclosure. *Psychotherapy: Theory, Research, and Practice, 26*(3), 290–295.

Jackson, A. M. (1983). Treatment issues for Black patients. *Psychotherapy: Theory, Research, Practice, and Training, 20*(2), 143–151.

Jordan, J. (1986). The meaning of mutuality. *Work in Progress, No. 23.* Wellesley, MA: Stone Center Working Paper Series.

Joyce, A. S., Ogrodniczuk, J. S., Piper, W. E., & McCallum, M. (2003). The alliance as mediator of expectancy effects in short-term individual therapy. *Journal of Consulting and Clinical Psychology, 71*(4), 672–679.

Kaslow, F., Cooper, B., & Linsenberg, M. (1979). Family therapist authenticity as a key factor in outcome. *International Journal of Family Therapy, 1*, 184–199.

Knox, S., Hess, S. A., Petersen, D. A., & Hill, C. E. (1997). A qualitative analysis of client perceptions of the effects of helpful therapist self-disclosure in long-term therapy. *Journal of Counseling Psychology, 44*(3), 274–283.

Knox, S., & Hill, C. E. (2003). Therapist self-disclosure: Research-based suggestions for practitioners. *Journal of Clinical Psychology, 59*, 529–539.

Lander, N. R., & Nahon, D. (1992). Betrayed within the therapeutic relationship: An integrity therapy perspective. *Psychotherapy Patient, 8*, 113–125.

Mahalik, J. R., Van Ormer, E. A., & Simi, N. L. (2000). Ethical issues in using self-disclosure in feminist therapy. In M. M. Brabeck (Ed.), *Practicing feminist ethics in psychology* (pp. 189–201). Washington, DC: American Psychological Association.

Mathews, B. (1989). The use of therapist self-disclosure and its potential impact on the therapeutic process. *Journal of Human Behavior and Learning, 6,* 25–29.

McCarthy, P. R., & Betz, N. E. (1978). Differential effects of self-disclosing versus self-involving counselor statements. *Journal of Counseling Psychology, 25,* 251–256.

Miller, J. B. (1976). *Toward a new psychology of women.* Boston: Beacon Press.

Miller, J. B. (1986). What do we mean by relationships? *Work in Progress, No. 22.* Wellesley, MA: Stone Center, Working Paper Series.

Peterson, Z. D. (2002). More than a mirror: The ethics of therapist self-disclosure. *Psychotherapy: Theory, Research, Practice, and Training, 39*(1), 21–31.

Ridley, C. R. (1984). Clinical treatment of the non-disclosing black client: A therapeutic paradox. *American Psychologist, 39,* 1234–1244.

Ridley, C. R., Mendoza, D. W., & Kanitz, B. E. (1994). Multicultural training: Re-examination, operationalization, and integration. *The Counseling Psychologist, 22,* 227–289.

Robitschek, C. G., & McCarthy, P. R. (1991). Prevalence of counselor self-reference in the therapeutic dyad. *Journal of Counseling and Development, 69,* 218–221.

Sue, D. W., & Sue, D. (2003). *Counseling the culturally diverse: Theory and practice* (4th ed.). New York: Wiley.

Terrell, F., & Terrell, S. (1984). Race of counselor, client sex, cultural mistrust level, and premature termination from counseling among black clients. *Journal of Counseling Psychology, 31,* 371–375.

Thompson, C. E., Worthington, R., & Atkinson, D. R. (1994). Counselor content orientation, counselor race, and black women's cultural mistrust and self-disclosures. *Journal of Counseling Psychology, 41,* 155–161.

Watkins, C. E., Jr. (1990). The effects of counselor self-disclosure: A research review. *The Counseling Psychologist, 18,* 477–500.

Wells, T. L. (1994). Therapist self-disclosure: Its effects on clients and the treatment relationship. *Smith College Studies in Social Work, 65,* 23–41.

Wetzel, C. G., & Wright-Buckley, C. (1988). Reciprocity of self-disclosure: Breakdowns of trust in cross-racial dyads. *Basic and Applied Social Psychology, 9,* 277–288.

chapter twelve

Engendering a new paradigm
Self-disclosure with queer clients

Jason Patton

Introduction

Experiences for the community of gender and sexual diversity (inexhaustibly, this includes bisexual, lesbian, gay, intersex, questioning, and transgender persons; Reicherzer, 2006), which I will call the *queer community*, represent unique challenges in a culture in which there are a given set of rules of how to act as women and men. For clients of this community, these unique challenges are best met by appropriate use of therapist self-disclosure in the therapeutic relationship. This chapter indicates a work in progress; it represents my journey, both personally and professionally, as a queer therapist who continually expands in relational definition.

There is a common, shared experience of what it means to be a part of the queer community that I sense when I am doing therapy with a client. The cultural identity we cocreate is one of resilience in spite of ongoing marginalization, stigmatization, and oppression. This identity serves to both motivate us to come together to weather these effects as a group in a community of resistance, as well as keep us from allowing ourselves to be vulnerable and intimate with each other. Perhaps the exploitation many of us have experienced as a result of exposing ourselves to the broader culture sets a precedent of keeping ourselves from fully investing in relationships.

Truly, I believe that contact, intimacy, and connection are things for which we yearn. However, we learn not to trust this drive. Often we have found that vulnerability with another person is dangerous. Vulnerability can lead to great pain and isolation if someone were to exploit our weaknesses. At the micro-level, this creates what relational cultural theorists have come to call the *central relational paradox*. We desperately need to experience connection—some might call this a form or extension of love—and acceptance from another person, but are also afraid that there are things about us that are unacceptable. These things, we often believe, are best left out of our relationships, unexposed. We fear that we would be rejected. In the end, we do not bring ourselves fully into our relationships, so the connections we experience are not as whole and rewarding as they might have been (Miller, Jordan, Stiver, Walker, Surrey, and Eldrige, 2004).

I am compelled to respond personally and professionally to this dilemma. In order to not participate in a culture of fear and isolation, I must actively confront it. So, I believe therapeutic, intentional use of self-disclosure helps create a safe space for clients to begin the process of tuning into the parts of their experience they may have left out of relationships for fear of loss and rejection.

In my work with clients of gender and sexual diversity, a common thread woven between our lives is of society-instilled shame. We are taught that we are unequal and unworthy of support. The things that make us different, in terms of our physical presentations, mannerisms, desires, and so on, make us *other*. If I am not comfortable sharing my lived experiences, how could I expect my clients to be? It would seem, or at least feel, disingenuous to set an expectation for others but not keep it for myself. Thus, I am apt to self-disclose these very things about myself, given the right set of circumstances with my clients. If it helps move therapy along, if it validates my clients' experiences, if it helps to strengthen their resources and helps create an ability to meet the desire to connect, then it is more than okay. It is essential.

In an effort to embody the kind of authenticity and vulnerability that can inspire impactful, real connection, I intend to use this opportunity as a forum to outwardly explore the complex interplay of gender, sexuality, vulnerability, and self-disclosure. Hopefully, we can come to a greater sense of clarity about ourselves and our ways of existing in the world through the process.

Gender and sexual identity constructs

There are innumerable ways of talking about and understanding gender and sexuality, so I think first a common language to speak about these constructs will be of great value. With some clients, I am likely to explore how they see themselves, in terms of gender and sexuality. If it seems pertinent and likely to help them come to a greater sense of awareness for themselves and how they operate as gendered beings, I may plot myself with them on the various continua. These continua reflect the complex interplay of sex, sexuality, and gender (Reicherzer, Steves, & Patton, 2007).

Birth-assigned sex or gender

First, birth-assigned sex or gender is what many people think of when they hear the word *gender*. When a child is born, a healthcare professional, generally a medical doctor, examines the child's genitals, and makes an assessment as to whether the child is a boy or a girl. This evaluation is generally based only on the presence of an apparent penis or a vagina. It should be noted, though, that these visual cues are not always entirely accurate. There are a number of intersex conditions that would be missed in this brief examination, if present. The term *intersex* refers to a sex-blended experience, in which the individual is genetically both male and female. For instance, the child may have a vagina with testicular tissue—an experience known as Androgen Insensitivity Syndrome. While these instances are relatively rare, there are more individuals who are intersex than one might imagine. The Intersex Society of North America (ISNA) estimates that approximately 1 in 100 people have some sort of sex-blended experience (ISNA, 2008).

As the examination of a child's genitals is sometimes cursory at best, healthcare professionals have often missed even outwardly visible signs of these blended features. These errors in assigned sex have often had dramatic, long-lasting effects on the affected individuals' lives. At my birth, the obstetrician examined my body and determined that I was male. Had I been born with ambiguous sex features, it is likely that the attending physician would have deemed an assignment surgery necessary. In these cases, a doctor often makes a judgment of the child's sex and removes the genitalia that do not fit. These surgeries were once thought essential in assuring an intersex child a normal, happy life. Often times, these individuals are unaware until they are much older that such a surgery had taken place. Many intersex people, their allies, and healthcare professionals believe these surgeries are far too risky, and that the decision to assign a sex should be available to the affected individual later in life.

Gender identity

Outside of birth-assigned sex or gender, a person comes to see herself/himself as a gendered being later in life (Reicherzer, 2006). One's *gender identity* is her or his core sense of being male, female, or of a blended or third gender. Those who do not consider their gender identities to be defined by and congruent with their birth-assigned genders can be thought of as *gender nonconforming*. Sometimes the term *transgender* is applied to people with nonconforming gender, even if they have no intention of transsexing their bodies.

Gender expression

Gender expression is another construct I often discuss with my clients of gender and sexual diversity. By degree, all cultures have implicit or explicit rules for how men and women may act without reproach. These rules include style of dress, appropriate affect and emotional responses, speech patterns, interaction styles, and so on. When exploring gender expression (Reicherzer et al., 2007), I have found it useful to work with clients to come up with examples of their understandings of these culturally prescribed ways of existing in the world. For instance, my clients often say that men should be strong, stoic, and concise in their choice of words. They often describe women as more nurturing, empathic, and loquacious.

At least in modern American culture, expressing gender in ways that are not consistent with commonly held understandings of what it means to be male or female can be quite dangerous. Imagine the vulnerability of a person with a birth-assigned sex of male who wishes to wear makeup and women's clothing. However, many other societies allow more leeway in what is considered gender-appropriate. In some cultures, a nonconforming gender identity and associated gender expression is something to be tolerated, even revered. For instance, many Native American tribes afford special status to these individuals, considering them to be of great spiritual wisdom and importance (Reicherzer, 2006).

Sexual orientation

Frequently, when talking about gender, clients bring up the topic of sexual orientation. There is a common misconception that gay men, for instance, are naturally effeminate and may someday wish to transsex their bodies. Those with same-sex-attracted friends and clients know this to be a falsity. Gay men who do not consider themselves to have a gender identity of female would be no more likely to undergo sexual reassignment surgery than would opposite-sex-attracted men.

Interplay of gender and sexual attraction

There are innumerable permutations of the complex interplay of gender and sexual attraction. In fact, sexual attraction may not be related to a client's gender at all. An example might be useful here. A person may be determined to be female at birth, later consider himself to be male and wish to transsex his body, and be male attracted. In these instances, it is easy to see how terms like gay or lesbian can be extremely limited. In the truest sense, he could well identify himself as a gay man, but to do so would be deemphasizing a good deal of his past lived experience as a birth-assigned female. It is precisely because of the exclusive nature of words such as gay, lesbian, and bisexual that I tend to say gender and sexual diversity instead.

Gender queer

I am struck by an overwhelming sense that even this particular way of looking at gender feels limited when I try to describe my own experience. I am more apt to call myself *gender queer, other gendered,* or *bigendered*. These terms are really trying to get at an experience of feeling like I fit into both male and female categories. When I consider this in terms of gender roles and gender expression, I think back to some of the associations my clients make for what it means to be a man or a woman. I am certainly not stoic, but there are times when I can hide my emotions pretty well; this is particularly true when I am feeling vulnerable or exposed. I am really quite nurturing and warm, at my best; although, I do not always live up to these aspirations. I'm relatively talkative and do not tend to use concise, to-the-point language, unless the situation calls for it. I usually wear clothing that is gender neutral, commonly considered unisex, or traditionally masculine clothing, but I probably more often wear brighter colors than most men. All of this means, to me, that gender is far too nuanced and rich to be one thing or the other. It can be both, perhaps neither. I believe I hold all gendered characteristics by degree, and that they are exhibited more or less depending on my mood, atmosphere, and so on. So, I believe gender can be fluid and plural for some people: fluid in an ever-changing and adaptive sense, plural in a non–mutually exclusive way.

While finding language to help give voice to my clients' experiences is an essential step in the process, it is by no means the end. Sometimes, it seems to be a daunting task: dangerous and painful. Perhaps an example is in order to help illuminate this process.

Case example: On being a man

The backdrop and setting for this example is a community counseling clinic, Waterloo Counseling Center (WCC), in Austin, Texas. WCC primarily serves the counseling needs of clients of gender and sexual diversity. Our clients are often referred to us from a number of local organizations because of our mission and because of our ability to offer services on a sliding scale. Clients presenting with concerns around gender are often referred to me by colleagues or a developing network of members of the trans community. Sometimes, these clients already know a bit about me and my understanding of gender before I meet them. In some ways, this makes our first sessions a little easier; they may be more comfortable with being more fully disclosing and apt to discuss topics that would be harder to broach if I were not "one of them."

F2M (female to male)

In this instance a client, whom I will call "Mark," was referred by another WCC therapist because she believed that I might be better able to meet his therapeutic needs. Mark presented with a desire to explore "gen-der stuff" and consider beginning a body migration (transsexing one's body) process from female to male. This was the only information I knew specifically about Mark before our first session. However, I did get the impression from my colleague that she was a bit uncomfortable with him at times, although I did not want to hold strong preconceptions of him prior to our first meeting. I did not pursue this as a line of inquiry when I met him.

Our first session together was pretty typical. We went through the necessary paperwork, and we talked about what kinds of things he might like to get out of therapy. He disclosed that he was a birth-assigned female, and had in almost all ways thought himself to be male "on the inside." I talked with Mark frankly about my concerns and relative dis-comfort with being considered a gatekeeper in the transitioning process and expressed my desire to participate with him in therapy as a col-laborator and advocate. Often times, clients will present with the notion that this therapy is just a "bump in the road," a hurdle to get over in order to qualify for the first steps of treatment, usually hormone therapy. Many of my peers and I have noticed that clients who come in with this set of preconceived notions have often been told by others who have gone through this process to put their best feet forward. They have been told to clearly state that they have always considered themselves to be transgender, that they have never questioned this assumption, and that after the process begins there will be no looking back. I think by talk-ing frankly about my wish to be seen as a collaborator and ally in his process, Mark was able to hear that he could bring himself fully into the therapeutic relationship without fear of being rejected for not being "trans enough."

It was clear to me from the beginning that Mark had little to no inkling that I considered myself gender nonconforming. I made a mental note of this and decided that if it were to become pertinent, I might consider sharing some of my own "gender stuff" with him in the future. It seemed to be more pertinent to talk about how issues of power might be present in the room, and how we might mitigate and navigate through these.

Power dynamics

One of the most salient things that came up for me in this first meeting, in regard to power, was how some of the dynamics of our relationship might ostensibly mirror his existence in day-to-day life. I assumedly appeared to him to be a well-educated, employed, white male. He was an unemployed, transgender birth-assigned female African American. Our shared regional culture was the southern United States, which presented its own complexity in racial context and history. To top it off, I was to see him and help evaluate his fitness to proceed through the transition process. I would inevitably be seen as not only the gatekeeper but also one with a good deal of unearned privilege. He acknowledged the frustrating and seemingly daunting prospect that this presented. We agreed to begin our work together, keeping this in mind. We negotiated terms that included his willingness to openly express when he noticed the presence of these elements in the room, so long as I was willing to address them within myself. We further agreed that frustration would likely emerge, and that we should give ourselves permission to bring this forth fully with the knowledge that nothing was too great for us to tackle together. To me, it felt like mutual respect and empathy, and I was honored to share this experience with him.

Feeling different

In our second session, Mark seemed more relaxed, as was I. He delved heartedly into his story. "What do you want to know?" he asked periodically. I expressed my desire to hear about the things that seemed pertinent to him in regard to his experience of feeling like a man who was born with female genitals. This took him to childhood experiences of first realizing that there was something "different."

Mark talked about his early childhood in fond terms. His mother and sister were strong figures, who treated him fairly while holding the expectations that he should become "a good Christian lady." His father was also a central figure who lived nearby, and they visited often. A number of aunts and uncles also had prominent roles in his childrearing. There was no recognizable event that stood out for him as epiphanic, in regard to his gender identity. Church became a weekly source of stress, as he was forced to wear dresses. He felt humiliated at the resulting attention he received.

I was finding myself increasingly in touch with the pain he was recalling as he described how, at age 12, he was mortified to find out he was becoming a woman. At the first sign of menarche, he became emotionally and relationally withdrawn. He hid his menstruation from his family

members, unwilling to speak of something that held such a high degree
of shame for him.

Condemned isolation

I was noticing, not for the first time, how often in our most painful
moments we further isolate ourselves from those who care about us.
He was feeling alone and scared, perhaps a confidant would have been
able to provide a space for him to express these emotions fully. Instead,
he was forced into further aloneness because of the compound shame
of feeling different, almost unworthy of companionship in his shameful grief. In a way, he was experiencing a sort of *condemned isolation*,
where we believe ourselves to be unworthy of connection with others
(Miller, 1988). Condemned isolation, for Mark, meant despair, loneliness, thoughts of self-harm, and withdrawal from previously rewarding
relationships.

Even if his intonation and gesticulation had not indicated it, his words
illustrated that this pain was still present, almost pressing. He made it
clear to me that he felt safe enough to share this most vulnerable period
of his life. As he continued, my inward response to his experience became
more and more intense. I found that tears welled in my eyes. It does not
happen often, but I do not believe I would be modeling authenticity if I
were to deny this away. I probably could have steeled myself against my
emotional reaction, but this would have felt incongruent.

There was a split second when my tuned-in response registered and
he almost stopped his story. Maybe this is when it could potentially be
dangerous, or at least less than optimal, for therapists to bring themselves
fully into the therapeutic relationship. Many of us have been warned that
in times like this, the client may want to stop her or his story and take care
of the therapist's needs. We have also been warned that a client could feel
further shame, that her or his emotions are unreasonable, and that there is
something wrong with feeling the way she or he feels. With this in mind,
I proceeded with full intent that he should feel joined and validated in his
story and remembrance. "I am so touched that you are sharing this with
me right now. I'm really feeling this with you, please go on," was enough
for him to understand my emotional response and desire for him to continue and he did.

We made a mental note of what it had been like for us to connect
over something that had been so hurtful in the past, and agreed to come
back to it, in some way, in the future. Mark missed the next regularly
scheduled session, but did leave me a voice mail message explaining
that he did not have a ride, and committed to seeing me the next week.
At our next session, he said that the last two weeks had been stressful,

and he wanted to talk about them before going back to our previous conversation.

A dangerous secret

Mark said that he had not told me everything about his current life, and that I needed to know more about him before we move forward. "My boys don't know I have a pussy," he continued. It took me a bit of time and further conversation to fully grasp the gravity of what he had just disclosed to me. Since Mark had been in high school, he had been rising in the ranks of a local male street gang. This particular gang is known in the area to be involved with transportation and distribution of illegal drugs and is considered to be extremely violent.

Mark further expounded on the difficult circumstances he faced in his gang. I was noticing how he seemed to shift occasionally in his speech between a sort of hypermasculine bravado and the kind of vulnerably disclosing style he had shown in our previous session. When talking about his boys, he expressed a good deal of pride. He had risen in the ranks to become a well-respected member.

For many transgender men and women, there is a strong desire to *pass* (Reicherzer, 2006), where they fit in society fully masking a birth-assigned sex that is incongruent with their presented gender identity. One's worth in this is often measured in how well one can pass without being found out. This is what Mark was doing with his gang. An added element of danger beyond regular disclosure was present here, though. Had he been found out, he would have risked a lot more than just exposure; he feared they might retaliate against him for his lie. This might have put his life at risk.

As we continued this conversation, Mark further disclosed a number of things that he had not yet shared with me or his previous therapist. "I'm about to be daddy," he said when we were nearing the end of this visit. I was eager to find out more about this, but as we were out of time, I was not able to delve into it sufficiently with him.

I was noticing that the dynamics of our relationship seemed to be changing with each session. I was not concerned, per se, as he seemed comfortable sharing with me, but there was something that felt as if it had shifted from our first meetings. The next visit confirmed this for me. He mentioned his girlfriend and their decision to have a child together. He talked about his "bitches on the side" as well. I made an internal assessment and mental note that for me, this disclosure was somewhat activating. This seemed like something to explore further in supervision. I also acknowledged that to address this immediately with him could be experienced as shaming or belittling of his worldview, so I decided to come back to it if it seemed relevant in the future.

Relational violations

The next few sessions seemed for me a whirlwind. He gave more specifics on how he had decided with his girlfriend to have a child, and about the number of clandestine relationships he was pursuing. I found myself increasingly numb and disconnected in ways that are not foreign, but extremely infrequent. When he talked about women as being crazy and in need of strong guidance, which he was able to offer, I had an illuminated realization of why I was experiencing pain in response to his words.

Even describing this period of our relationship now feels vulnerable. I felt hurt and excluded, but had not really had a clear understanding of why this was. These were felt as *relational violations*. Essentially, relational violations are any acts that are hurtful to a person and a relationship (Dooley & Fedele, 2004). Had I not struggled with my experience to explore the roots of my emotional response, I believe we would have been at risk of what I can only describe as a relational rupture; without addressing these concerns it would have been impossible for me to participate fully and not feel exploited. When he used words that to me felt misogynistic and reflective of a power-over patriarchal system, part of my experience of feeling gender-blended was invalidated. The part of my self that is feminine heard that my femininity is unworthy, that it needs to be kept under close watch and is incapable of strength and personal power.

Deciding to disclose

When I was able to recognize what was happening for me, it took me to a place of greater understanding of his experience. After supervision and personal reflection, I decided that a disclosure of this experience seemed clinically sound. I told Mark that I needed to share with him some things that had been coming up for me in the last few sessions. I first explained how I acknowledge myself to be gender queer. He seemed mystified, at first, as to how I could identify as being of both genders. He was immediately able to identify with my experience of feeling *other*, though. Although our experiences and identities of gender were markedly different, our shared awareness of the pain and complexity in our shared queerness brought us into connection.

This moment of contact created an immediate, tangible shift in our ability to join in our differences and similarities. Mark shared with me his boys' views on women, and how he had changed over time in this respect. He described his father's displeasure with Mark's treatment of women in his life. Mark's father was trying to teach him how a strong man is one who can feel pain and who knows how to treat women as equals.

We arrived at a mutual understanding of how adopting a hypermasculine persona took care of some of Mark's needs to protect himself. This identity allowed him to pass, to feel like he had made it. In this constructed masculinity, he was able to feel both respected and admired. However, these things came at a cost. Constructing an identity of invulnerability, centered solely on what it meant to be a man, did not allow him much flexibility in how he could experience his emotions. He had adopted and internalized a worldview where men are capable of a limited set of emotional responses. Here, men were able to feel anger, frustration, and joy only in reference to physical pleasure. This served to keep him from fully experiencing his relationships. A result of this was a series of unsatisfying, nonmutual relationships. I recognized that Mark's acknowledgements here represented a vulnerable disclosure. In some ways, my vulnerability had invited him to more fully represent his experience.

Mark took with him the knowledge that, for some people, identities need not be solely based on a central, idolized understanding of what it means to be a man or a woman. To do so is to adopt a potentially limiting *controlling image*, a stereotypical understanding of how people should fit roles in society that indicate a range of possibilities of how one can act appropriately and how much potential growth they have, serving to keep social power and hierarchy in its current order (Collins, 1990). In transitioning out of our work together, Mark decided to continue thinking about where he is with all of this. From here, my sense is that he will be actively constructing a gendered identity with a greater sense of clarity of how he operates in relationships with others in his life.

Concluding comments

I took from this interaction a much more nuanced conceptualization of how gender impacts our lives. The richness of one's experience is made up of a complex interplay of identity markers, such as race, socioeconomic status, level of education, geographical location, and so on, that come together to present a unique theater in which we play out our gender roles. My relationship with Mark affirmed my understanding that vulnerability invites vulnerability. That is, when I am able to bring myself more fully into the room, clients are brought to greater awareness and feel safe in disclosure of their own experiences.

References

Collins, P. H. (1990). *Black feminist thought: Knowledge, consciousness, and the politics of empowerment.* Boston: Unwin Hyman.

Dooley, C., & Fedele, N. (2004). Mothers and sons. In J. Jordan, M. Walker, & L. Hartling (Eds.), *The complexity of connection* (pp. 220–249). New York: The Guilford Press.

Intersex Society of North America. (2008). http://www.isna.org.

Miller, J. B. (1988). *Connections, disconnections, and violations. Work in progress, No. 33.* Wellesley, MA: Stone Center Working Paper Series.

Miller, J. B., Jordan, J., Stiver, I., Walker, M., Surrey, J., & Eldrige, N. (2004). Therapists' authenticity. In J. Jordan, M. Walker, & L. Hartling (Eds.), *The complexity of connection* (pp. 64–89). New York: The Guilford Press.

Reicherzer, S. (2006). *The grounded theory of the new gender episteme: Transgender subjectivity deconstructs the power, privilege, and pathos of mental health diagnostics.* A dissertation published by St. Mary's University.

Reicherzer, S., Steves, M., & Patton, J. (2007). *Transgenders, Vestidas, Hijra, Kathoey: Responding to cultural expressions of gender identity.* Vistas 2007. American Counseling Association.

section four

Treatment variations

chapter thirteen

Family therapist/family member
Family dynamics at work and at home

Fran Gerstein

Introduction

Although my family members do not seek contact with my patients, sometimes their worlds collide. At times, my husband is watering the lawn
as someone pulls up in front of our house. Other times my young adult
children may, in their comings and goings, see someone in our driveway.
Once in a while, a patient is coming out of the bathroom and spots one
of my family members in a hallway. My husband and children are used
to this sort of interface. And I strongly suspect that patients who would
be disturbed by this kind of exposure to my family weed themselves out
quickly and seek other therapists.

From the inception of my private practice, some 20 years ago, I have
worked out of a home office. Because it's been my priority to maximize
time with my family, this setup is best for me. It's cozy, and over the years
I've been able to make dinner, help with homework, check in on my kids
between sessions, or be involved in personal matters.

Home practice setting

I live on a quiet suburban block. My office is situated at the back of the
house, in what was originally a small garage. To get to my office my
patients walk down a driveway and then a stone path lined with flowers.
As I don't have a waiting room, they wait on a bench situated outside my
office window (when weather permits). The office has a separate entrance
so they come and go without having to enter my family's living space. If a
patient needs to use the bathroom they use the bathroom next to my den.
If my daughter or son is hanging out in there watching TV, I make sure
the coast is clear and/or scoot my kids out for a moment. In spite of this
occasional, potentially awkward overlap of my professional and private
lives, I try to maintain sufficient work/home boundaries. Thus, my family

has been long instructed by me to maintain a courteous, nonintrusive demeanor when they run into my patients. I've never had a major problem with this setup, at least not that I know of.

Because my patients know my kids and husband from afar, some ask questions indicating an interest in my family life. It's not unusual for me to hear, "Where is your son going to school?" or "Is your daughter home for the summer?" I may express curiosity as to why they're asking, but almost always answer directly without giving more information than seems necessary and then ask how they feel about my response.

For many years things have gone well in my family life. And so I have been able to share basic facts comfortably. But this changed when my husband and I encouraged our son to take a leave of absence from school because of academic and emotional problems he was evidencing. All of a sudden my patients' heretofore harmless questions hit up against my Achilles' heel.

Practice models

Although I was trained in psychoanalytically oriented psychotherapy in the late 1980s, and consider myself primarily a psychodynamic therapist, I have since been learning as much as I can about structural family therapy. I can now say I am familiar with two somewhat opposing models regarding therapist self-disclosure and some of the inherent contradictions in these models are overt; others are covert.

Psychoanalytic trainings

My psychoanalytic training emphasized a stance of empathic neutrality, which, according to Gill (1982), is defined as

> giving equal attention to all the patient's productions, without prior weighting of one kind of material over another, and confining oneself to the analytic task, that is, abstaining from deliberate suggestion. (p. 63)

So I acted nonjudgmentally to what my patients had to say, accepting all thoughts as equally important, in the service of eliciting unconscious material. This neutrality included not revealing more about myself than was readily apparent. It was widely thought that knowing too many specifics about the therapist would inhibit the transference, although what this meant often seemed rather mysterious. As Gill (1982) states in his seminal work, *Analysis of Transference*, "The concept of transference is itself somewhat unclear" (p. 9). Regarding the even more enigmatic issue of countertransference, I was to notice the feelings my patients elicited in me but was not specifically told what to do with them. I knew I was to overcome them in some way, but even the experts seemed confused. According to Tansey & Burke (1989), "The question arises as to what Freud meant by 'overcoming' countertransference. Did he mean eliminate the countertransference response, which is to be regarded only as an impediment deriving solely from the analyst's unresolved conflicts; or did he mean attempt to analyze and understand the experience, thereby reducing its intensity?" (p. 11).

Mostly, what I surmised was that an unanalyzed countertransference could become too good (love or erotic feelings) or too bad (hateful feelings) and in either situation, the therapist was to terminate the case and refer it to someone else. In order to ensure that these dangerous countertransferential feelings didn't get out of hand, the therapist was supposed to be in his own therapy (and sometimes also a training analysis) in addition to undergoing supervision with a more experienced therapist and/ or peer group. More often than not, countertransferential feelings were considered the province of the therapists' own pathology and were to be analyzed into submission, so they did not interfere or tamper with the purity of the transference.

Therapeutic neutrality showed itself in other ways, as well. On an unspoken level, I remember noting how my psychoanalytic supervisors arranged their offices. They often had elegant but neutral furnishings, nothing considered too touchy-feely or personal. Their belongings conveyed little sense of belonging to anyone at all, presumably so as not to impede the patient's free associative thoughts.

Structural family therapy trainings

I've always been fascinated by my patients' unconscious conflicts and found interpreting them helpful, but when I decided to specialize in eating disorders, I wanted to not only address people's intrapsychic struggles but also understand family dynamics, because I had learned that one of the hallmarks of anorexia is that the identified patient is often the symptom bearer for the family; it is the unconscious way the family conspires to express its dilemmas.

So, I turned to a consultation group made up of structural family therapists who helped me to understand that the anorexic is merely trying to adapt and live within a system that encourages her to regress and thus express herself in this particular way. Minuchin, the father of structural family therapy, states, "The individual who lives within a family is a member of a social system to which he must adapt" (p. 9).

I noticed that, in my family therapy group, people were less pathologizing of families and somewhat looser about their revealing the details of their own personal lives, in general. It was unusual *not* to see family pictures on these therapists' desks and it seemed that personal affects were often prominent in their office decorations. Likewise people talked about their families more in supervision, and sometimes offered their patients examples based on their own personal family dynamics. Some went a step further to eschew diagnosis of any kind, considering it akin to labeling. This attitude certainly had its roots in the family therapy movement. Minuchin and Fishman (1981) indicated that "...fortunately for family therapy, therapists have not been able to develop diagnostic categories for families that can pigeonhole some family forms as normal and others as deviant; with any luck, we never will develop them" (p. 262).

Another angle my family therapy group pointed out was that by my working individually with my eating disorder patients, I could, in fact, sabotage their mothers' helpfulness. This went along with some of the ideas of the feminist theorists, namely Steiner-Adair (1991), who says in her chapter

> Another danger I see for therapists working with eating-disordered women is that a therapist may present himself or herself as the perfect mother...I see this played out in therapy when a therapist sets himself or herself up as the ideal or perfect mother, in opposition to the patient's mother, and the therapist becomes invested in maintaining this position. (p. 240)

Integration of models: Toward a personal philosophy

I believe people suffer due to conflicts in both their intrapsychic and interpersonal worlds, so I continue to straddle these two worlds of psychotherapy. As a compromise formation, I work with young adult patients both individually (so that I can better understand their unconscious conflicts) while also scheduling family sessions (so that I can assess how their symptoms play into their family dynamics).

As I've gained more experience as a therapist and eating disorder specialist, I give myself permission to divulge two facts: The first fact is that I struggled with an eating disorder as a teen and consider myself to be fully recovered. My purpose in sharing this is to give hope to eating disorder patients and their families, particularly if they've heard recovery from an eating disorder is nearly impossible. The other fact I share is that

I, too, am a parent and, thus, understand the complexity of raising teens and young adults in these times. For a long time I was able to say, with certainty, I felt good about my parenting. But in the past year, I began to have my doubts.

Work/home boundaries

It was serendipitous that I got a case that challenged me on these two personal levels at the same time. A young woman, named Amy, was referred to me when her college roommate noticed that she'd lost weight, become increasingly withdrawn, and had stopped attending class. The roommate deemed it necessary to notify Amy's parents. Once Amy was home her parents noticed a lot of cuts on her legs. Amy admitted she'd made them with a razor and further offered that while at school she'd made a suicide attempt with over-the-counter pills. When Amy continued to be despondent and couldn't promise she wouldn't hurt herself again, her parents had her admitted to an inpatient unit where she was treated for bulimarexia and suicidal ideation. She stayed in the hospital for 2 months, yet the hospital staff felt she'd made little improvement in that weight gain was minimal and her connection to peers and staff was fair, at best.

Upon discharge, Amy continued to manifest signs of depression and an eating disorder, staying in her room all the time, and refusing to eat with or speak to anyone in her family. Although she was due to return to college, her parents forbade it and Amy had little reaction. She seemed impassive about school, her family, her future; that is, about everything in her life. If coerced to speak she had one topic she wanted to talk about: the end of the world.

Naturally her parents were worried. They didn't know if they should hover or let her be. Either way, they were afraid she'd try to commit suicide again. And, to make matters worse, Amy was unable and unwilling to make any promises about her safety. She was clear that if things continued to seem this bleak, suicide was, at least, an option. Deeper and deeper cuts began to appear on her legs with greater frequency. Under her parents' scrutiny she was getting worse, not better.

My sessions with her were hardly an oasis. Although Amy was a young woman of few words, at best, her ability to withdraw and shut everyone out was staggering. Coming to therapy was clearly a form of torture for her, and by proxy, for me. I would ask her a question and then wait what seemed like an eternity for her response. I would look at the clock and expect it to be near the end of our session, when we were only 10 minutes into it.

After gathering some psychosocial information from her family I began to form some hypotheses. I posed these thoughts to her in an attempt to make sense of her maladaptive behaviors and to try to understand her symptoms as coping mechanisms gone awry. Her cutting seemed to be a form of repetition compulsion. As a young child she had been hit by a car, had broken her hip and leg, and had to undergo emergency surgery. According to her parents, she had barely reacted and had rather gone numb. Perhaps she had dissociated and her medical trauma became lodged within her psyche as a body memory, that is, something she had no language for, but rather enacted control over by cutting herself.

Her binging and purging was a form of self-mutilation, but also expressed her rage at her parents for not being able to help when she was in pain, both psychically and physically. Like many young adults who are having a difficult separation struggle, she was deeply ambivalent toward her parents, especially her mother, in that she both resented them and was utterly reliant upon them. Minuchin and Fishman (1981) refer to this as a *"pas de deux"* family, an intense family style which fosters mutual dependence and mutual resentment at the same time.

To make matters worse, Amy had for many years struggled with social anxiety and obsessive-compulsive disorder. This manifested itself in that after having interactions with people, Amy would ruminate about them in her head and falsely determine she'd said something inappropriate. She would then turn to her mother, tell her about the incident and ask her mother repeatedly to go over it with her. Her social anxiety further fueled Amy's tendency to isolate herself. As uncomfortable as it was to be around people, the aftermath was even worse and, rather than becoming less needy, she needed her mother more than ever to sort things out and reassure her.

As many young women do, Amy had unconsciously used her anorexia to lose body fat and to stall her menses. In effect, she was bringing her body back to a prepubescent state. This was not only a way of forcing her parents to once again care for her, but also served to keep sexual feelings at bay. Because Amy had felt so inadequate socially, she tried to make up for it with what was probably pseudo-hypersexuality. She was extremely attractive and had always attracted boys. So as to gain some sort of social acceptance, she found herself unable to say "no" to sexual advances. Also, Amy was a people pleaser. Orbach (1985) states, "The anorexic may feel shut off from intimacy and close contact; the anorexic may have been trying to meet the sexual needs of her partners and unable to call up her own desires" (p. 99). So even though girls her age weren't terribly interested in her, the boys were. This was additionally shameful for her as her parents were baffled as to why so many boys called the house. They'd question her about it, and she, of course, found it humiliating.

As a child Amy was treated for her excessive shyness. She'd seen a child psychiatrist who told her and her parents that Amy had a condition known as social phobia. Amy and her parents seemed concerned about this condition as if it were something of a sentence and immutable. It struck me as something I might be of help with once I developed more of a therapeutic alliance with them.

In our family sessions, I was able to look at Amy and her parents through a family therapy lens and see how Amy's behavior disengaged and isolated her from the rest of her family: "The girl, who has been treated by her parents as a sick, weak, obedient child, is controlling her parents, putting both of them in a position of helplessness and incompetence" (Minuchin, 1974, p. 103). Not only was she separate; she was powerful. She ruled the entire household in that her parents needed to stay close to home, lest she cut, purge, or attempt suicide. So vacations were postponed, dinner engagements cancelled and family routines revolved around her as the family attempted to follow her eating schedule (which was impossible to follow) and tried, in vain, to get her to talk about something nondepressing.

It was here I decided to self-disclose about my eating disorder. Much of my disclosure was directed at Amy as a way to say, "I haven't been exactly where you've been, but I have a general sense of how you feel." It also reassured Amy's parents, at least on a superficial level, that I, too, had been in a state of despair from an eating disorder and had spent much time isolating. Yet now I was doing quite well in my life.

During one particularly difficult individual session with Amy, I decided to let her in on some of the more intimate details of my eating disorder. I did this by reading aloud an article I had written about my own recovery. The article described how, as a teen, I'd been shy and self-conscious about my tallness—stuff I knew Amy would especially relate to. This intimate self-disclosure, directed toward Amy, seemed to have the intended effect. In later sessions, when I asked her for feedback on whether she felt understood by me, she frequently referenced the article. My sense is that she trusted me and felt I had a vested, personal interest in helping her. I also decided to share an incident having to do with my daughter, who had been quite shy too. But at the age of 12 she announced to us, "I'm ready to stop being shy now," and we were impressed by her ability to take charge of it. I let Amy know that I thought she had more control over it than she knew.

Self-disclosing about my old self was easy since my past seemed distant. Besides, it had been remedied. I could easily withstand my feeling that Amy was, in some ways, similar to how I had been. Likewise, sharing a light-hearted story about my daughter was also pretty risk-free.

But, in terms of self-disclosure, things became infinitely more complicated for me when we asked our son to take a leave of absence due to poor
school performance and concerning behavior. Now, just like Amy's parents, I, too, had a child living at home without a plan. Not wanting to stay
in his old room, our son lived in our basement, in a makeshift space he'd
sectioned off for himself. He was lost and confused. His sense of futility
pervaded our household, making us doubtful of the inherent wisdom of
our decision to keep him home with us.

I was living my life in stereo. I'd be in a session with Amy and her
parents. They'd ask me, "What have we done to cause her to struggle so
much?" "What if she never gets past this?" and more complex questions
like "How can we help?" and "How much crap should we put up with?"
Then I'd close my office door, enter my own living space, and hear the
same questions whirling around in my own mind. It was like a house of
mirrors where every therapy session with Amy reflected some aspect of
my own confusion. For me, doing therapy had been a respite from my
woes, but with Amy's family it was a magnification.

My twin roles—mother and therapist—were dichotomous. As Amy's
therapist I had the luxury of being able to step back and see that if her
parents made age-appropriate demands, parented her as a team, and
accepted where she was at, she would eventually grow developmentally.
But I was struggling with serious doubts about my husband and I being
able to do this for our son. I found myself saying to Amy's parents what
people were saying to me: "Your child is having a developmental crisis,
but she will be OK." This was infinitely easier to say as a therapist than
to hear as a parent. After all, how does a parent launch a child who is too
confused to be launched?

I held on to certain tenets, both personally and professionally. The first
is that parents cannot force development. Rather they must set boundaries
and parameters that encourage it. Because of this, parental authority must
prevail in the home. Also, parents should honor their children's steps
toward separation, no matter how shaky, since each person/ child, alone,
is responsible for his decisions, no matter what his excuse or background.
Often this means a parent should sit back and let a child fail or flail without bailing him out.

After several weeks of sessions where I felt my life was being lived in
duplicate, I shared with the family that I was having my own problems. I
told them my son had to leave school and was lost and that I knew what
it was like to live with a confused child. I also told them that the self-
doubt and fears that haunted them haunted me too. In addition, I noticed
a similar dynamic between Amy's parents and me and my husband.
Amy's mother tended to be more anxious and alarmist about Amy and
her self-destructiveness, which was complemented by her father's sense of

distance and denial. This not only led to arguments between them, but it was hard for them to be on the same page in terms of setting boundaries and limits. Amy's mom wanted her to have dinner with the family every night, whereas her dad said that as long as she ate he didn't care where it was.

On the home front, I noticed the same sort of patterns. As my anxieties about our son escalated because I was home with him all day observing his frozen stance to the world, my husband would imply I was overanalyzing things. So, as part of my self-disclosure to Amy's parents I also let them know it was hard when spouses were not on the same page. I mentioned that my husband and I often disagreed on how to parent our son. I was a softy and he tended toward authoritarianism. When things went wrong with our son, we blamed each other instead of holding our son accountable for his behavior. I made it clear that it was important to try to listen to each other and make sufficient compromises for several reasons. First of all, it's a good way to show young adults that agreeing all the time is not always possible, but that in adult relationships people come to halfway points. In addition, it helped Amy's parents form a united front and also consult each other more about things, also creating more closeness and understanding between them. Finally, it was a way to help Amy's parents hold Amy more accountable to herself.

At this point I spent some time with just the two of them. We worked in vivo on their finding compromise formations. For instance, because they couldn't decide on where Amy had to eat dinner, they compromised and told her she had to have dinner with the family several days a week and could do her thing on other nights. As I witnessed them bolstered by my support, I, in turn, gained the strength I needed. I finally decided to actually take the advice I was dishing out. I put faith in the idea that we parents needed to toe the line, accept our children's thoughts and opinions as their own, and see their suffering as a part of life, not as an outcome of something we'd done wrong. I let them know that not only were we parents all in this together, but that we, as humans, had to suffer to find ourselves and grow.

Final reflections

I always kept my comments about my troubles to Amy and her parents general. I knew early on that Amy's mother tended to be overly involved and caretaking and I wanted to make sure she didn't feel the need to caretake me. Were I to elaborate, it could have been a slippery slope. I needed to stay in the role of advisor and expert so as to avoid confusion on all our parts.

At this point in the therapy Amy's parents seemed more relaxed when they came to see me. Their heretofore tight shoulders seemed looser; they sat closer together on the sofa and gave each other more eye contact. It seemed they felt less like "bad parents" and much like my husband and me, parents trying to do better.

I believe my decision to self-disclose, especially my decision to disclose about my son, showed me the wisdom of letting my patients know that while being a therapist I am in the process of leading my own, complex family life. This enhances my humanness and the idea that we are all in this together. In real life, no parent gets a guarantee regarding the happiness or safety of our children. Therefore, we must learn to live with anxiety and also do our best to set appropriate boundaries to facilitate their growth and development.

Ultimately I agree with Minuchin & Fishman's theory that "the family is the natural context for both growth and healing, and it is the context that the family therapist will depend on for the actualization of therapeutic goals" (p. 11). The next time my son walks past Amy on my driveway, perhaps I'll be tempted to introduce them. I've learned a lot from both of them and their respective families.

References

Gill, M. (1982). *Analysis of transference, volume I: Theory and technique.* New York: International Universities Press.

Minuchin, S. (1974). *Families and family therapy.* Cambridge: Harvard University Press.

Minuchin, S., & Fishman, H. C. (1981). *Family therapy techniques.* Cambridge, MA: Harvard University Press.

Orbach, S. (1985). Accepting the symptom: A feminist psychoanalytic treatment of anorexia nervosa. In D. M. Garner & P. E. Garfinkel (Eds.), *Handbook of psychotherapy for anorexia nervosa and bulimia* (pp. 83–104). New York: Guilford Press.

Steiner-Adair, C. (1991). New maps of development, new models of therapy: The psychology of women and the treatment of eating disorders. In C. Johnson (Ed.), *Psychodynamic treatment of anorexia nervosa and bulimia* (pp. 225–244). New York: Guilford Press.

Tansey, M., & Burke, W. (1989). *Understanding counter-transference: From projective identification to empathy.* Hillsdale, NJ: The Analytic Press.

chapter fourteen

The perils of rigid adherence
A look back at a group

Meredith Barber

Introduction

"Can anyone give me a ride to group next week? My car will be in the shop." So began a seemingly innocuous request by Laura, a member of the weekly therapy group I led. But the request made me sit up and pay close attention. From the time I began leading the group a few months before, I had made the rules quite clear, and one of them prohibited contact between members outside of group. I was somewhat terrified at the first challenge to my authority—I was a novice group therapist, and my knowledge was mostly theoretical.

How should I handle the suggestion? Should I restate the rules? Discuss the members' feelings about the rules? Interpret the new developmental stage the group was entering? Ask myself whether the rule truly applied?

The importance of rules in group therapy is the subject of this chapter, and specifically the perils of adhering to rules too rigidly. I examine two types of rules—the rules that group members need to follow and the "rules" of sound group therapy technique. With the benefit of hindsight, I explore how, as a novice group therapist running a weekly outpatient group at a hospital for women with eating disorders, I tried to adhere religiously to the rules. I also explore the consequences of adhering to them as if they were commandments. In reality, the rules are guidelines, not commandments. Here, though, I present them the way I understood them when I ran the group, and I explain their logic.

Common group psychotherapy rules: For leaders
Thou shalt bring all material from the there
and then to the here and now

One of the basic tenets of group therapy is that the group is a social microcosm. Members act in the group the same way they act outside it.

Therefore they will eventually bring all their interpersonal issues, conflicts, and dramas into group. According to Yalom and Leszcz (2005), one of the most important skills of the group therapist is to help members bring their problems into the "here and now" so that the group can be most helpful. Let's say Elaine has difficulty expressing tender feelings with loved ones. She will almost certainly have difficulty expressing them with group members. For Elaine, one of the best uses of group is to practice expressing tender feelings. Her difficulties therefore become more alive and accessible. Other members can benefit too. If Mary has difficulty tolerating tender feelings, she can be challenged to accept Elaine's expression of tender feelings toward her. If Susan is reporting anger at her partner, it would be a great use of group if the other members could give her real-life feedback on the effect of her anger, because they are likely to have been targets of that anger.

Talking about what is happening in vivo is very different from normal social interaction and can take some adjustment. Therefore, the process of shifting from the there and then to the here and now is initially disconcerting for clients, and a hard skill to learn for therapists.

Thou shalt maximize member interactions

Unlike individual therapy, which has only one in vivo relationship to explore (the one between the client and the therapist), group therapy entails multiple interactions. The group leader should encourage peer interactions rather than just the relationship between the leader and each individual member. This is another hard skill to learn, and many beginning group therapists tend instead to conduct individual therapy with one member after another as the other members observe. Although that approach has some therapeutic value, the use of the group is missing, and group therapy works best when the group is used (Brabender, 2002).

Thou shalt ignore symptoms and focus on relationships

The best use of group is to work on relationships (Yalom & Leszcz, 2005). For instance, even in an inpatient group, Yalom advocates steering away from discussing symptoms. Instead, he helps patients translate their symptoms into interpersonal issues. Let's say Jack is depressed. In Yalom's model, the therapist would say that the group is not the ideal place to discuss his depression. The therapist would point out that Jack has other places—individual therapy, for instance—to explore his depression. Instead, she would ask Jack to think of a way in which his *interpersonal relationships* might be aggravating that depression. With that guidance, Jack might wonder whether his isolating and pushing others away is abetting his depression. Then the therapist would encourage Jack to find a way to invite another into his interpersonal life *right here in the therapy group*. Jack's goal for that group therapy session would be to connect with one other person.

Thou shalt not self-disclose

Another rule is that the therapist should not reveal personal information about herself. One main reason for not self-disclosing in a group is to avoid causing group members to view the therapist as too fragile to help them. They not only might question the leader's ability to take care of them, but also might feel the need to caretake the leader. Particularly in early stages of development, when the group is not yet cohesive and members still idealize, and are still quite dependent on the leader—as opposed to the group itself—precipitous self-disclosure may prompt members who are worried about the fragility of the leader to pull back from their investment in the group.

Common group psychotherapy rules: For members

Thou shalt be on time, attend all sessions, and give ample notice of termination

In outpatient groups, rules about absences and lateness are common, as they affect the entire group, not just the therapist and one client, as in individual therapy. There are rules, too, about terminating—if a member decides that group is not for her, she must give the group ample notice so that both she and the group can explore their feelings about her leaving.

Thou shalt not engage in extra-group socializing

Many therapists feel that all interactions between group members outside of group should be limited (Brabender, 2000; Rutan & Stone, 2001). The notion is that if two people develop a relationship outside the group, the outside relationship becomes more important than the therapeutic relationship. Because they want to protect their outside relationship, they become less willing to be honest and confront each other within group. They lose each other as therapeutic agents. Let's say Elaine tells Mary a secret about herself—that she's having an affair—but hasn't shared it with the group. The next time Elaine talks about her failing marriage in the group, Mary is in a bind. If she confronts Elaine about the affair, and shares the information with the group, she risks losing her as a friend.

If she keeps quiet, she honors the friendship but is of no use to Elaine as a group member. Mary becomes complicit in Elaine's stagnation in her marriage.

The application of rules

As a novice group therapist and as someone who desperately wanted to do the right thing, I took the above rules—the ones for the members to follow and the ones I considered to be good practice—seriously. I enforced the no-contact rule outside of group. Lateness and absences were always explored, and I worked hard to bring group content into the here and now. I kept an eye on fostering member interaction and, like Yalom, encouraged members to discuss how their interpersonal problems might affect their symptoms rather than to focus on the symptoms. Finally, I did not reveal much personal information about myself in group.

Consequences of an unswerving adherence to rules

As a result of following these rules of good technique, I believe my group was effective—a safe, supportive place where people healed. They learned about their interpersonal selves by exploring with other group members, and they practiced new ways of relating. Generally, the women left the group with many fewer eating disorder symptoms than they entered with.

Although the group was a curative place, my rigid adherence to the rules led me to miss many opportunities to make it even more effective. Too often I let the rules overshadow my intuition and attentiveness to my clients and their needs.

One example of my being too rigid occurred when group members said they wanted to structure time at the beginning of each group to do a "check-in." The idea was to guarantee that each member got airtime to let the group know what was going on for her. Members said that sometimes an entire 90-minute group would go by and they would never find the opening to let the others know what was happening. I was opposed to the suggested change. I felt that it would enable them and that they needed to learn to speak up about their needs without the aid of a structure. I felt that structuring the check-in would be giving in to the part of them that could not advocate for themselves. I was happy to spend time exploring why group members felt they needed a structured group, but I was not in favor of changing the structure.

In retrospect, I was clinging to my ideal of where I thought the members should be versus where they were. If I had accepted what they were telling me—that they were unable to advocate for themselves in the way I wanted them to and, ironically, were advocating for themselves by asking for a change in the group structure—I would have praised them for speaking up about what they wanted, rather than push them toward an ideal I held.

Anxiety behind rigid adherence

One reason I adhered so strictly to the rules was anxiety. The leader of a therapy group is responsible not only for her actions but also for the multitude of interactions the members have with one another. Group therapy can be exciting, but it also raises the therapist's anxiety much more than individual therapy does.

My anxiety level was a gauge that determined the extent to which I would cling to the rules. For instance, when someone acted out in the context of the group—by not attending or terminating early or coming late, for instance—I often felt personally challenged. When my anxiety level was heightened, my primitive inner reaction was to feel manipulated and powerless. At those times, I tended to think that my only options were to give in to the acting-out behavior or to set a boundary. Because I didn't want to ignore the acting-out behavior, I generally responded with a boundary. If someone didn't show for group, I'd respond with the widespread practice of charging for the no-show.

Having a rule about charging for a no-show and sticking to it is good practice, which I'm not criticizing. The problem was that I practiced it punitively when I was feeling powerless and felt that instituting a rule was my only recourse. When I was feeling less anxious and more grounded, and the same situation presented itself—a member not showing for group—I could explore the behavior with the member (when she returned) or encourage the group to explore the acting-out behavior. The issue of whether or not to charge became much less loaded and sometimes almost irrelevant.

Group therapist self-disclosure

Another option when I was feeling powerless and in a bind would have been to share my feelings with the group. Ordinarily, I tended to keep my struggles to myself. However, I could have empowered the group by being more open about some of my conflicts. Together, we might have been able to come up with more creative solutions.

With regard to a chronically absent group member, what if I had said this: "I'm not really sure what to do here. I know we have a rule about coming consistently and yet Mary Anne is frequently absent. I know that I tend to be personally challenged when people are not present, and I don't want that anger to make me act punitively. In addition, I believe that if group members challenge Mary Anne about her absences, you would have much more of an impact than if I challenge her. I think I might be feeling all the resentment and anger for the group when someone is absent, and that might explain why no one else seems bothered by it. So, I need some help here—what should we, as a group, do about this?"

By stating my frustration and asking for help from the group, I would have been placing the responsibility where it should have been—on the entire group. That would have freed me to lead them in their exploration of Mary Anne's lateness rather than carrying the responsibility myself. The idea of handing the responsibility to the group is a basic tenet of good group therapy technique and actually represents traditional rules. It is ironic that had I broken the rule about self-disclosure, I would have been following the rule about empowering the group.

I recall another session when disclosing my frustration could have helped. One of our members was severely depressed. I spent most of a particular session conducting individual therapy with her in front of the group. I knew it wasn't the best use of the group, but I was too nervous to hand the situation over to the group, thinking that my interventions would be better than anyone else's. Meanwhile, however, my interventions weren't working. We were in a bind: She was stuck in her depression, and I was stuck in trying the same thing over and over. In retrospect, I wonder what would have happened if I had been open and honest with the group about how I felt. What if I had said: "I'm frustrated and worried about Betty. It doesn't seem as though any of my interventions are working. How can we together help her?" That would have shifted something in the group. I would have empowered them and showed that I trusted them. I would have been demonstrating my belief that the group really is powerful and that together we could help Betty in a way that I alone could not. Again, handing responsibility to the group is good therapy. I could have elevated the group work by self-disclosing.

Along with sharing my struggles, I wish I had shared more of my positive feelings with the group. I loved the women in the group and was moved by watching them grow, heal, and support one another. I found it inspiring that they were willing to repeatedly take risks and to share their vulnerabilities and triumphs. Yet even though I believe that the experience of being appreciated builds self-esteem, I rarely expressed my feelings of admiration and gratitude. In addition, because these women carried serious diagnoses and often felt pathologized, sincere acknowledgment might have elevated their journeys toward health. Looking at oneself and one's history with honesty demands courage and determination, and the sanctity of that work needs to be appreciated.

I also would have been modeling the sharing of positive feelings and thereby encouraging them to do the same, both inside and outside the group. This more balanced approach toward self-disclosure in group therapy meshes with the theory, which is nuanced. Many factors need to be evaluated, including group development, type of group, and content of the disclosure. (Dies, 1983)

Designing the group differently

As a novice group therapist, I was painfully aware of how little I knew. I felt obligated to follow the "fake it till you make it" admonition of 12-step programs. Whenever I helped a member translate a symptom into an interpersonal issue, or brought a member's interpersonal issue into the group, I did it the way I imagined a highly skilled group therapist would. But while I was busy pretending to be a master therapist, and striving for my image of how a perfect, high-functioning group should be run, I missed many cues about what the group really needed.

If I had listened to the members more, I probably would have designed the treatment differently. According to Brabender (2002), when designing a group, one must be clear about the goals and tailor the group design to the population and the setting. Brabender divides goals into four categories—interpersonal change, skill acquisition, intrapsychic change, and symptom reduction. They are all interrelated, and change in one often leads to change in others. Nevertheless, Brabender suggests that it is helpful for group leaders to prioritize their goals. For myself, I regarded interpersonal change as primary (and believed it would lead to symptom reduction). If you had polled the group members, however, I suspect that they would have cited symptom reduction as their main concern.

The discrepancy between my goals for them and their own goals explains some of the frustration we all experienced. For instance, although I wanted them to provide loving feedback about the effects of their behavior on one another, they were extremely hesitant to give one another honest feedback. I was disappointed that the group did not conform to my idealized image of how effective groups are "supposed" to behave. I stubbornly kept trying to get them to "open up" rather than seeing that they had more immediate and pragmatic goals to achieve.

If I had modified the group design so that it reflected the members' goal of symptom reduction and not my imagined goal of interpersonal change, we would have focused much more on symptoms and would have experienced less frustration. Perhaps the members would have felt better served if we had checked on symptom status each week and then used the resulting information to explore related interpersonal issues.

Reflections

In my examples of how I would have run my group differently, I have aimed to integrate both rules and intuition into group psychotherapy and to achieve a balance between the two. It's important to pay attention to one's population and intuition rather than adhere to rules rigidly. If we follow rules at the expense of our flexibility and intuition, we run the risk of not responding to our clients' needs—as I did. The traditional rules and principles represent a useful anchor or point of departure. On the other hand, every group has unique characteristics waiting to be discovered. Attempting to force a group to fit some universal, textbook model is a formula for frustration. A more effective approach is to listen to the group members and one's own intuitions, selecting the relevant principles and modifying the rules accordingly.

The commandment with which I struggled the most was the one about no extra-group socializing. Although I believed that the rule had merit and I could intellectually defend it, something about it gnawed at me. I suspect that I stuck to it partly because I feared losing control of the group. The idea that my group members were out cavorting with one another, unsupervised, raised my hackles. To compensate for my inner doubts about my motivation, it was the rule I was the strictest about.

Also, there was a very strong argument to be made in favor of extra-group socializing for this population. The reality was that both inside and outside group, members had great difficulty reaching out to others. They needed social supports, and they especially needed a network of people who understood eating disorders. Part of me believed that members could benefit from extra-group contact and that the advantages outweighed the potential problems.

My own hesitation about the rule gave group members the opening they needed to challenge me about it frequently. Laura's early ride-seeking behavior, mentioned at the beginning of this chapter, was the first of many such challenges.

The rule was even questioned by colleagues. In all other levels of care and all other weekly therapy groups at the hospital, contact outside group was allowed and sometimes encouraged. My adherence to the rule ignored the entire setting.

After prohibiting extra-group contact for about 5 years, I relinquished control and decided to allow it. I educated members about the pitfalls (and advantages) of outside contact and required them to report all instances of it, so that we could explore feelings about it. I felt that the new policy represented a better balance of group theory and the unique needs of the population.

The result of my experiment surprised me. Once I gave up fighting with group members about it, and the onus was on them to make contact with one another, they rarely did. All the energy had gone into arguing with me about it. Therefore nothing much changed for the group members outside of group, but it did free up energy within the group to discuss the real issue—why they were isolating from one another. I found myself in the unaccustomed position of encouraging and challenging them to reach out to one another, which was a much more productive use of our time and energy. In the end, once I gave up control of something I felt was a commandment, and instead paid attention to my population and intuition, I gained much more control over the group.

References

Brabender, V. (2002). *Introduction to group therapy.* New York: John Wiley & Sons.

Dies, R. R. (1983). Clinical implications of research on leadership in short-term group psychotherapy. In R. Dies & K. R. MacKenzie (Eds.), *Advances in group psychotherapy* (pp. 27–78). New York: International Universities Press.

Rutan, J. S., & Stone, W. N. (2001). *Psychodynamic group psychotherapy* (3rd ed.). New York: Guilford Press.

Yalom, I., & Leszcz, M. (2005). *The theory and practice of group psychotherapy* (5th ed.). New York: Basic Books.

chapter fifteen

Creative expression in service of others

Reflections on transparency in art therapy practice

Shaun McNiff

Introduction

The expansive literature generated by the arts therapy disciplines has underscored the way in which these creative media have increased the breadth of communications within the psychotherapeutic process. By and large the writings of arts therapists have concentrated on the creative expressions of others. Far less attention has been given to the corresponding growth of possibilities for the self-expression by therapists within various arts modalities and the resulting influences on the experience of therapy.

In this chapter, I will focus on the expression of art therapists when working with people with visual art and, more particularly, on my own practice. Consistent with my commitment to arts integration in therapeutic practice (1981, 2004), I will make references to other creative media and how they help us understand the multisensory dimensions of the arts therapy experience and how expression in every arts modality unavoidably involves varying degrees of personal revelation. Before exploring the particular aspects of self-disclosure by art therapists within therapeutic practice and efforts to research the dynamics of art and healing, I would like to briefly discuss how the arts therapies overlap with the more comprehensive domain of verbal psychotherapy.

Verbal disclosure within the arts therapies

Within the verbal realm we can define self-disclosure in a relatively circumscribed sense as the literal communication of personal experiences, thoughts, and responses to situations. Those of us who use the arts in therapy tend to talk just like verbal therapists, so we must also make judgments about what we say and do not say within a therapy session. There is a general sense in the arts therapy community, perhaps in keeping with the larger psychotherapeutic field, that our primary purpose in relation to all communication is the well-being of the people we serve. Ideally we strive to navigate within the therapeutic process in a disciplined and empathetic way, doing our best to further the well-being of others rather than satisfy our own needs for self-expression.

As someone who works primarily with groups, I appreciate the importance of restraint in leadership; how saying less can generate more in terms of others' creative expression. My verbal communications about what I feel and experience are generally focused on what is happening in the present moment rather than my past or experiences outside the group. I see my primary role as a keeper of the creative space, as a guide and companion, and as a disciplined and attentive witness to what others are doing in their expression. Communications about what I perceive and feel in relation to the expressions of others and the nuances of action within studio groups are always intertwined with how I strive to fulfill leadership responsibilities.

Those of us who work with the arts in therapy can perhaps maintain a modicum of verbal expression in a natural and comfortable way because people within both individual and group settings tend to be engaged with various forms of artistic expression that occupy attention. Verbal expressions of what I observe in a session are thus connected to the ebb and flow of the artistically oriented space and what is needed to further its impact. Generally, this therapeutic environment does not demand much from me in terms of personal revelation. I find that the more I can step aside, the more room I leave for the expression of others.

Yet I will in certain circumstances pointedly describe how I feel about a particular situation and generally people in my studio groups want to hear how I react to what they are expressing. To the extent to which psychotherapy involves a process of intersubjectivity and learning more about ourselves through the perceptions of others, this sharing of what therapists observe and feel can be an essential component of the work.

Artistic expression as an ongoing process of self-disclosure

The engagement of the arts in therapy and perhaps more essentially the perspectives toward communication that the arts bring to therapy significantly expand the discourse regarding the nature and use of self-disclosure by therapists. When we look at experience through the lens of an artistic consciousness, there is sensitivity to what is conveyed through the postures and gestures of the body, the tone and cadence of the voice, the way in which a space is organized, and other sensory dimensions of our interactions with others. Therefore, within the context of artistic perception therapists cannot avoid self-disclosure when interacting with other people because we will inevitably show and reveal things about ourselves in relation to how we move, act, and convey emotions in the most elemental expressive activities.

The use of the arts in therapy thus generates many new questions related to what therapists reveal about themselves when working with others. This is especially true when engaging performing arts disciplines such as dance, music, vocal expression, and dramatic improvisation, where the arts modalities require therapists to become involved in various ways that range from demonstrating methods to direct participation in expressive activities.

Dance therapist Vivien Marcow Speiser emphasizes how within dance and movement therapy "the instrument is the body which is always responding and you can't turn it off. It is expressing itself all of the time." She describes how her methods of practice involve a constant mirroring of another person's movement with her own (personal communication, February 19, 2008).

Mitchell Kossak, a musician who practices expressive arts therapy, calls attention to how he exercises a "dual level of attunement" to both the needs of another person and his personal artistic involvement as they enter the "creative water together." Both he and Marcow Speiser state how their self-expression is always focused on service to the other, enhancing spontaneity, and furthering the overall flow of creativity and the resulting emergence of therapeutic contents.

I asked Kossak, a jazz musician and vocalist who focuses on improvisational expression in expressive arts therapy, whether he can completely let go when playing music with another person during sessions. He again stressed the practice of dual awareness and continued with how he might model letting go, for example with drums, for someone who can benefit from this.

I asked how the making of improvisational music with another person involves self-disclosure. "There is a kind of intimacy," he replied, "that cannot be avoided. It is about closeness and saying, it's OK to get close, let's get closer, let's play together—we can get soft together, intense, and share lots of emotion—the lines between therapist and client get blurred in the music, but I still hold the responsibility as therapist. I take the risk to show my creative process, a deeper inner expression, and the range of my feelings, my humanity" (Kossak, 2008).

In my conversations with both Kossak and Marcow Speiser, they kept emphasizing how their artistic expressions with others in therapeutic settings are absorbed in the spontaneous immediacy of the present moment and that their self-expression is an integral element within the therapeutic process. The realization that our physical expressions and gestures are "always responding" to the situation at hand contributes to a more comprehensive sense of interpersonal communication in therapy.

Why therapists make art in their sessions

Art therapists are increasingly interested in the role that their personal artistic expression can play within the therapeutic process (Moon, 2000, 2007; Fish, 2005). Where a large sector of art therapy practice grew from more traditional psychotherapeutic methods which emphasized withholding personal expression, the increasing preference for studio environments and a greater appreciation of the art therapist's identity as an artist have changed many of the basic assumptions about how therapists become involved in the therapeutic experience. In this respect the art therapy experience is progressively corresponding to the overall structure, atmosphere, and activities of the studio.

Within the art studio environment, as contrasted to the more conventional therapeutic office or consulting room, it is thoroughly natural for people to make art alongside one another. This process of simultaneous work with art materials is now commonly called "responsive art-making," a method of practice involving therapists in the creation of images as a way of supporting the therapeutic experience or communicating through artistic media within sessions. Reflective art is also being utilized by art therapists within supervision and as an ongoing medium of self-inquiry.

Artistic participation in the studio involves therapists in what can be viewed as a process of parallel expression and cocreation. These interactive practices have also emerged from the discipline of play therapy and the more general area of psychotherapy with children where there is a long pattern of therapists joining children in creative activities, and where different forms of artistic expression complement and in some cases transcend verbal communication.

Play therapy—art with children

Well before art therapists became seriously involved in discussing the practice of responsive art making, the psychiatrist Robert Coles described how he would draw alongside children who made pictures in his sessions to help them relax and lower self-consciousness and inhibition (McNiff, 1976, pp. 123–124).

In my conversations about art therapy with Coles during the mid-1970s, he described a number of different reasons why his artistic expression in sessions may have been useful to the children with whom he worked. He felt that they often felt a sense of "relief" when encouraged to make art alongside an adult and not experience pressure to talk. Interactive drawing was also helpful when children resisted expression or kept repeating the most stereotypic forms.

He described his artistic ways of engaging children who were feeling stuck:

> The only way I can deal with them is in a nonverbal way, by noticing what the child is drawing and responding with my own drawings. If I see a child who is being stereotypical, I go out of my way to fill my paper up with a blazing sun, which any child can do, or just put color on the paper without any interest in form or structure, which is very easy for me because I'm not very good at form and structure anyway! (p. 124)

He goes on to emphasize how he is "constantly responding" to the child's art with his own and "adjusting" to his sense of what is needed in the moment. Sometimes the child's proficiency with art challenges him to "work harder" in his responses and in other situations he will intentionally lower the threshold of his drawing skills to be more empathetic. These ways of responding simultaneously to a person's ongoing artistic expression with our own, in keeping with the dance and music interactions described above, can be viewed as primary modes of communication and support within art therapy.

When I spoke to Coles, who describes himself "as no great artist" but as someone who likes to draw (p. 123), about these methods of practice, I was impressed by the ease of his graphic expressions and how his attitude was distinctly different from the more formal and restrained demeanor that many art therapists tended to exhibit at the time. We art therapists might consider taking ourselves less seriously, diminishing our self-consciousness, and developing the ability to engage art materials in more playful ways.

As Winnicott stated, individuals really should not be doing this work with others unless they are able to let go and really play. Winnicott perceived psychotherapy as interactive and "overlapping" play and felt that "only in being creative" can a person discover "the self" (1971, p. 54). It would appear that both Coles and Winnicott place more emphasis on being able to play and become involved in creative expression than focusing on what they disclose about themselves. The larger goal, and this coincides with recent developments in studio art therapy, is one of establishing a creative and safe space, an overall atmosphere of imagination that supports participants in their own creative expression (McNiff, 1995). The studio becomes a kind of slipstream that enables people to do things that they could not do alone. Therapists are less concerned with what they reveal about themselves and they are more focused on creating an atmosphere that supports the creation of others. They find that their own involvement in creative expression may at times further the making of an effective therapeutic milieu.

Shared art-making with adults

Winnicott's description of the therapeutic process and the more general play space is very much in sync with these approaches to art therapy. The goal is one of activating a person's creative expression and letting the process unfold and carry us where we need to go. Because the role of the therapist is one of cultivating this space that acts upon people, personal artistic expression can be used to further this objective.

Although I will from time to time become involved with interactive art experiences with others, my artistic expressions generally do not directly respond to what other people are doing in sessions. I have a tendency to focus more on parallel expression. In this respect I view the making of art objects as an individual inquiry that we may do simultaneously. This way of working can be viewed as one of many styles within art therapy where others, like Bruce Moon, will often relate directly to another's expression with paintings (2007).

In the group art studio I find that there are always subtle forms of interaction and influence taking place. In keeping with what Coles said about drawing spontaneously to help a child's expression become more imaginative and free, I am keenly aware of how my way of moving with materials may affect others. The same applies to the contents of expression. If I am free and open and willing to be unusual and intimate in what I express, others may feel the same license to create.

Therapists making art during sessions can in this respect demonstrate and model more spontaneous, imaginative, and personal artistic expression. People generally approach artistic activities thinking that they must execute preexisting ideas and images and so I might display through my own quick gestures and simple movements how to build a picture without knowing the final outcome at the beginning.

As students repeatedly say to me, how can I expect to help a person to do something that I will not do myself? In this respect the artistic expressions of therapists can break the ice, relax inhibitions, and assist others in feeling more comfortable in taking risks.

The art therapist's self-image as an artist

One of the most significant barriers to transparent and ongoing cocreation in the art therapy experience is the feelings of insecurity that art therapists sometimes have about their own artistic abilities, which tend to vary greatly. I venture to say that many art therapists do not always feel confident about using their self-expression to serve the expression of others. There might be a sense of inferiority in relation to one's skills or experience and fear of disclosing this potential inadequacy. I differ from many within my discipline in that I see art therapy as both a profession and a modality, and I welcome people from outside the arts who want to give their clients these opportunities for expression.

When students ask me whether their skills as artists make a difference within the arts therapy experience, I refer to people like Robert Coles and I adapt Winnicott's "good enough mother" idea to being a "good enough artist." The spectrum of art therapy experiences is endless and there is room within our discipline for people with varying degrees of skill with artistic media. For me, quality expression within therapy has more to do with authenticity and being "good enough" with the materials of art.

Graduate students and beginning therapists need to become familiar and comfortable with their artistic expression, they need to know their capabilities as well as their limitations and realize how their art will add to the interplay of transferences, perceptions, influences, and ongoing communications that form the basis of therapeutic environments. I encourage the same kind of awareness toward a therapist's personal art making in sessions that is applied to the use of spoken language, striving for the best possible aesthetic interaction between self-expression and restraint.

On the basis of my personal experience, both as an art therapist and as a trainer, I feel that the major challenge facing beginning therapists is the vulnerability, discomfort, and uncertainty commonly felt when sharing their own artistic expressions. Consequently, training programs will often make ongoing self-expression by students a major and ongoing part of the educational experience. The training process places great emphasis on continuous presentation and responses to personal artistic expressions. We all need to know more about how our expressions affect others, how we feel and react when others respond emotionally to our work, and generally develop the ability to ground ourselves when interacting with others in this way, especially when showing our most personal artistic expressions. Continuing education and professional supervision in art therapy similarly focus on these core issues.

Priscilla's challenge and invitation

My most intense personal experience with the issue of self-disclosure as an art therapist occurred in the early years of my practice in relation to these questions regarding self-confidence and my self-image as artist and art therapist.

I entered the field of art therapy as a serious young artist immersed in the trends of the art world and attempting to find my place in it. I found that the soulful, spontaneous, and personal art made in the art therapy studio that I ran within a psychiatric hospital was distinctly different from the more conceptual paintings and sculptures that I made in my own studio. Over time, as I have shown in various publications, my own artistic expression was significantly influenced by the expressions and styles of the people whom I engaged in art therapy (1989, 1992). As I helped others access their unique and personal styles of expression, the process began to rub off on me and I started to find my own innate ways of expression.

However, in the beginning of my art therapy work I felt a definite gap, as I said above, between what we were doing in the hospital studio and my personal expression. Priscilla, one of the patient-artists with whom I worked very closely, kept asking me to show her my art. She was a capable painter who made vibrant, sensuous, colorful, and imaginative pictures reminiscent of Van Gogh, Gaguin, Cezanne, Munch, and others (Figure 15.1).

I knew on a certain level that her art was more personally developed than mine. But I was her art therapist, and perhaps a bit uneasy about being challenged in relation to my artistic ability.

When she asked me to show my art, I said the standard things about how I was there to help others with their expression and not to present my own work; that the purpose of the art studio was not about me. I never considered bringing my personal art to the studio. I had convinced myself that this separation between my roles as a painter and as an art therapist was essential to the professional integrity of the latter function where I did not want to bias the people with whom I worked. There was some degree of truth to this feeling since art students will often select teachers whom they admire and strive to express themselves in related ways. On another level, I perhaps sensed that my large abstract paintings were out of sync with the pictures being made in the hospital studio.

I also felt that I needed to keep clear borders between my work as a painter and as an art therapist. I am sure there was a significant degree of self-protection at work in that it would have been difficult if Priscilla and others in the studio did not understand what I was doing in my art, or even worse, not like it. But protecting my feelings was far less significant than the concern that negative judgments about my art could impair my

Figure 15.1 Christopher by Priscilla.

impact as their art therapist. Since Priscilla and I worked together on such a regular and personal way within the studio, I also felt the need to keep a certain distance and detachment, and maintain my role as someone who was there to help her.

On a certain level I wondered whether Priscilla, who was about 10 years older than me, was testing to see whether I could really paint and draw. I told her that I studied and painted in New York City with prominent artists like Theodoros Stamos, but this only increased her persistence in wanting to see what I did.

Over time I came to realize that Priscilla longed for a community of artists and I believe that she was genuinely interested in relating to me as a fellow artist, and that perhaps in this particular case my role as her art therapist may have called for this. In many ways our work together, which continued for over 10 years, grew into her vision and I must say that my overall image of myself as an art therapist has unfolded in keeping with her idea of fellow artists working together within a studio environment.

Painting with Priscilla

After leaving the state hospital, I returned for a number of years to paint with Priscilla and other artists in a studio environment. I also continued to work together with them in a special community art therapy program sponsored by the Addison Gallery of American Art where we conducted weekly sessions within one of the country's finest small museums.

Artists in the studio drew and painted portraits of me and I did the same with them; as they became more adapt at painting according to their innate styles and preferences, I experienced corresponding effects in my own art (Figures 15.2, 15.3, and 15.4).

My drawings and paintings of patient-artists within the studio combined perceptions of their gestures and qualities with my own ongoing and unintentional self-portraiture. I have observed how this self-presentation or interpretation occurs with everything I paint, males and females, and even animals, trees, and other elements from nature. All of my artistic expressions are apt to carry traces of psychic DNA.

Although, as Winnicott suggested, it may be best for therapy if we can help people discover their own fulfillment in living creatively and then "finish with us and forget us" (p. 87), I can say that the reverse has not been the case for me, especially in relation to my early and formative experiences. A number of the patient-artists had a major and unforgettable influence on my life and art. Through my experiences with them I learned how to more completely integrate my artistic expression with inner and outer experience.

Reaching comfort in some degree of mutuality

As I became more secure and comfortable as an artist and art therapist, I did not feel the same need for distance between personal expression and my professional work with others. If someone did not like my art, the negative reaction might be engaged as part of the ongoing therapeutic process. I also felt that my expressions became part of the larger studio

Figure 15.2 Anthony.

and therapeutic interplay. Participants enjoyed having me join with them and they were intrigued with what I did. I also discovered how my art did not seem to exert bias of any kind in relation to the expression of others in the studio. Each of us worked in our distinct ways and my images were viewed as simply part of the overall therapeutic community of images in the various groups I led.

When people in my studios ask questions about my art, I attempt to be open with them. In keeping with my research into the nature of artistic interpretation, the stories and accounts that I give about my artistic expressions can never give an absolute and definitive explanation of a picture's meaning (McNiff, 2004). My interpretations are reflections upon the

Figure 15.3 Danvers Man 1.

nature of an artwork and its particular expressive qualities. Words and
personal statements about pictures have more to do with how we respond
to them, how they affect us, what we see in them, and so forth. When
interpreting my art in this way, I try to be transparent, doing my best to
make contact with whatever the qualities of the image may be. Again, I

Figure 15.4 Danvers Man 2.

see myself as modeling how to candidly, sensitively, and imaginatively relate to images.

I encourage people within my studios to freely make their interpretations of my pictures; tell their own stories; and respond to expressions of my imagination with theirs. I discover how people may at times find more personal meaning in my picture than in their own and vice versa.

We respond to art with art in ongoing cycles of expressions intended to enhance the circulation of creativity, which is the primary medicine of the studio.

Maybe this is what Priscilla was trying to get across to me in the first years of my practice.

Fears of self-revelation and avoidance of self-absorption

Another impediment to art therapists openly showing their art within therapy sessions has been the long history within the mental health field of viewing artistic images as "printouts" of the artist's inner life. These diagnostic interpretations have generally focused on psychopathology and a pervading sense that whatever you draw or paint can and will be used against you.

From the start of my work in art therapy I did not accept these often idiosyncratic ways of interpreting art which were at odds with what I knew about the process of creation. Thus my early reluctance to show my art to Priscilla was not influenced by unwillingness to have my work evaluated in this way. Priscilla herself did not recognize the validity of these often projective approaches to art interpretation which she described as hurtful.

Moving beyond the posture of analyzing others and becoming part of the creative process may help art therapists establish greater empathy for the experience of others. In my experience the fixation on psychological contents lying below the surface of experience is tied to an inability to see and understand what is disclosed and presented on the face of our expressions. Perhaps the notion that deep emotions are tied to the past and hidden within the recesses of the psyche can be viewed as a defense against opening to the uncertainty of new and unplanned situations. I like to emphasize how depth is on the surface of expressions and my experience constantly affirms how the deepest psychological states are accessed by attentiveness to what we do and feel in the present moment, which can never be reduced to formulaic labels. Artistic expressions will always communicate dimensions of experience that extend beyond present awareness. In art therapy we move naturally between making spontaneous expressions and then reflecting on them as a dynamic process of discovery.

Although the long history of psychology's efforts to decipher codes of artistic expression has yielded no reliable mode of translation, I feel that these ingrained attitudes continue to play a role in relation to the degree to which art therapists are comfortable in freely showing their art to others.

Do we want to subject ourselves to the same disclosure of psychopatho-
logical contents that many within our discipline purportedly identify in
the works of others?

Self-disclosure of work in print

I took my biggest step in relation to self-disclosure as an art therapist when
I decided to use my own art in books that I wrote about the work that I
do—*Depth Psychology of Art* (1989) and *Art as Medicine: Creating a Therapy
of the Imagination* (1992). I was keenly aware that by showing my art in
this way I was making myself accessible to the kinds of interpretations
that I challenged. I had moved beyond my reluctance to disclose my art
to Priscilla and was now showing it to the world. However, I sensed that
doing this full disclosure would help to end the speculative diagnostic
practices that have had such a long-standing influence on art therapy and
the public perception of how art is used in therapy.

I wanted to use my own art as a basis for examining the psychology
of art and art therapy methods because I was increasingly uncomfortable
using the art of others to do this. I also felt that I could get much closer to
the phenomena being studied through these firsthand encounters with the
creative process. In these books I established methods of personal artistic
investigation that led to the publication of *Art-Based Research* (1998b) and
the creation of a rapidly expanding field of inquiry.

In researching the process of imaginal dialogue with artistic images
in *Art as Medicine,* I felt that "by using my own pictures, I can take risks,
speak freely, and publish the contents of intimate dialogue" without
using "another person's private expression to elucidate my methods"
(1992, p. 4).

When I presented my art in this public way I was more concerned
with the perception of self-absorption than disclosure. I described how
my goal was not to show myself and the contents of my private musings
but to illustrate the life of the imagination and to demonstrate how to
engage pictures and psychic images in the most intimate and poetic ways.
I have realized through this comprehensive disclosure that my "confes-
sions" within image dialogues are forms of creative and imaginative
expression just like all of the other art objects that I show to the world. My
experience also suggests that transparency tends to moderate the demand
to uncover.

I have found the same to be true in sharing intimate creative expressions within the arts therapy studio where we aspire to use all of our
creative resources in sensitive ways to further the flow of imagination and
feelings of satisfaction in relation to the impact of the creative process.
The expression of our sensibilities and responses to others is thus part

of an ongoing movement of creation that thrives on the mixing of varied, unique, and strong ingredients.

A circulation of creative energy

The painter Edvard Munch described how art involves an opening of the heart and communication of emotion in a way that can be helpful to others (Tøjner, 2003). In a similar vein C. G. Jung felt that healing comes from the realization that we are not alone in our struggles. These observations from both art and depth psychology suggest that therapy can benefit from the most open communication between therapists and clients with regard to their respective life experiences and perceptions.

I have also learned from my practice of the arts in therapy that art heals through the flow and exchange of creative energies that act upon us in ways that cannot be planned in advance. As I wrote in *Art as Medicine*, "the medicinal agent is art itself…an infusion of imagination and awareness rather than a specific answer" (1992, p. 3). Honest and well-intended communications and exchanges of expressions can be viewed as enhancing this circulation of creativity.

Repeatedly I observe how the creative process finds its way through the thickets of our emotional lives in ways that are inaccessible to the linear movements of verbal and analytic explanation. Within this context I view the artistic expressions of therapists as simply part of the process, part of the larger dynamic of discovery and creative transformation that I have learned to admire and trust (McNiff, 1998). Deep artistic healing happens when both clients and therapists let go and trust the wisdom of the creative process and the psyche's own power to treat itself.

References

Fish, B. (2005). Image-based narrative inquiry of response art in art therapy. Doctoral dissertation, Union Institute and University.

Kossak, M. (2008). Personal communication.

McNiff, S. (1976). Art, artists and psychotherapy: A conversation with Robert Coles. *Art Psychotherapy, 3*(3–4), 115–133.

McNiff, S. (1981). *The arts and psychotherapy.* Springfield, IL: Charles C. Thomas.

McNiff, S. (1989). *Depth psychology of art.* Springfield, IL: Charles C. Thomas.

McNiff, S. (1992). *Art as medicine: Creating a therapy of the imagination.* Boston: Shambhala.

McNiff, S. (1995). Keeping the studio. *Art Therapy: Journal of the American Art Therapy Association, 12*(3), 179–183.

McNiff, S. (1998a). *Trust the process: An artist's guide to letting go.* Boston: Shambhala Publications.

McNiff, S. (1998b). *Art-based research* London: Jessica Kingsley.
McNiff, S. (2004). *Art heals: How creativity cures the soul.* Boston: Shambhala Publications.
Moon, B. (2000). *Ethical issues in art therapy.* Springfield, IL: Charles C. Thomas.
Moon, B. (2007). *The role of metaphor in art therapy: Theory, method and experience.* Springfield, IL: Charles C. Thomas.
Winnicott, D. W. (1971). *Playing and reality.* New York: Basic Books.

chapter sixteen

The therapeutic relationship in motion

A dance/movement therapist's perspective

Elise Billock Tropea

Introduction

Movement is self-revelatory. Most humans are fairly astute at reading body language and automatically gathering information about a person by how they move in their body. Are they angry, tense, assertive, or passive? Are they sad, tired, joyful, or in pain? Without a word being said, much is revealed about a person in movement, so even as the dance/movement therapist may not intend to disclose a particular aspect of him- or herself to the client, it happens. In this treatment modality, therapist and client move together, watching and observing each other, interacting nonverbally. The therapist's nonverbal cues are there for the client to read, constituting unavoidable self-disclosure. Unavoidable self-disclosure is different, however, from therapist movement strategies that are more intentionally self-expressive and disclosing. In this chapter, both will be considered.

Any look at the role of self-disclosure in psychotherapy must first take into account the nature of the treatment modality. By definition, "Dance/ Movement Therapy (DMT) is the psychotherapeutic use of movement as a process which furthers the emotional, social, cognitive, and physical integration of the individual" (ADTA, 2008). A dance/movement therapist makes choices about how to move with a client in the service of furthering his or her treatment goals. This is distinctly different from moving freely, as on a dance floor, which is done either purely with the intention of self-expression or as a social activity. Just as therapists who talk freely about material irrelevant to their clients are being countertherapeutic, the same holds with the physical self-expression of the dance/movement therapist. Thus, moving in a self-disclosing, self-expressive way must be connected to a therapeutic goal, and its therapeutic value needs to be assessed. There are many techniques that movement therapists use; some are more disclosing of the therapist's inner self than others.

Traditional "talk" therapists are certainly aware of the power of the nonverbal realm and utilize it to a degree, just as movement therapists utilize the verbal realm to a degree. Let us compare the two therapies in the dimension of therapist self-disclosure. Talk therapy is typically conducted with both parties seated, relying more on the spoken word as the main medium of treatment. Therapist self-disclosure happens when the talk therapist decides whether or not to say something that is self-revelatory; the therapist can ask the client whether or not the therapist's disclosure was helpful. By contrast, the whole process of self-revealing through movement is a fairly nebulous process, because while something is always being communicated nonverbally, precisely what is being conveyed and received on a nonverbal level is uncertain. In talk therapy, the verbal therapist decides how much facial expression to show—some may choose to have as much neutrality as possible, attempting to show little emotion—other therapists, or the same therapist at different times, will choose to share their emotional response through facial expression—to smile or laugh with a client, to shed a tear in response to the client. The DMT also makes choices about how much expression to show, but as Geller (1974) points out, "In contrast to the relative anonymity, passivity and affective neutrality of the [traditional] psychotherapist's role, dance therapists are frequently called upon to be as active, exposed and physically involved as their patients" (p. 14).

Likewise, DMT clearly has a verbal dimension as well. DMT involves the same verbal self-disclosure issues as talk therapy, and talking is very much a part of the process, especially with higher functioning clients who typically rely on language as self-expression. Thus, in my practice with verbal clients, words play an important role, especially in the earlier stages of treatment. In essence, the language aspect of the connection can most often help regulate the level of "intimacy," thereby allowing the client time to find her/his comfort level, helping allay the awkward feelings that moving can stir. An important goal of DMT is to facilitate a fluid balance between verbal and nonverbal self-expression. My DMT training included in-depth training about psychodynamic theory and practice. I continue to believe that in the verbal dimension, judicious and attuned self-disclosure can be helpful. I do err on the side of caution, being careful about what I disclose, and mindful of the effects of verbal self-disclosure.

In this chapter, I will focus on the efficacy of DMT with children who do not typically use the spoken word for communication purposes, children who have been diagnosed with pervasive developmental delays

(PDD) and autism. I will explore how unavoidable and purposeful therapist self-disclosures manifest on a nonverbal level. In my case study of
Karl, a latency-aged boy with autism, I will review some basic tenets of
dance/movement therapy assessment and treatment, particularly as they
relate to therapist self-disclosure as a component in the therapeutic process. As clients reveal themselves through their bodies, both while moving and in stillness, so too, does the therapist.

DMT training and body awareness

DMT training teaches the therapist to be aware, first, of her own style and
preferences of movement. For example, my preference for typically navigating through the world may be one of quickness; directness and use of
my own weight as I cross a street, weed a garden, or even engage in conversation with a friend. If someone observed me in these actions, they would
sense intentionality, clarity of purpose, and economy of movement, in order
to accomplish these movement tasks. In understanding how my own natural movement preferences are read, and what they convey, I learned to be
mindful of what I am transmitting on a nonverbal level and how my movement dynamics (i.e., nonverbal self-disclosure) might impact my client.

Once grounded in sound knowledge of nonverbal aspects of communication, the dance/movement therapist is aware and able to broaden
her movement repertoire, move away from her own preferred movement
styles, and is then, as Sandel describes it, free to "straddle a delicate balance between spontaneity and self-control" (p. 110). Spontaneity, when
a therapist decides it might be an appropriate intervention, is a form of
purposeful therapist self-disclosure, as the therapist decides to see if the
client is ready to respond on that level. A therapist creating a movement
of her own (as opposed to only mirroring the client's movements) says
something about who she is and thus is a self-disclosure. In doing that,
just as in verbal therapy, there is the possibility of the experience revealing or expressing "too much." In verbal therapy, revealing something the
client doesn't want to know, or attempting to relate in a more mutual way
than would be truly beneficial to the client, is an example of "too much."
The analogous error of "too much" in movement therapy translates as a
movement experience that precipitates sharing too much affect, or expecting too much mutual creativity when the client is not ready for that. Doing
so would exemplify self-disclosing without attunement, and would be
unlikely to be helpful. A DMT thinks about this dimension of the therapeutic process, and using sensory awareness (an intuitive sense of the
meaning of the other's movement), makes choices about what is disclosed,
when it is disclosed, and evaluates whether or not therapist movement
disclosures were, in fact, therapeutic.

Kinesthetic empathy: Knowing each other intuitively

Kinesthetic empathy, which we all possess to some degree, is the ability to feel and understand another person simply by being in physical proximity or contact with that human being. When we recognize a smile or a gesture of another human being, and we sense what was meant by the nonverbal gesture, we are engaging in kinesthetic empathy. As we observe another's movement repertoire and "try it on" in our bodies or even imagine what it would feel like to execute that movement, we know what the other's intention is, to an extent. Through that process we gain an intuitive understanding of the other.

Recognizing that a person just smiled at me can mean a lot of things; we interpret its meaning by extrapolating from both our own experience of smiling along with our history of reading others' smiles over the course of our lives. The act of smiling contains nuances. For example, a smile could have myriad meanings, depending on the context: the person is happy, the person is reaching out and being friendly; conversely, the person could be attempting to manipulate the other (if the smile is purposeful and insincere), and so on. We recognize the meaning of each other's gestures by knowing what it feels like to do it, and also by considering its context. These are fairly high-level social skills that most people possess and simply take for granted and seem to happen spontaneously without thought or effort.

If we think for a moment of how we learn these skills in the first place, picture an adult relating with an infant. Early attuning behaviors are, for the most part, natural responses on the part of the adult. She mirrors and amplifies what she sees and hears the infant doing, adding expressiveness along the way. The adult finds herself making infant sounds, similar to the ones she hears the baby making. The baby laughs when the adult mirrors the baby's expressions, and gradually, the two build a rapport that is uniquely their own. We adults delight in this playfulness and in the building of reciprocity, one movement and sound at a time. Coupled with touch and in relationship with another, the infant learns interaction.

DMT taps into this fluid cycle of nonverbal understanding, beginning with the basics and building up to the highest level of nonverbal communication.

> As DMTs, we listen with our bodies, listen, as well, to the words, while observing and sensing areas in the body [where tensions] are held. We acknowledge without physically or behaviorally changing [the] body. Instead, we employ methods such as

amplifying, modulating or mirroring the movement behavior, suggesting ways of broadening the repertoire of the children, and in doing do introduce new coping skills. ... It is through this same process that we help clients to heal emotional wounds, learn new communication skills, and become more adept with the experience of feeling alive in their bodies. (Tropea, Dulicai, Freeman, 2008, pp. 352–353)

Children with special needs: Autism, Asperger's, and PDD

Children on the autistic spectrum have varying degrees of skill deficits in kinesthetic empathy, and thus, the typical relating that begins in infancy does not work in the usual way. Children with these differences do not respond relationally to mirroring and amplifying—instead, they remain absorbed in their self-stimulating movements patterns such as rocking, spinning, and fluttering their hands. In recent years the work of neurobiologists such as Gallese (2007) and Iacoboni (2008) has yielded major breakthroughs in the concept of body/mind interconnection. They posit that "mirror neurons" are the biological basis for socialization skills, self-awareness, empathy, and morality. Rizzolatti, in a lecture reported by Robinson (2008), explained that instead of a complex cognitive process, mirror neurons may allow for an automatic understanding of another's actions:

> "How do you understand what's happening when you see someone grasp a cup of coffee?"...This visually observed action is immediately transmitted to the motor cortex, and since we know what it means to grasp, we have this immediate comprehension that does not require a complex cognitive computation. Mirror neurons are really a mechanism to translate sensory information into a motor format....The value is that the system allows predictions. By replaying the action, we understand the intention of another person. If you see somebody grasp something, you can guess the next step using this mechanism....And, it is that ability to guess the intentions, and in a larger sense, the mental state of others that is so impaired in autism. (Robinson, 2008, p. 21)

Thus, DMT is an excellent modality for treating this population. These children have extreme difficulty expressing themselves verbally, as well as deficits in reading the nuances of nonverbal communication. The dance/movement therapist is able to make a beginning connection by entering their world and gently attuning to their movement. Children with autism are trapped into isolation using stereotypical behaviors (such as rocking, finger fluttering) to self-soothe. DMTs skillfully address these issues by more deliberately teaching the mirroring and amplifying skills. The processes that did not develop automatically can be taught when a therapist carefully crafts experiences that bolster the child's ability to grasp the nonverbal realm of communication and the intention that it reveals.

To accomplish this growth process, the dance/movement therapist begins by using movement as an attempt to join with the child, to enter her world and convey to her that we do understand a little bit. In so doing, we make a powerful statement that honors her movement as the communication it truly is. DMT pioneer Blanche Evan states, "The object is first not to change the body of the client but to let the client become freer and freer in exposing the body that she has" (Rifkin-Gainer & Evan, 1982, p. 11). Using their expert understanding of body language and how to mirror properly, DMTs relate nonverbally with the child in ways that untrained people are not usually able to do.

My early experiences working with children with autism provided me with a compelling understanding of nonverbal communication at its most basic level. If I were to miss the pure movement of my client and offer instead my own self-expressive version of the communication, I would miss the opportunity to connect in any meaningful way to the child. When I responded that way—expressing myself, or making a move that was not attuned—she let me know in the moment by seeming imperviousness to my presence. Her lack of response let me know I was not connecting and needed to read and replicate her body language precisely in order to respond in her language of movement.

In fact, in some cases, we can unwittingly drive a wedge into developing a relationship by merely mimicking a gesture or a movement without embodying the qualities fully. Think for a moment how alienating it can be when your attempts to communicate a thought or feeling are misinterpreted or misread by another. Though speaking the same language, it can feel as though the interchange happens in foreign tongues. Simple repetition of what the other has said, devoid of intonation, lacking any clear intention, can often result in creating frustration, and, after several attempts at making yourself heard, you give up the hope of being understood. Thus, as movement therapists, we have to be careful not to create that experience in our clients, particularly with children on the autistic spectrum, who struggle with being understood and are isolated. If we don't match them, we simply add to the alienation they already experience. In these moments, the DMT must "check in" with herself, and determine to what extent and how her own movement style and affective state—nonverbal self-disclosures—have influenced the quality of the connection. The DMT is careful not to bring her "mood" into the session because that will affect the way she expresses herself in her body. Since the body is our instrument and the common communicator, we, just as dancers do, must warm up prior to entering the movement space with our clients, clearing out our own material to make way for clear connection.

Nonverbal observation in assessment and treatment

In order to accomplish exquisite levels of movement attunement, DMTs rely on well-honed observational skills to both assess and treat clients. I will explain a little bit here, in order to help the reader understand the case study, as I will share my observations of Karl's movements in these terms. "Effort/shape" is a system for notating body movement, providing researchers and therapists with a common language—it defines how the movement is done, rather than what is done:

- *Flow* refers to the degree of tension accompanying a movement on a continuum from free to bound and, according to North (1972), is associated with feeling.
- *Space* refers to the quality of attention to movement displays on a continuum of direct (single-focused) to indirect (multifocused) and, according to North (1972), is associated with thinking and organizing.
- *Weight* refers to the quality of how weight is used in relation to gravity on a continuum from strong to light and, according to North (1972), is associated with differentiation of self and intention.
- *Time* refers to the urgency or lingering pace of movement on a continuum from quick to sustained and, according to North (1972), is associated with making decisions (doing).

Thus, matching another's body movement successfully requires that we recognize the coordinates of movement along these dimensions, and translate to our own body, the actions to encompass these qualities. Through that method, the therapist may enter into relationship with a client, regardless of her/his developmental level of functioning. We each have our own unique preferences as moving beings. Think for a moment of your own style. For example, as you sit in front of your computer prepared to respond to an e-mail, do you most often approach the keyboard with a sense of directness, using a firm touch accented by a rhythmicity of quickness, or do you notice a lightness in your fingers as you type? How might your movement approach to typing change with the content before you? Think how different your movement approach would be accepting an invitation to a party hosted by a good friend, as opposed to responding to criticism you have just received from your boss. As you continue, what do you notice about how you are holding your body? Shoulders? Wrists? Breath? In short, how do you move in general, and to what extent does your affective state alter your body? Thus, your movement and body language is a direct expression of your emotional state at the time.

Now that you have the basic understanding of how DMT proceeds, I will share with you about my work with Karl.

Karl: A case example

My work with Karl began when he was 7½ years old, 2 years after his diagnosis of PDD NOS, sensory integration deficits, and mild to moderate autism. His parents had trained in the Son Rise Program (SRP), one specifically designed for children with autism, and had, at the time of my introduction to his therapeutic team, been actively engaged in home-based treatment. Son Rise is a play-based approach that begins where the child is utilizing activities that originate with the child. The concept of joining with the child is the cornerstone of the method. As stated in the program mission,

> Autistic children can become very focused on their particular areas of motivation, often to the point of being termed "obsessional" or "preservative." Many traditional approaches have tried to steer children away from their areas of motivation in an attempt to broaden the child's range of interest. The SRP instead recognizes these interests as doorways into that child's world, a means of forming a connection to become the foundation for more spontaneous and flexible social exchange. (Son Rise Program, 2008)

I had not worked with a child in treatment in his home up until this time, and I wondered if such a shift in venue might constitute a boundary crossing and have an adverse effect upon his treatment. Typically, going into a home could create a problem, because a therapist working with a child in his home could be misperceived, and could cause confusion. What is the therapist doing there? How is their role to be understood? I was reassured to see that they had created a separate room for his therapy, lessening confusion for Karl as he transitioned from this space to the rest of his home. The space was purposely devoid of "clutter" and stimuli that could easily distract him. Props, such as balls of varying sizes and textures, stretch cloths, scarves, blocks, puzzles, art supplies, books, and music were readily available though stored away from the moving space. My concerns were allayed, seeing that much thought had been put into ensuring that he would understand our relationship in the context of his healing.

Our early sessions reflected Karl's intense need to remain separate from me, often tolerating my presence as safe only from a distance of 6 feet or more. I mirrored his movements in my own body, picking up his activities and trying them on. I was careful to match his engagement rather than offer new activities of my own design. In essence, I joined with him supporting his private world as "good enough."

During our once-a-week 45-minute sessions, Karl would often retreat under a cloth or into a corner of the room. His use of available space was severely limited. Eye contact during this time was fleeting at best. While Karl had developed speech, he still fell far behind peer developmental norms in expressive aspects, especially regarding intentionality as it related to social connection with others. He exhibited difficulty in fluid movement when engaged in locomotor activities and often struggled with balance throughout the sessions. It was not unusual for Karl to lose himself in his own rituals (e.g., stacking blocks in a ritualistic manner or playing by himself in fantasy reenactment of collapsing buildings later connected to his fascination with natural disasters such as Pompeii and tidal waves). I joined him from a distance, mirroring his movements, affect, gestures, and his use of speech.

As the relationship began to grow, Karl was able to tolerate closer physical contact with me, engaging more consistently through eye contact and with it the beginnings of reciprocity, seen in his growing willingness to include me in his favorite activities. When he retreated under the cloth, he was now able to allow me to join him, and to eventually use that cloth, then others as a prop as he moved to music. We began turn taking, first, he led and I followed, and as the sessions progressed Karl became comfortable enough to allow my leadership and to offer suggestions at times. We explored movement qualities of effort/shape and he began to use this shared movement vocabulary as well as to slowly put names to the feelings they evoked. He had made excellent progress, too, in the area of gross motor planning and balance as we played with stretch jersey, pulling with force, at times, and then shifting its quality to sense the light touch and its effect on the material. He began to spontaneously play with the props I introduced and would delight in creating his own "dance" for me, his audience. At times, he would invite his mother to watch, and afterwards he would share what the dance was about. "I am the king, taking care of the people." "I am moving like a volcano and I feel powerful." "Now it is your turn." And I would move, often replicating his dance as he watched. He knew his role as observer and took it seriously as I "attempted to do just what he had done." He was almost always able to remind me when I had left out an element or added something that wasn't his. At one point, he remarked, "You don't look like a king when you are moving. You look like a queen." I responded, "You are right. I felt like a queen, not a king." Karl was truly in present time in this moment. He was able to notice me and to feel my movement dynamics, to differentiate mine from his.

My choice to move with him as my observer, allowed him to "see" his own movement style, and to sense the difference between him and me. My nonverbal self-disclosures became more deliberate as his ability to attune grew. Pure replication of his movements gave way to reciprocal "dancing" where I offered my own sequences as he observed. We had begun a slow and steady progression into mutual authenticity.

A year later the sessions were markedly different in content and in the level of mutuality between us. As Karl became more at ease with the available moving space, he delighted in exploring and moving out into the room. I was becoming his witness, moving less with him, observing and offering feedback to him about what I saw in his improvised dances. The need to mirror him lessened with each session. Karl was making remarkable progress in his home-based program where joining with him was the cornerstone of treatment. He had grown very close to his support team, was integrating more with his siblings, and relating well to several children whom he had come to seek out.

DMT in his home terminated after 2 years as Karl began to need less time in his home-based safe space, and began attending a private program where he was fully included with children in a regular education setting. He had discovered a real interest in dance and enrolled in a hip-hop class at a local dance studio. A year later, I received a call from his mother asking that I consider seeing him at my studio to continue the kind of improvisational creative movement we had begun to grow. These sessions took place over a period of one year and were distinctively different from our early meetings. Our session began with conversation, as Karl sat on the couch. I encouraged him to speak about his week, asking questions that would then inform his movement theme.

One particular example illustrates the shift in the treatment technique and in Karl's use of DMT. He told of a trip to Florida with his family, of getting stuck at sea in the middle of a rainstorm, with his father at the helm of a catamaran. He shared his fear and his relief when they finally came ashore. He then put his story and his feelings into a 3-minute piece, choosing music that matched his theme. Using a large stretch cloth, Karl began his dance, curled tightly under the material.

He had, from the earliest sessions, been drawn to the colorful stretch cloth. Where once he had used it solely to withdraw, he had by this point found very creative ways of incorporating it into his movement improvisations. Barely moving at first, he slowly found his way onto his feet, swaying as if he were buffeted by winds and wave, the cloth held in one hand. As he began to make use of the available space, he shifted to being the wind and the sea, using strength and quickness, the cloth now purposefully draped around him as a stately robe. The cloth stunningly transformed, at one moment from the rolling waves, to the next, a royal cape. There was an ease and flow to his movement and a full complement of movement dynamics that matched his emotions and affective state. As the session ended, Karl spoke briefly about his dance, sharing his delight in its creation, pointing out how good it felt to be "that strong."

In subsequent sessions, Karl continued to expand his movement repertoire and to utilize the time together to explore his feelings, ideas, and his creativity.

Concluding comments

Karl's developing sense of his own body, his growing kinesthetic empathy with another, and increased verbal self-expression allowed him to use the DMT session to fully embody and release the fears and anxiety he experienced while on the boat. He had truly discovered his own ability to cope with and regulate his affective self in that moment. I and others with whom he worked entered into Karl's isolated world, first joining him on a nonverbal, kinesthetic, relational level. In doing so we were able to help him learn attunement to himself, others, and the world around him.

In a recent conversation with Karl's mother, she enthusiastically shared the progress of her 15-year-old son, highlighting his passion for clothing design. She spoke of their frequent trips to New York to attend fashion events, as he continues to develop an already impressive portfolio of his renderings. I couldn't help but remember his ingenious use of that stretch cloth during our sessions and his creativity.

DMT demands a willingness on the part of the therapist to travel to the unspoken realms of another. Self-disclosures, as they occur in this treatment modality, reveal the greater dimensions of disclosure of things not said in words. There is great potential for connection by being present together in a physical way, in a safe way—modeling the way for these skills that clients may bring to their everyday lives after they are able to do them with you. Moving one's feelings can open new pathways that allow for greater coping skills to emerge.

References

ADTA. (2008). *What is dance/movement therapy?* Retrieved August 5, 2008, from http://www.adta.org

Gallese, V., Eagle, M. N., & Migone, P. (2007). Intentional attunement: Mirror neurons and the neural underpinnings of interpersonal relations. *Journal of the American Psychoanalytic Association, 55,* 131–176.

Galles, V., Keysers, C., & Rizzolatti, G. (2004). A unifying view of the basis of social cognition. *Trends in Cognitive Sciences, 8*(9), 396–403.

Geller, J. (1974). Dance therapy as viewed by a psychotherapist. In *Writings on body movement and communication* (pp. 1–22). Columbia, MD: American Dance Therapy Association.

Iacoboni, M. (2008). *Mirroring people: The new science of how we connect with others* (1st ed.). New York: Farrar, Straus, & Giroux.

Laban, R., & Ullmann, L. (1971). *The mastery of movement*. Boston: Plays.

Levy, F., Fried, J., & Leventhal, F. (Eds.). (1995). *Dance and other expressive art therapies: When words are not enough*. New York: Routledge.

North, M. (1972). *Personality assessment through movement*. London: MacDonald and Evans.

Rifkin-Gainer, I., & Evan, B. (1982). An interview with Blanche Evan. *American Journal of Dance Therapy, 5,* p. 11

Robinson, R. (2008). How mirror neurons help us understand insights of others and are impaired in autism. *News From the AAN Annual Meeting, 8*(12), 20–21.

Sandel, S. (1993). The process of empathetic reflection in dance therapy. In S. Sandel et al. (Eds.), *The foundations of dance/movement therapy: The life and work of Marian Chace*. Columbia, MD: Marian Chace Memorial Fund, American Dance Therapy Association.

Sandel, S., Chaiklin, S., & Lohn, A. (Eds.). (1993). *Foundations of dance/movement therapy: The life and work of Marian Chace*. Columbia, MD: Marian Chace Memorial Fund.

Son Rise Program Web site. (2008). Retrieved October 6, 2008 from http://www.autismtreatmentcenter.org/contents/reviews_and_articles/research-child_centered.php

Tropea, E., Dulicai, D., & Freeman, W. (2008). Applying dance/movement therapy in school settings. (pp. 352–353). In R. Christner and R. Mennuti (Eds.), *School-Based Mental Health: A Practioner's Guide to Comparative Practices*. NY: Routledge.

section five

Therapist losses and personal challenges

chapter seventeen

Nobody gets to see the wizard
An interview with Dan Gottlieb

**Dan Gottlieb, Andrea Bloomgarden,
Rosemary B. Mennuti, and Catherine McCoubrey**

Introduction

Dr. Daniel Gottlieb is a psychologist and family therapist who is much loved and heeded in the Philadelphia listening area due to his public radio call-in show. Since he began broadcasting in 1985, his renown and stature have grown through his newspaper column (recently relinquished), four books, frequent professional appearances, and his Web site, as well as his private practice. When Dan was invited to share his experience of self-disclosure in these pages, he wanted very much to contribute his thoughts on a subject so close to his heart, but he did not have the luxury of time and energy for the writing process. After living with quadriplegia from a highway accident nearly 30 years ago, Dan is watching his body begin to "wear out," as his physician says. So he invited the editors to his home office on the wooded crest of a gentle hill to interview him on self-disclosure.

As his nurse led us down a long gallery of artwork to an open living area with a freestanding stone fireplace and large windows, we responded viscerally to the peace and beauty of Dan's personal environment. The generous, aesthetic spaces also enable his mobility in his wheelchair. We were shortly settled in his comfortable office, where Dan showed us his assistive technology that has aided his considerable productivity. Throughout the interview, Dan's speech was animated by his facial expression and expressive gestures, in spite of the limited range of motion in his upper body. Although Dan can't hide the outward signs of his disability, he has chosen not to hide his inner life, including the daily consequences of his profound injury. His extraordinary perspective on therapist self-disclosure is rooted in an affirmation of his brokenness and the fullness of his experience. He strongly believes that the power of healing comes from genuine connection between two human beings, rather than from a power-over relationship between doctor and patient. During our interview, Dan shared personal life events, as well as experiences with his clients, to illustrate the evolution of his psychotherapeutic philosophy.

The young professional

As a therapist in training, Dan learned about professional boundaries and observed how staff in clinical settings separated themselves from patients. Although he was intuitively uncomfortable with viewing people in treatment as being different from himself, he wanted to belong to the community of mental health professionals, so he tried to share their point of view. "I tried to identify with the staff, and I wanted to, but I [really] identified with the patients. When [the staff] got together and talked about 'those people,' I was uncomfortable. And I was more comfortable when I was in a session with one of 'those people.'"

Dan shared some of his personal history that shaped his sense of belonging to provide a background to his quandaries as a young therapist. As a child, he always felt different. "I felt it growing up. I felt it as a therapist. I felt different, and it felt awful, and I desperately wanted to feel like one of the kids. And I thought if I achieved enough, accomplished enough, and produced enough then [I would belong]. So I worked my ass off, and I became supervisor very quickly, and I got offered a job as regional director in a community mental health center substance abuse program. I had a really big job, and I was 27 to 28 years old, and I had a very big job. Supervisor of some 30 people, and I still did not feel like I was one of the kids." Dan thought differently about the clients than many of his colleagues did; he saw them as people not unlike himself, but that didn't match the prevailing notion of being a good therapist. "And I was good, I mean I was told that I was a good therapist, and in hindsight, I was pretty good for somebody at that age." At that time, Dan was still fighting his sense of feeling different.

The accident: Another form of different

"And then 'my accident': I was crippled, dependent, helpless. I was 33 years old, and I knew I would never be one of the kids."

"I was acutely suicidal right after the accident, and I am lying in ICU again, and I am wearing a halo vest. I don't know if you have ever seen one of them. They are the grossest apparatus, I would say; a metal bar literally gets bolted into your head, and you are like that. So I am in bed staring at the ceiling, and my only wish was to go to sleep and not wake up, and I hear a voice say, 'You are a psychologist, aren't you?' and I said,

'Yes.' She said, 'Can I talk to you?' Because of this apparatus, I could not turn my head."

"I never saw her face. She sits down, and she tells me about a significant loss she has just endured. Her boyfriend, if I remember it, and she is in agony, and she is suicidal, and we chat, and I listen, and I know what she feels, because that is what I feel—that kind of desperation—and I did not know what I said, but I knew, and she knew that I knew, and at the end I referred her to someone, and she moved on. And I knew. I closed my eyes after she left, and I said I can live with this. I know I can be of value. She showed me that I could be of value."

"But those three words—'please help me'—saved my life." As Dan became well enough to rebuild his life with quadriplegia, he grew to embrace his differences, free from his prior efforts to conform to the professional community at large. Finally he could be himself; he had to be. "The image I have is that my neck broke, and my soul began to breathe."

In his most recent book, *Learning From the Heart*, Dan describes wondering in the aftermath of his accident if he was even human anymore. He was in excruciating pain and suicidally depressed. More than the shock, grief, rage, and terror of his trauma, "what was most painful and most terrifying was feeling disconnected from my fellow human beings. Over the next several weeks [right after the accident, in the hospital], I began to wonder what it really meant to be human...to cope with the terrible sense of alienation, I began to simply notice what humans (they and I) did; how we acted and reacted, how feelings worked, and how thoughts and feelings played off one another...I needed to do this to reassure myself that I was still one of them. And yet, deep down, I knew that although I might be one of them, from this point on, I was different" (Gottleib, 2008, pp. 1–2).

In learning to accept his physical condition, which promised to set him still further apart, Dan discovered a deeper sense of sameness and connection through the spectrum of human emotions that we all experience, regardless of our condition. By shedding his desire to be "one of the kids" and simply being himself, his relationships to his clients came into accord with his initial perception of the shared human legacy that held them together. Dan also realized that when we hope and try to be someone other or better than we think we are, instead of living in the moment and being as we are, we open ourselves to despair. We can be so busy chasing something else that we miss our own lives and never feel good enough.

Freedom to connect

Sharing his own stories of pain, shame, terror, and love, of wrestling with his desire to fit in, to be someone else, to badly want something other than what was happening, allowed Dan to make healing connections with other human beings, who carried their own intimate knowledge of these experiences. It is in that connection of shared experience that people help each other to not feel alone, to feel validated in their pain, and to be part of the human family. When we are ashamed of our vulnerabilities, we risk assuming false identities to mask our flaws. By letting our guard down and allowing ourselves to see and be seen by another, we invite deeply resonant connection, healing, and meaning into our lives.

"I [began] to experience the freedom of not belonging." Dan no longer felt like he had to conform; in fact, even if he wanted to, he couldn't. "People would walk into my office, and they would know, and I would know that they knew, and it was a different relationship right from the beginning. It was more tender, it was more open, it was less bullshit and less defensive."

Dan told us a story to demonstrate his point. "It was evening and I was working with a young girl—woman, 17. She was sitting right where you are sitting, and I forgot what the issue was about, something about shame, about looks, weight, I don't know, whatever. She was gorgeous, like most kids are." But of course, she was striving to be something other than what she thought she was—she wasn't satisfied with herself because she wasn't living up to her own expectations of what she thought her body should look like. "So I am there listening, wrestling with my helplessness and my paternal impulse to say something stupid and reassuring, and my eyes go down to the floor while I am thinking, and I see on my lap that my catheter leaked, and my pants are soaked, and in that flash I am thinking that if it were anyone else over there—a man, a grown woman, a boy, anyone else—it would have been better, but for some reason, that was the most humiliating situation for me. And I looked up at her, and she could see the shame in my eyes, remorse from shame, and she knew why, and I mean she saw that my pants were wet, and without saying a word, she came over and just held me, and she put my head on her chest and just held me, and I let her. And she sat down, and we knew, and we both felt the same thing, and it was nothing to be cured, because that's what humans do. I peed in my pants, and I get crazy inside, but I can't change it."

At the next appointment, Dan processed what that experience was like for her. "You know we talked a good deal about shame and what it was like for her, and I talked about what it was like for me, and … we talked about when she pees in her pants, metaphorically." Dan continued, "At other times I have peed in mine literally and metaphorically, and it normalized it. I mean that is what much of the work is about. When you open yourself as a human, you normalize an awful lot." So Dan used that experience, first to allow her to connect with him in his humiliating moment, and then, to open the discussion about the many humiliations that she faces, that we all face, and in doing that, he allowed that awful experience for him to become an opportunity for connection between two human beings. Had he done something else in the moment—perhaps called his nurse, ended the session, pushed her away when she had tried to reach out to him—the alternative might have had an entirely different effect, disengaging and alienating them from each other.

Among Dan's observations of human nature that he offered over the course of the interview was our need to be "important," our striving to be something more than we are, and the pressure and pain caused by expecting such "importance" of ourselves. "I'll tell you this story. A man came to me who had been in analysis for 16 years, and [he] came to me for [a] consult in his mid-60s, and he said that he felt like a failure. He felt like a failure as a man and a failure as a patient. He said, 'All my life I felt like I am not very important in this world, and I have been working on this forever in therapy, and there is no change.' He said 'I feel like a failure.' And I said to him, early on, (he is [here] 10 minutes), and I said I have got good news and bad news. I said you are not a failure; your perception that something is wrong with that is the problem. You are just not very important in this world. And he laughed and he cried. And he laughed again." Dan went on, "I feel deeply that I am not very important. I think in the broad scheme of things, who I am isn't important at all, and everything I do matters."

The apparent contradiction between personal humility and significant action illustrates Dan's use of paradoxical ideas to get us to embrace the opposite poles of our experience, to own all the parts of ourselves. We may not feel important in the ideal sense toward which we strive—to be good, to be attractive, to be accomplished "enough"—yet everything we do, if we are in the moment, does matter. How we treat others matters; connecting with other human beings matters. Dan's earlier observation of the lethal nature of hope to push us into a future that can never be reached and away from the present moment in which we might experience real connection is another example of his paradoxical, therapeutic guile.

Dan remembered his first patient, Flora, who had carried a diagnosis of schizophrenia for 35 years. Many people assume that people with schizophrenia are totally out of touch with reality, without recognizing the limits of their cognitive distortions and their often-heightened interpersonal perception. As a newly minted psychologist, young Dr. Gottlieb entered his first appointment with Flora with trepidation, wondering what he was going to do to help her. He had the title, he had the power, and he was supposed to know what to do. "I was 23 years old, and I thought that I was going to help, and she comes in, she shuffles in, and she sits down. She is tearing paper. She has got a sheet of paper that she is tearing. I did not want to interrupt her, and all I know is that this last

50 minutes is all I really know about therapy. And she is tearing paper, and I don't want to ask her [what she is doing]. I am too afraid that I will screw something up. She gets up, and she shuffles towards the door, and she turns towards me at the door, and she says, 'You know something?' she says, 'You are full of shit,' she says, 'and I have the papers to prove it.' Fabulous! So you can imagine what kind of relationship we had after that. I mean, I was full of shit, and she knew I was full of shit, and now I knew that she knew, and I did not have to pretend that I was not full of shit, and we could just hang out, and we had a great relationship." Dan's relationship with Flora presaged what he came to know later through his accident: that we are all human, that facades are not particularly useful and are often harmful, and that masks of shame can cause separation and prevent healing. In their stead, self-disclosure begets mutual self-disclosure, connection, and healing.

Dan went on to explain the power of shame and the use of self-disclosure as a potent antidote. "I think what prevents all connections is shame, and pretense which is based on shame, and the only cure for shame that I have ever known is disclosure. It is the only way I know to cure shame." As an example, he told us "another ungodly fluid story….I gave a lecture at a middle school, and I went there by myself without help. I am giving a lecture, and I looked down on the floor, and I saw that my bag, my catheter bag, was leaking on the floor. It was a puddle. And I have to drink a lot, so I knew that puddle was going to get a lot bigger, and I am 15 minutes into a 1-hour talk, and I am dying up there, I am dying up there. And then after the lecture is over, people come up to the stage to shake my hand to thank me, and I am watching them walking through it. And I just want to die. I rush out into my van, and I just cried and cried and cried from shame. And for about a year after that, at every lecture I gave, I told that story. And that is how I do my life, not just therapy."

For Dan, pretending is a source of falseness and disconnection from one's true self that causes real suffering. When we pretend to be better or less than our true selves, we are implicitly living in shame, denying what is real and accurate. Able-bodied therapists have the ability to appear as though we could never soil ourselves, we are always clean and perfect, we never smell bad or look undignified, and we can appear to be professionals who mostly have it together. We don't live with the risk that our catheter could leak at any time, spoiling our show and exposing us to embarrassment and humiliation. We live with the privilege of hiding our fallibility, even though we can become lost in our own hiding places. Dan has no such place. "I can't pretend I am not crippled, dependent and helpless; I can't pretend that I don't pee in my pants; can't pretend that I'm not scared. I can't, *can't* pretend that I am big and strong." Since his injury, Dan has arrived at an attitude of love and gratitude toward his body, as it is, and for its heroic effort to cope with its imposed afflictions. By embracing his own distressed body, Dan helps others to accept their imperfect selves and to face their limitations and challenges appreciatively. He does not pretend to be a great healer who will solve their problems or cure their ills.

Besides his physical condition, Dan reported that he is open with his clients when something big and important is happening in his life. "I talk about my life very openly, and my struggles. When my sister was dying, most of my patients nurtured me through it. The day she died I got a call at eight o'clock in the morning. She lived up in central Jersey, and I had a patient at 8:30, and I could not cancel in time. It was a man, he is obese, and I am sitting in the hallway, and he walked up. As he is coming up, he stopped 30–40 feet away, and he said, 'It happened, didn't it,' and I said, 'Yeah,' and he came up to me, and he put my head on his great big belly and just stroked my face, and I held him, and I cried and cried and cried. I even got snot on his shirt. He didn't mind." We questioned him further, asking him to describe how it affected their relationship and this man's therapy. "Well it was, I hate to say this, but it was no big thing to him, because that was just an extension of the nature of our relationship. So I think me allowing him then to nurture me through this changed the relationship. That is therapy."

Dan is fairly matter-of-fact about the sorts of things that happen to him; they are the same sorts of things that happen to his clients, and he makes no bones about that. By allowing a client to support him in a vulnerable moment, Dan shares the roles of giving and receiving empathy and makes room for the sense of connection between them to grow. This mutual exchange is also a legitimate activity of psychotherapy. In his willingness to be vulnerable and real, he gives his clients the opportunity to sense their value to him, in relationship, as they are, not for their accomplishments or neediness, but because of their empathic connection with him. An invulnerable therapist, who never appears to have anything go wrong in his life, "treating" a client who is seen as a sick patient only perpetuates dominant and submissive roles and prevents therapeutic change. As Dan told a psychoanalytic society several years ago, "our patients call us with the perception of [their own] 'pathology.' We schedule an appointment with them with the presumption of pathology. And maybe the problem is the perception and presumption, because you can always find it, you can always find it."

Dan does not view some people as sick and others as healthy. We are all part of the human family; each of our lives travels along the continuum of human experience, facing the same basic existential issues as we go. We have the capacity to really hear and understand each other, and on common ground, we can learn from each other and help each other to heal. Flora, the veteran of schizophrenia, taught Dan about the importance of being down to earth and real with clients. Therapists learn from their clients, growing and healing in therapeutic relationships without crossing boundaries or reversing roles that would betray the primary commitment to the client's well-being. The presenting symptoms or problems do not define a client for Dan, nor do they imply that the client has nothing to offer him in their work together, as if therapy were a one-way street. When Dan's clients have helped him through his losses and humiliations, they, too, experience the power and gratification of giving. More importantly, they have received an opportunity to connect on a deep and intimate level with another human being, which is what therapy is all about.

Our connection

Early on in our meeting, Dan told us, "Hippocrates said that inside of every patient is a doctor that can heal them, and Gottlieb says, inside of every doctor is a patient, and unless all four are present, there is a lie in the room." This captures Dan's view on therapist self-disclosure. Healing cannot take place when the therapist is in hiding. A client can only have a genuine human connection with a therapist who is fully present and willing to share and reflect on his or her own experience of being human. This does not mean that therapists talk excessively about themselves, or fail to focus on the client's needs and reasons for being in therapy. In Dan's practice, self-disclosure is at the heart of the paradoxical gift that he offers his clients, an authentic connection with those aspects of himself and his experience that are the most useful and meaningful for their work together toward the client's goals.

As we approached the end of the interview, Dan said, "I want you to look at the sign outside my door that I have way up on top of the door. A lot of people do not notice it. Will you go [look]?" Andrea walks out of the office, turns to look above the door frame, and laughs. Roe says, "What does it say?" Andrea answers, "Nobody gets to see the wizard." Dan adds, "No way, no how. Because there isn't one. That is where self-disclosure starts." Dan shows us his business card, too. Instead of a litany of his impressive credentials, it simply said, "Dan Gottlieb, Human."

In the cool-down from the interview, Dan talked with pleasure about his writing career. He was anticipating the imminent publication of his latest book, *Learning From the Heart*, which includes a chapter on psychotherapy, and the airing of his public television special in conjunction with the book release. Dan also described his satisfaction with the popularity of his book, *Letters to Sam*, addressed to his then-6-year-old autistic grandson, in whose life Dan revels. Near the end of our visit, Dan noted with wry humor the coincidence between his increasing signs of success and physical decline. He spoke again of living in the moment, closely attuned to nature's cycle, so visible outside the large windows of his office.

As we left Dan's home and walked quietly to our car, we shared a sense of sober exhilaration after sitting with a man whose intimacy with his mortality allowed us to experience our own; our vulnerability and our strength, our common humanity as wounded and healing souls.

chapter eighteen

Confronting life's adversities
Self-disclosure in print and in session

Dana L. Comstock

A therapist's adversity

My journey with therapist adversity and self-disclosure began in April of 1998, when I was faced with traumatic pregnancy complications. Midway through my pregnancy, and much, much too early, my first daughter, Samantha, was born still and premature. One day I was on the treadmill of life, earning my membership into the "mommy club," and the next I was alone is an abyss of despair. The process was emotionally and physically grueling. Just when I began to fully understand what was happening to me, I was hit with an onslaught of grief, immobility, and despair. From the moment I discovered I was in trouble, I had to abandon all professional responsibilities including the university courses I was teaching, as well as the clinical work I was doing at the local Rape Crisis Center (RCC).

Initially, my colleagues at both the university and the RCC explained my absence to students and clients as best as I, myself, understood it: "Dr. Comstock is facing serious pregnancy complications. We aren't sure how serious things are at this time. She is in the hospital. If the baby survives over the next 24 hours, she'll need surgery and will then have to stay on bed rest for the remainder of her pregnancy. She won't be returning to work until after she delivers her baby." This initial disclosure was the "best-case scenario." Maybe I was naïve, or perhaps in denial, but I was not able, nor did I feel the need, to share my fear of the fact that I might lose my baby.

The complications that slammed me midway through my pregnancy involved the painless dilation of my cervix, which put my baby at risk for infection and premature delivery. The diagnosis of "incompetent cervix" was humiliating, but there was a possible intervention: a "rescue cerclage." My only hope was that after a day or so in the prone position (feet elevated above head), gravity would pull everything back into place (namely the gestational sac) at which time a "rescue cerclage" could be placed around my cervix to keep it closed.

The placement of what is referred to as a "preventative cerclage" is not an uncommon procedure. When an expectant mother has an incompetent cervix (which can only be diagnosed once the problem presents itself in the same way mine had), the cerclage is placed at the end of the first trimester *before* any cervical dilation. In my case, the intervention required a rescue cerclage because I was in my second trimester and already 2 centimeters dilated. The risks of the procedure are too numerous to mention, and the pregnancy outcomes, according to my research, left me with very little hope.

Although the surgery was successful, I was at a high risk for an intrauterine infection. I remained in the hospital for another week on strict bed rest before being discharged. My memory of this period is that my department chair at the university and the clinical director of the RCC would get briefings on my condition from my husband or mother, which were then communicated to students, clients, faculty, and the university community. It was made clear to everyone that I wasn't up for any phone calls or visitors, and everyone respectfully kept their distance. I also recall the beginnings of a sense of isolation that resulted from my complete absorption into trying to stay vigilant of any changes in my body. My reality during this time was that at any moment my water could break and that a premature delivery would be inevitable.

After a week in the hospital had passed, I was sent home. Home health care was arranged so that I could continue with intravenous antibiotics. My job was to pray, wait, and be on alert for any signs of infection or loss of amniotic fluid. The only news I had to share at that time was that I'd reached a significant milestone. My obstetrician explained that because I'd made it a full week, "in theory," my chances of carrying to term were equal to that of someone who'd had a preventative cerclage. It looked like it was time to settle into a new routine, which, for me, involved staring at the ceiling or the maple tree just outside the bedroom window. My students and clients seemingly went on about their lives. There wasn't anything anybody could do for me. A doctoral teaching assistant was assigned to wrap up the last few weeks of my courses, and new therapists were assigned to a very small caseload at the RCC.

There's just no easy way to transition into what happened next. Within days of returning home, I began to suspect I was leaking amniotic fluid. Then, a low-grade fever set in. Shortly after, my lower back began to hurt. My complaints to the after-hours on-call obstetrician were dismissed as a possible kidney infection which "must be a result of the catheter used during surgery." Knowing full well a catheter hadn't been used in surgery (I had specifically asked), I decided to leave this man alone for the rest of the night and decided to wait it out and pray for relief. Throughout the night, the fever got worse, and the back pain slowly became unmanageable even with the low doses of Tylenol I'd been taking in the hope that everything was just my imagination. As the hours passed, I *knew* I was in trouble and felt helpless to do anything about it.

Being that I was (and still am) a therapist, a "caregiver" by profession, I made an irrational decision *not* to call again (are you ready for this?) until the clock had reached a reasonable hour at which a man might get up to play a game of golf. By 5:30 a.m., I'd had all I could take and rationalized it might be an appropriate hour that a man might get up to *shower* in order to make it to a 7:00 a.m. tee-off. During this call, I announced I was headed to the hospital. I was admitted but wasn't actually seen by a physician until 10:00 a.m., during which time I was in labor with my cerclage in place. The risks involved in *that* scenario are deadly. During my initial assessment, an ultrasound showed that my baby had died, most likely due to an infection. I was given an epidural for pain, the cerclage was removed, the amniotic fluid was indeed full of infection, as was my body, and I was given Pitocin to intensify my contractions.

I was, at the time, particularly afraid of the actual delivery. Fortunately, the hospital assigned me an obstetrical grief counselor. She took care to explain to me and my family what the baby would look like, encouraged me to hold her after she was born, and coached me through what I could expect during my recovery. Samantha was delivered at 8 p.m. that evening. We held her, took pictures, stamped her footprints on a mock birth certificate, and cried. My grief counselor kept telling me I was "going to be okay" because I was "doing all the right things." I secretly kept asking myself, "How can anybody do something so 'right' that feels so awful?" Exhausted, I surrendered to the idea that there just wasn't any "sensitive" way to go about the business of helping someone through this kind of loss and held little expectation that anybody could truly help me.

Disclosing the loss

Students at the university were told by the faculty that I had lost my baby and the clinicians at the RCC shared the news with my former clients. I was too distraught to talk to anyone directly about my loss. For a time, my grief seemed insurmountable. I retreated into a routine of sleeping and sobbing. After growing tired of "going it alone," I sought support and spent the summer doing intense grief and trauma work and began taking medication for postpartum depression. To complement my therapy, I began sorting through the growing pile of cards and letters I'd received from students, from people I knew only professionally, and from former clients who reached out to me while consumed with their own pain. The latter moved me the most. I felt, and still feel, that this meant something powerful about the mutual healing process that takes place in *all* relationships, even therapeutic relationships.

Relational-cultural theory would suggest this is "mutual empathy" in action. Mutual empathy, the key to healing from the RCT perspective, is the experience that we *matter* to another. In therapeutic relationships, mutual empathy unfolds when clients are empathic with how their experiences move or impact their therapists through the responsivity of the therapist (Jordan, 2000). For me, one of the most challenging things about working with sexual trauma survivors was that it was often difficult to cocreate mutual empathy in therapy. Clients often felt reserved, mistrustful, easily reinjured, worried that their stories would or had "contaminated me," all of which were healthy and expected responses, especially in the early stages of therapy. As a result, it was hard for them to sense how their stories impacted me, particularly when, paradoxically, some worked to protect me from their traumas altogether!

I was deeply moved that so many of my clients had the courage to reach out to me during one of the most vulnerable times in my life. And having done so eventually provided us with a means to explore a relational competence they did not believe they had prior to my loss. Their courage, in particular, motivated me to get better and back to work. I took a lot of strength from *their* responsivity and courage.

Docking the ship after the storm

Reemerging back into my professional life as both a professor and therapist came the fall of that same year. Although I felt ready to return to life as usual, I had practiced, *at length*, a script of how I'd address my absence. I had anticipated this task would require negotiating the curiosities, as well as the legitimate needs and concerns of my students and of the clients with whom I would resume therapy. I truly had no idea what to expect, but was keenly aware of how raw and vulnerable I felt. My diagnosis of "incompetent cervix" (not "overanxious cervix," or "really-ready-to-have-the-baby cervix") really took a toll on my self-worth. Call me anything, but not "incompetent."

I was also aware of how uncomfortable I made some people. It just so happened that shortly before returning to the university, I made a trip to the local mall. By chance, I ran into a current student. My genuine response at the sight of her was one of excitement. I think I might have even called out her name. Her response, it appeared, was one of horror. Perhaps she hadn't worked on *her* script, but what had once felt like a mutually warm fondness suddenly felt like two naked strangers were being forced to have a conversation simply because there wasn't anybody else around to talk to. After a brief exchange of small talk, she bolted. That hurt, pure and simple, and I wondered how many other experiences like this one awaited me. How much energy would I have to expend putting others at ease when I was the one that had dealt with so much pain?

Upon my return to the university, I was aware that our department had changed. The handful of students with whom I anticipated I'd feel most safe had graduated, and new ones had been admitted at both the master's and doctoral level. I had no sense of who knew what amongst the newcomers. For those still in the program, I returned with a degree of guilt for having disrupted the rhythm of their education, particularly in relation to students whose dissertations I'd been directing. Some had moved on and had gotten another dissertation director; others had replaced me "temporarily" and were curious to know if I felt up to the task. There were also others who were seemingly unaffected by the whole thing and we simply picked up where we left off, just business as usual.

Although I understand there is a continuum for everything, the latter response took me off guard. In higher education, there is, at least from my experience, a certain objectification of professors (I find this to be true of therapists as well). I find that often we're treated as if we're not human (ask any professor if they've ever truly had their feelings hurt by a student evaluation), or if we are perceived as human, we're *superhuman*. There's very little ground from the masses. What I learned was that all the time and energy I put into my "script" was useless. Most students who wanted to speak to me about it had written me during my absence, so their sensitivity and my gratitude was the springboard for our reconnection. And it was the same with most of my clients. In nearly every exchange with clients, we dealt briefly with what happened and moved on. But not after we explored what their reaching out had meant to them and to me particularly in relation to how little self-worth most of them had felt to have.

My adversity was a time for my trauma clients to exercise the reality that they *did* have something to offer to the world, that they weren't "damaged goods," and that they'd changed in a big way with one small step in reaching out to me. And I had been healed, in part, as a result of their effort and was able to demonstrate that, in fact, I did *not* get "contaminated" by them or the stories many were then able to share for the first time.

We were able to truly make use of the opportunity to explore what relational-cultural theory (RCT) refers to as the "central relational paradox," particularly what it means for trauma survivors: We all have a yearning for connection, but for trauma survivors in particular, movement toward connection triggers terror (rather than manageable fear, or vulnerability) as most have been betrayed and abused by loved ones, or people they or their families had trusted. As a means to maintain emotional safety, clients (just like the rest of us) exercise strategies for disconnection. Such strategies are to be honored by the therapist and constitute a practice that takes a great deal of patience, empathy, presence, and a sincere effort to contextualize their responses (versus pathologizing them).

It didn't take me long to give up my strategy for disconnection: the script. Its sole purpose was to protect my vulnerabilities, which ultimately kept me out of connection with everyone I came into contact with. I wanted to express my gratitude to those who had reached out to me, and that simply couldn't be done with a script. RCT holds that any time we work toward maintaining an image, we move away from the possibility of connection. The other option is authenticity, which, from the RCT perspective, gives you many more response options than a simple script. Sometimes that meant I said to someone in the hall, "Hey, I got your letter, thank you, that meant a lot." Other times, I privately shared how rough things had been with students in my office and then spent time listening to *their* stories of loss, stories they'd been out of touch with until they'd learned of mine.

In every scenario, I never lost sight of the fact that relationships with students in higher education, even in graduate school, need to remain transparent. Specifically, it is naïve to think that you can, or should, disclose something to a student and expect it won't be shared with other students. It is unfair, perhaps even unethical, to even make such a request. With my clients, the impact of my loss was discussed in a manner as to how it had impacted them, and/or our work in therapy and those explorations felt really different in the context of my now being a "touchable" therapist, versus being perceived as "untouchable" prior to my loss. The remainder of this chapter will focus on self-disclosure in relation to a therapist's loss in the context of a culture in which people are uncomfortable with those who are grieving. It will address the impact of the nature of "losses made public," as well as how the need to remain transparent impacted my decision to write publicly about my experience.

Cultural and professional prohibitions against the disclosure and visibility of grief and vulnerabilities

An important lesson for mental health professionals struggling with self-disclosure is that some people, *many* people, are very awkward around issues of loss as well as issues related to vulnerability, particularly the vulnerabilities of the therapist. This is an *extremely* taboo subject and it is a rare thing to use "therapist" and "vulnerability" in the same sentence (Comstock & Duffey, 2003). I would argue that the mental health profession's prohibition and fear around self-disclosure mirrors that of the broader culture's difficulty with vulnerabilities, which is further complicated by theoretical orientations, namely psychoanalysis, that call for neutrality in the therapist. I would also argue that this "neutrality" is demanded of *many* theoretical orientations, including systems theories, as an unspoken necessity.

There is a plethora of research on grief in our culture, and I, like most, was reemerging from basically having gone "underground." Our culture's issues with taking note of those who are vulnerable, coupled with the reality that some people, including clients, are just simply not always going to care about their therapist's life adversities, make for a complexity of complications to negotiate in making the decision to self-disclose.

My reemergence back into my professional world was frightening. I was feeling raw and overwhelmed over the myriad ways in which I might, with my new history in tow, be received. Quite frankly, I was dreading the whole experience and never again wanted to feel what I'd felt that day in the mall! As I shared in the previous section, once I gave up my "script," I was able to reconnect with students who were at all kinds of different phases of their education. The majority of my clients, most of whom were dealing with PTSD, had emerged from the period of my absence with a renewed sense of resilience. Our work shifted to a deeper level as my loss had created an opportunity for them to also explore how life can turn on a dime. In many cases, our work moved from feeling stuck in past traumas to exploring the opportunities of the present, whether they be relational, professional, or familial in nature.

It is important to add here that my clients' experiences and responses to my infant loss were much like those reported by Miriam Greenspan in her 1986 publication titled "Should Therapists Be Personal? Self-Disclosure and Therapeutic Distance in Feminist Therapy." Greenspan, one of the very first feminist scholars to write on self-disclosure in therapy, shared how she returned to work and dealt with the loss of her infant son, Aaron, who was born very ill and subsequently died at 2 months of age. Because of her writing, I sought out to interview her to learn more about how she processed the loss of her son with her clients. I also want to add that because Miriam was (and is) a sole clinician who sees clients in her home office, she, alone, was the one to make the calls informing her clients of her son's birth, his health problems, and ultimately his death. During our interview in the summer of 2001, she shared:

> It was as if a sudden dose of real reality hit hard and became a part of the therapeutic process. Obviously, when I came back, my child's death was the subject that was on the table. There was no way to avoid it. My clients were all very, very concerned about me. I felt they were very compassionate and very respectful.

They wanted to know how I was doing, but were very careful in that they always expressed: "I don't know how much you want to talk about this." It just humanized the therapeutic relationship and broke through the fiction of psychotherapy that the therapist is some kind of superhuman being and is there only as the total transference object for the client or patient . . . there to be a mirror for you. You know, I never did that kind of therapy anyway. The book I was writing (*A New Approach to Women and Therapy*, 1983) was very much opposed to that whole model (laughing) and this experience really brought it home!

I think that the reality of what happened in my life broke through the clients' fantasies of having a "protectress" that is all-powerful. That became grist for the mill. Everybody seemed to be dealing with that. They were concerned with whether or not I'd be able to talk about their feelings in relation to this painful destruction of their illusions. I think they were very relieved when they found out that, yes, I could. They were also very relieved that I could be a human being with them. That I could say: "Yes, my son was born with a brain injury and I don't know why. He was with us for two months and I loved him very much, and I miss him very much" . . . and could cry, and did cry. There wasn't a single client I spoke to that I didn't cry with. There was just no way I was going to sit there and try to distance myself from what I felt. Here I am trying to teach them to be with their emotions (laughing), so it made no sense to stifle my own!

They could see me crying, the tears came through, and then the tears stopped, and then we continued. It didn't interfere with the work. If they were feeling bad for me or wanted to protect me, they would tell me, and we would work on that. For the most part, it was absolutely some of the most fruitful work my clients did, especially in terms of their vulnerability and fears. All of that talk about whether they were there to protect me from feeling bad was very helpful. We could then look at how they went about their relational business in other places. (Comstock, 2008, p. 184)

It is important to note that like Greenspan, I, too, took about a 3-month respite. But *unlike* Greenspan's (1986) experience, my return to my professional life came with the announcement that I was "expecting," again. This is a significant point in that it seemed to "band-aid," in a sense, the depth of my previous loss. Had my previous loss disclosure not come with the "Oh, and another baby is already on the way!" the nature of "coming back out" into all aspects of my professional life might have been remarkably different. I would have been different, and different in ways I can only speculate. Happy endings are not always the norm when therapist self-disclosure is related to their own life's adversity.

My subsequent pregnancy afforded me a buffer, of sorts, that made it appear that this traumatic phase of my life was, perhaps, behind me. I had a diagnosis for my previous loss that, although it would mean yet another absence (bed rest for 5 months during the latter phase of my subsequent pregnancy), there was a strong likelihood I would get that "pot of gold" that was lurking at the end of yet another journey. I did, in fact, carry my daughter, Julianna, to term and her arrival in March of 1999 marked a new beginning for me, as well as the belief that my traumatic loss was behind me.

My subsequent pregnancy and anticipated bed rest also coincided with the end of my contract work with the RCC. The remainder of my time with the agency, and former clients, marked a period of closure for some, and a transition to another therapist for others.

The initiation

When Julianna was about 2 years old, I ran into Dr. Jeffrey Kottler at a professional conference. While catching up on the events that had transpired in our lives over the past couple of years, he invited me to write for a column he edited, "Finding Your Way," in *Counseling Today* (the American Counseling Association's monthly newsletter that is disseminated to approximately 43,000 members worldwide). The nature of the column is fairly straightforward and his request and directive were simple: "Dana, why don't you write about how the impact of losing Samantha shaped your 'finding your way' as a counselor? I think you have something valuable to share that would help other counselors dealing with similar circumstances." I accepted without hesitation, in part because working with this *New York Times* best-selling author and editor was a chance of a lifetime and besides, I *did* need publications and this was only supposed to be a six-page double-spaced essay, right?

At the time I began putting the essay together (and my wheels began immediately turning!), I was not focused on the long-term implications that the telling of my story might have on my professional life but was rather focused on the intensity of emotions that resurfaced during the writing process. At this point in time, I was relatively fearless, ready to put it out there. I had read Annie Roger's *A Shining Affliction* and Lauren Slater's *Prozac Diary* and had a deep appreciation for the precedent that had already been set. I had also read Slater's *Lying: A Metaphorical Memoire* and had had many fantasies about one day asking her, as a client, if she really did "that" in the hotel room on that snowy evening, which turned out to be the last time she would see her writing mentor and lover.

In a nutshell, I was familiar with and held a deep appreciation for the impact that their self-disclosure through their writing, and that of many others, had on the development of mental health professionals, both those who were seasoned and those in training. My work from the RCT perspective also emphasizes the value of authenticity in relationships. The opposite of authenticity is the movement toward an image. In this case, creating an image of the perfect therapist who could handle anything that came her way was a movement out of and away from connection in every relational context in my life. This image, which was increasingly familiar, was one I could no longer tolerate, so I began to deconstruct this image by putting together the first essay that would tell my story.

There is always a "story behind a story," and as I began to write that seemingly harmless six-page essay entitled "The Initiation," about the traumatic loss of my premature, stillborn daughter Samantha, intense memories, both emotional and physical, resurfaced. I had bodily sensations that were so intense during the writing process that I actually produced breast milk at one point. The intensity of emotion through the revisiting of that experience might have been enough to ward off any and all future invitations to discuss the issue (including this one!), much less write another word on the topic. It is important for readers to understand *I did not put that piece together alone*, but did so with a great deal of support from my editor in what RCT refers to as the creation of "courage in connection." Had it not been for his belief in how my experience would benefit counselors and mental health professionals around the world, I'm not sure I could have completed the task. I *know* I would never have written it in the first place, much less have thought of such a project as becoming the cornerstone of my life's work.

Self-disclosure in print

In December of 2001, my essay, "The Initiation," was published in *Counseling Today*. Cards, thank-you notes, and acknowledgments of my courage trickled in, but not to the degree that matched the intensity of the effort it took to create that publication. I had built up an expectation of reader responses that mirrored my emotional fallout of the whole experience, including the writing challenges. My editor assured me that he, too, rarely gets much feedback from his reader audiences following the publications of similar types of writing. He shared that in his experience, the level of vulnerability never seems to match the responses from readers. The good news is that I was confident that most dated issues of *Counseling Today* ended up in the trash can, or at least mine had. And while this was a fleeting source of relief, I soon learned that a collection of articles from Kottler's "Finding Your Way" column, the most frequently read column in *Counseling Today*, was being compiled for a book to be published by the American Counseling Association (ACA) that would come out the very next year (Kottler, 2002).

In a flash, the script I had now imagined I'd share with clients and students about writing the piece, which had gone something like: "Sometime back I wrote an article about the psychotic grief I experienced; I wish you could have read it, it might have helped you in some way" had to be scrapped. It now read: "You know, in 2001 I wrote an article in Kottler's column in *Counseling Today* about the psychotic grief that took over me after the loss of my stillborn, premature daughter. It's still available through ACA if you'd like to order the book; in fact, our library has a copy." This brings me to a very important point about self-disclosure in print: Clients (and the students I counsel through the adversity that arises during their education) have the *choice* to learn about their therapists' (or professors') adversity that is not afforded to them through verbal disclosures that come during sessions.

Self-disclosure in print provides clients a "choice" as to whether or not they want to know more about me and allows them to determine readiness, if ever, and also allows for an opportunity to explore what it might feel like to learn about certain aspects of my life. Self-disclosure in the traditional sense (on-the-spot, in-the-moment sharing), provides very little opportunity to prepare clients for what they might hear, and subsequently, there is a risk that a great deal of time will be spent processing what has been shared *after* the disclosure. I also feel there is something about the "invitation" to read about my life adversity that gives them a sense of safety and respect, which, in my experience, fosters mutuality in that they actively participate in taking the work in whatever direction my "print disclosures" might offer.

Self-disclosure in session

That latter was exactly what happened in my work with a client whom I'll refer to as "Carin." The obstetrical group that had supported me through my previous loss and subsequent delivery of my first live birth referred Carin to me. As a result of my being a therapist who'd survived such a traumatic and sudden loss, I began receiving, and accepting, invitations extended to me from the medical community through my obstetrician to train nurses, hospital professional staff, and clergy in how to best assist obstetrical patients with pre- and perinatal loss and trauma. I also agreed to accept private clinical referrals from this obstetrical group, which primarily included women who had suffered similar losses, and in some cases, much, *much* worse. Carin was among them.

She came to see me following the death of her 2-month-old son, Noah. My work with her is featured in *How Connections Heal: Stories From Relational-Cultural Therapy* (Comstock, 2004), the first RCT casebook published by Guilford Press. In the chapter, entitled "Reflections on Life, Loss, and Resilience," I begin by noting the convergence of our life circumstances and the context of Carin's pain:

> The themes woven throughout this case stem from the convergence of my life circumstances with Carin's. It is about the challenges we faced trying to connect through impenetrable grief, our mutual strategies for survival, and our growth and resilience.
>
> For Carin, Noah's death was devastating, untimely, unjust, and so much more. She and her family had already suffered the loss of her first baby, a daughter, "Meg," who was stillborn at full term. After Meg, Carin had a son Benjamin, who was 2 years old when we began our work. Noah, her third child, began having problems shortly after birth. Before his death he had suffered through several surgeries to correct bowel obstructions, and was suffering from other neurological problems that caused him to have frequent seizures.
>
> During his short life his seizures became progressively worse, turning into infantile spasms, as many as 20 a day. . . . Interestingly, he was given his first dose of an experimental drug, which did seem to work, the same day he died. (Comstock, 2004, pp. 83–84)

It was on that note that we began our work.

Carin was a reluctant client. Following Noah's death, she was found unconscious next to bottles of vodka and Tylenol. As a result, she was admitted to the hospital for a suicide watch. Reluctantly, the hospital staff allowed her to leave the facility only long enough to attend her son's funeral and was given the directive to return *immediately* following the service. Instead, she decided she needed some "rest," which landed her *back* in the hospital.

In the interim, her treating psychiatrist "fired" her as a patient. Her family all seemed to think she was unstable, overreacting, and crazy. Her husband feared she'd hurt herself again. No one seemed to understand her, and before she'd be allowed to step one foot out of the hospital, she had to secure mental health services. Her former psychiatrist didn't want anything to do with a noncompliant patient, the hospital didn't know what to do with her, and her family was unprepared to care for her. So, after one call from her obstetrician, "tag," I was it. Initially, her husband did most of the sharing while Carin dropped tears and silently stared at her feet. After he made sure I understood the full extent of the poor choices she had made during the previous few weeks (which only intensified the stress on his relationship with his own family), he left us alone having entrusted me in her care. In response to what I'd heard, I validated the pain she'd endured and closed my initial comments with an encouraging, "Carin, I too have lost a baby." My sharing with her the little bit I did about myself was a way to gain her trust. It worked.

She began to disclose that she blamed herself for her son's death. It seems the night he died, the tip of his nose had rubbed raw against the lining of the bassinet in which he had been sleeping. "He suffocated," she lamented, "And there's no place in heaven for mothers who kill their babies." Ironically, she immediately began talking about getting pregnant again. Her obstetrician warned, "She needs 6 months between babies!" By her accounting, Noah had been born in July and January was her "qualifying" month. She conceived on her first try. Her obstetrician was as frightened as I was: Would she make it through the first trimester? What will happen to her mental health if she miscarries?

In spite of the fact that she made it through the hurdles of her first trimester, we continued to wrestle with her self-blame. Now, let me be clear, by no account did I consider this my best work. Lucky for Carin, I was under the supervision of Dr. Judith Jordan, one of the founding scholars of RCT, and was completing advanced training in RCT through the Jean Baker Miller Training Institute's Practitioner's Program. For months, it seemed Carin and I went in circles with her self-blame. There were, of course, many disclosures *related to my experience of her* during the course of therapy, which are addressed in detail throughout that chapter.

Note: Self-disclosure does not always involve therapists sharing information about themselves with their clients. In many cases, self-disclosure comes in the form of the therapist sharing their experience of the client in the here and now. From the RCT perspective, self-disclosure is a form of responsiveness (versus reactive or impulsive sharing) that is intended, through a process of anticipatory empathy (thinking through how what you want to share might be received by the client *before* a disclosure is made), to keep the relationship moving. As we were stuck most of the time, I took many liberties to share my sense of helplessness, my frustration, my desire to help her and sometimes my fear for her. Her postpartum depression, coupled with early pregnancy anxieties (not to mention her grief) turned into psychosis. One day I got a call from her. She was hiding in a closet in her home, certain that the police were watching her house with the intention of taking her son away.

That was a turning point for both of us. A point that had come to a head, in part, because she had yet to learn of the autopsy results of Noah's death. She called me the day we learned the coroner had prepared the report and asked if I'd call the coroner directly to get the results for her. The report was straightforward: "Noah had nodes in his frontal lobe, he died of a catastrophic seizure." The coroner (now known as "Dr. G," the coroner featured on Discovery Health's *Dr. G: Medical Examiner*) even encouraged Carin to call her if she had any questions. I immediately called Carin back, eager to share the news I was certain would change the course of our therapy from that point forward. I could sense her on the edge of her chair. After sharing what I anticipated to be the most liberating news of her life, she all but accused me of lying.

My response: "Are you saying that the coroner, the pediatrician, your obstetrician, and your therapist all got together to concoct a story to save you from the fact that you really did kill your son?" Without hesitating, she responded: "Yes." At that point, I surrendered. I knew I'd have to ride out our dueling perspectives. For the first time I truly understood I needed to give up my need to prove her wrong, but on some level, she seemed to need my objections to her self-destructive narrative.

At this point, it wasn't like my "narrative" didn't have any credibility, but neither did any of the other professionals', so I didn't take it personally. Never mind the cause of death was determined by one of the best coroners in the country. In hindsight, I believe that had I disclosed more about myself she would have dismissed my perspective in a heartbeat. And it wasn't that I couldn't relate to her: I, too, had blamed myself, even my own body, for the loss of my baby. I, too, experienced fleeting, psychotic grief. I, too, got the shaft by well-paid medical professionals. I, too, felt the irrational need to conceive again before many people held the opinion I had completely grieved the loss of my daughter, Samantha. I, too, had made some really irrational decisions during some very potentially deadly times. I, too, had isolated myself, and felt estranged from my family. But I'd made it to the other side; that's all she needed to know during the course of our work.

In the end, she delivered a healthy 10.6-lb baby boy. After a short respite, she returned to therapy and, in one of those "full-circle moments" that are so rare in the work that we do, she disclosed to me that she needed to believe she had caused Noah's death, otherwise she'd had been unable to tolerate the vulnerabilities of her current pregnancy. The idea that a random birth defect would resurface once again was too much for her to handle. In a flash, it all made sense.

Conclusion

At the end of our 14 months of work, I received an invitation to write a case study for *How Connections Heal: Stories From Relational-Cultural Therapy*, which was to be the first casebook illustrating RCT principles in action. I immediately thought of Carin. Because there had been so much shame in so many phases of her work, she might possibly refuse to consent to such a project. I asked her to think about it, and assured her that I, too, had written about my previous loss and that I was happy to share those publications with her, if she was ready. I made it clear I wasn't asking her to do anything I, myself, hadn't already done (she'd seemed to have set our lives apart, not knowing the full extent of my experience). Her response was an enthusiastic "yes" to everything. Her response went something like this, "Are you kidding? I'd love to read about your experience! I remember you shared you'd lost a baby too during our first session, but after that, I was too afraid to ask any more about it. And if what I went through might help someone else, then I *want* to do it, even if half the people who read it might think I'm really crazy."

Carin was a very talented creative writer, which was one of the reasons I wanted her story told, in part, in her own voice. I also believed that she could express much of her experience better than I could. So, instead of putting her in a position to edit *my* work (which does have the potential to be quite time consuming!), I let her take the lead in what she felt most important for the world to know about her experience. I even offered her professional credit, under a pen name of her own choosing, but she refused.

In the meantime, I had done some quick research on the process and impact of case study publications and discovered that since around 2000, clients had been using what their therapists had written about them in the actual process of therapy (Kantrowitz, 2005). I also learned that many clients had historically been *very* unhappy with what they read (Clifft, 1986). All of the research had been done on clients whose therapists were practicing from a psychoanalytical perspective, so I created my own road map from the RCT perspective (Comstock & Duffey, 2006).

As Carin was a person, (versus a "case"), I *invited* her to be a part of the process. I proposed a structure for us to meet, free of charge, and at her convenience, to spend some time revisiting our work together as an "extension" of our therapy. I also assured her that nothing would be published without her full review and consent of the final draft. I had a lot of questions for her, and she for me. First, she had *never* detailed for me the horrifying sequence of events the night Noah died that set the stage for so much of her trauma around his death. Her detailing of that night set a dramatic stage for the remainder of that chapter. As the drafts evolved, seeing her experience on paper was healing for her in that, "The whole thing *was* real, look at what I survived!"

We also processed what she learned about my frustrations, and despairing at times from reading through the emergent drafts. We talked about the many courses our work together could have taken. Once, during our consulting together, I asked her point blank, "What would it have been like for me to have just thrown up my hands and to have said, 'Okay, so you killed your baby, where do you want to go from here?'" She shared she would have been devastated. This point illustrates that the cocreation of case studies from the RCT perspective means that:

> clients are given an opportunity to co-author their experiences, which can lead to a sense of empowerment. At the same time, counselors are given an opportunity to learn from their clients, to be accountable to their clients and to their profession, and to set the stage for rich dialogue and authentic representation of the counseling process. . . . demystifying how the life of the therapy impacts the life of the therapist can lead to a deeper connection and increased clarity of the client's experience of personal growth and the therapeutic relationship. (Comstock, 2007, p. 3)

In the end, we created a wonderful project that has made a difference in the training of many professionals. What once seemed like an insurmountable period in Carin's life, she can now "hold in one hand." Carin has moved on with her life. She even had another son without so much as one hour of therapy along the way. The lessons for me regarding self-disclosure are these: (a) Listen, sometimes for a long time, before you disclose; your full attention may mean one thing at one phase of the therapy and something completely different at a later time; (b) Pay attention to the context of your client's story and their quality of presence; not all clients are emotionally present to take in anything you share, and some may even feel violated that you've turned your attention to yourself rather than focusing on them; (c) From the RCT perspective, exercise anticipatory empathy and give forethought as to how what you will share might be received before you speak; (d) When in doubt, stay silent, buy yourself some time, and check in with clients if there might be anything about your life that might be useful to them; (e) Be open to the idea that we, as therapists, are all fallible; we make mistakes. If you sense you mistimed a disclosure, check it out with your clients and encourage them to share with you what it felt like; (f) Avoid using "blanket rules" and never resolve not to answer any questions posed by clients in the event they request information about your life and experiences; (g) Make sure to keep your disclosures transparent by never leaving a client feeling like you've told them something you've never told anyone else. Lastly, *write* about your experiences. Don't set your life apart from the struggles of your clients.

References

Clifft, M. A. (1986). Writing about psychiatric patients. *Bulletin of the Menninger Clinic, 50*(6), 511–524.

Comstock, D. L. (2001, December). The initiation. *Counseling Today*. International Newsletter for the American Counseling Association.

Comstock, D. L. (2002). The initiation. In J. A. Kottler (Ed.), *Counselors finding their way* (pp. 31–34). Alexandria, VA: American Counseling Association.

Comstock, D. L. (2004). Reflections on life, loss, and resilience. In W. Rosen & M. Walker (Eds.), *How connections heal: Stories from relational-cultural therapy*. (pp. 83–101). New York: Guilford Press.

Comstock, D. L. (2007). A relational-cultural theoretical approach to co-creating case studies. Unpublished manuscript.

Comstock, D. L. (2008). *Therapist adversity and the life of the therapist: Perspectives from Miriam Greenspan*. Routledge Publishers: Taylor & Francis.

Comstock, D. L., & Duffey, T. (2006). Relational complexities and case presentation construction: Co-creating opportunities for mutual healing. *VISTAS Online Counseling Library*. Alexandria, VA: American Counseling Association.

Greenspan, M. (1986). Should therapists be personal? Self-disclosure and therapeutic distance in feminist therapy. In D. Howard (Ed.), *The dynamics of feminist therapy* (pp. 5–17). New York: Hayworth Press.

Jordan, J. V. (2000). The role of mutual empathy in relational-cultural therapy. *JCLP/In Session: Psychotherapy in Practice, 56*(8), 1005–1016.

Kantrowitz, J. (2005). Writing about patients: IV. Patients' reactions to reading about themselves. *Journal of the American Psychoanalytic Association, 53*(1), 103–129.

Kottler, J. A. (2001). *Counselors finding their way*. Alexandria, VA: American Counseling Association.

Walker, M., & Rosen, W. R. (2004). *How connections heal: Stories from relational cultural therapy*. New York: Guilford Press.

chapter nineteen

For your client's sake
Practicing clinically
constructive self-disclosure

David C. Treadway

Introduction

"And how are you?" That was my opening line for decades ... until I got cancer. Then it belonged to my clients. When I opened the door to the waiting room, they jumped to their feet, startled. As if they'd seen a ghost.

"Are you doing OK?" they would ask in hushed tones.

My shrunken body, hairless head, and gaunt face without eyebrows or lashes revealed more about my being ill than any self-disclosure I could offer. Hiding behind my boundaries as a therapist was not an option. My clients saw the truth.

Under normal circumstances many of us, clients and therapists alike, collude in not recognizing a reality: We, therapists, are simply flawed and limited human beings struggling to make do in our own lives.

Not "if," but "when" and "how much"

Throughout much of the past 100 years extending as far back as Freud's psychoanalytical psychotherapy, there has been an ongoing debate about the use and misuse of self-disclosure in therapy. This discussion about how much of one's own experience, thoughts, and values are clinically appropriate to share masks a simple truth. In many respects, self-disclosure is truly not a choice. It's always a matter of degrees of self-disclosure. We reveal ourselves the moment a client is referred to us: our gender, our degrees, frequently our age and ethnic background. In the very first phone call, we show our interpersonal style, state of calmness, sense of humor, and level of empathy. And when our clients are in our offices, we are even more exposed, as they note what we wear, our hairstyle, our weight, and how we decorate our offices. In the first session, they are checking us out every bit as much as we are assessing them. So regardless of how much we choose to say or not say about ourselves, in our every word and action, consciously and unconsciously, we are self-disclosing.

In addition, we are often going through our own life issues that are frequently transparent to our clients like illness, or pregnancy, death of a relative, and sometimes divorce, even the successes or failures of our children if we practice in a small community. In these circumstances, our lives are even more of an open book. The choice isn't whether to tell our clients; it's when and how much.

So the heart of the matter is not whether we self-disclose. Many of us are unsure about how much information about our own lives—our personal experiences, successes and mistakes, beliefs and values that they wouldn't otherwise know—to share. And how and when do we share in a way that serves *their* needs not ours? We know from many clinical studies that the main determinants of a successful therapy are not our theoretical approach, years of experience, or type of training. The most important variable is the relationship with the therapist. Within that relationship, how much does it help or hurt the client for the therapist to share of themselves?

The answer is: it depends on the client. That's what makes clinically effective use of self-disclosure an art, not a science. Each client is different.

A therapist's tears

One day, early in my career, I was a rehab group leader and asked a tough ex-con, who had been in the group for 6 months, what the most important moment in treatment was for him. Mind you, it was the early 1970s; we had met for 3 hours a day, 4 days a week, and had thrown every encounter group/gestalt technique possible at the poor guy. I expected him to pick one of his many "cathartic breakthroughs." Without a moment's hesitation, he looked at me and said, "The most meaningful moment I've had was that night when you had to discharge Carl from the group and you cried." That unintentional self-disclosure somehow allowed Jackson to know how much I cared and it mattered to him. My tears turned out to be a gift to him.

However, there was also the time when I was treating an older woman and her husband in couple's therapy and she shared for the first time in her life the details of having been sexually abused by her father when she was a girl. The story was so heartbreaking that my eyes filled with tears. I thought it was an incredibly tender moment between her, her husband, and me. She never came back for another session. Later I found out from her husband that she had said she didn't want to deal with a guy who couldn't handle her trauma history. So much for the gift of my tears.

Each client is different.

Pros and cons of self-disclosure

My professional life began in a culture in which clinical use of self-disclosure was highly valued. My first clinical job was in an addictions rehab center, Eagleville Hospital, where half the therapy staff were uncredentialed recovering addicts and alcoholics and the rest of us were master's-level counselors. I saw the therapeutic impact of therapists being able to say, "Been there, done that." I could see how inspiring a recovering therapist could be and also saw the extraordinary healing power of the 12-step-tradition programs in which a healing community is created by people helping each other as peers rather through the hierarchical medical model I was trained in.

When I became a family therapist and began to treat parents who were much older than me and when I had not become a parent yet myself, I could see how much easier it was to work with folks if instead of operating from the one-up "expert" position, I simply acknowledged my lack of hands-on experience and asked them to educate me about their experience of parenting as we learned to work together.

Sharing our limitations, failings, and uncertainties can empower our clients to be less judgmental and self-critical about their own human frailties. We put ourselves on the same level, rather than leaving them in the chronic one-down stance of the doctor-patient relationship. When we ask for our clients' input about the therapy and what might be most helpful, we are inviting them to collaborate in their own healing and to partner with us in the work, which also empowers them by valuing their perspective and expertise on their own lives.

Self-disclosure can be a healing gift. It can also be a boundary-violating, insensitive, inappropriate self-indulgence. Clients don't need to hear about our lives just because we want to share our thoughts or feelings with them. Too much mutual sharing can cause the therapy to become more like a friendship and that undermines one of the central tenets of therapy: that the client is encouraged to focus entirely on their needs and issues without having to be emotionally careful or care giving with the therapist. Clearly, as my clients were responding caringly to me about my cancer, there was a possibility that my issues would make it difficult for them to utilize our therapy optimally.

Suggested guidelines

However, learning how to use self-disclosure skillfully has been a challenge for me long before I got sick. Here's the model for thoughtful client-centered self-disclosure that guides me when I consider explicitly sharing a part of myself for the sake of my client. It is always an experiment that has to be conducted very carefully.

1. Hypotheses: First, I have to make some assessment about what's going on in a session—how open the clients are, if they are stuck in a rut, if they are defensive in relationship to me. I ask myself, what's happening right now and is it working? For example, I was once working with an alcoholic and his wife in a demonstration interview where he clearly felt on the spot. As the session progressed, I could see he was becoming more and more defensive and was feeling ganged up on.

2. Goals: It is essential to have a clear idea about what your client's goals are and what your goals are. This clarity allows you to assess whether a session is going well or badly. We have to adjust on the fly to realign to our goals or even change them. In the demonstration interview above, one of my goals was to help the couple and their therapist work collaboratively on the alcohol issue without it becoming more divisive or adversarial. They had told their therapist that they wanted to achieve that also.

3. Strategies: After reviewing what's going on in the room at that moment and how it aligns to our goal, we have to choose an intervention. In this case, with the husband feeling ganged up on by the wife, their therapist, and me, the big-shot consultant, I could have chosen to challenge the wife more or even the couple's therapist. That might have reengaged him, but I decided to do that later and choose to begin with self-disclosure. I had learned earlier in the session that Paul, the alcoholic, had grown up with an alcoholic mother as had I. So, in response to Paul saying, "I'm no dummy. I don't need to be lectured," I leaned forward in my chair and said in a soft voice, "Yes, Paul, you don't need to be lectured. And I don't blame you for getting annoyed. After all you grew up with a mother with a serious alcohol problem, much more serious than yours. I grew up with an alcoholic mother too, and I can remember just how mad I could be about all the people who tried to help but couldn't do anything but say platitudes and give lectures. That used to really piss me off, too."

4. Outcome: The key element of assessing self-disclosure is to watch like a hawk for the outcome of your sharing. Does the client respond well? Does it seem to intrude on the session? Does it help change the tone or feeling of the session in a positive way? Or do people glance at their watches or come back with "Well, what I was saying . . ." I waited for Paul's response to see what the outcome of my sharing would be. He looked at me for a moment and then said, "Well, I know what you mean. It does piss me off when she starts bossing..." Then he paused and matched my self-disclosure with his some of his own, "Look, I came in here on the defensive, because after all it's me doing the drinking." And then he laughed, and we were back on track.

But self-disclosure is always an experiment. If the client doesn't respond, don't take it personally. Just move on. Try something else. I sometimes have to remind myself that the therapeutic relationship is about the clients' well-being, not my own. It's not their job to reassure me if I share something about myself and it doesn't seem to resonate with them.

The therapist has cancer

All these issues about useful self-disclosure were amplified when I was so sick I couldn't hide it. When my clients looked at me with great concern, I would respond openly and directly. I gave them as concise and optimistic a report as I could. Invariably, one or both members of the couple would be like Bret and Elliot.

Bret was a blond, perky, cheerleader type, now a soccer mom in her 40s. Despite three kids, she was in great shape and looked very pretty with skillfully applied makeup. She was disappointed that Elliot didn't seem the slightest bit interested in a sexual life.

"Well, Dr. Treadway, it just doesn't seem right for us to launch into our difficulties around intimacy when you're dealing with something really enormous."

"Listen, guys, obviously my illness does puts everyday problems in perspective. Hopefully, you can utilize that awareness to be more tender and appreciative toward each other. This time in my office should be the one place where you feel like you can truly open up about the pain you carry and the struggles you have."

"You've got to admit it's pretty hard to deal with our sexual difficulties given what you're going through," chimed in Elliot, ignoring my reassurances.

So the session, which had barely begun, felt stuck. I didn't have any choice about disclosing about my illness. But I did have choices about how to respond to their genuine care for me and the ways it was blocking them from being able to utilize their session. I could either persist in encouraging them to focus on their own issues or, perhaps, help them by choosing to self-disclose even more.

Which I did.

I rolled my chair a little closer to Elliot and Bret. "I need to be clear about something. I love my clients. I love my work. I hate being sick. Frankly, having the opportunity to work with you guys on your intimacy issues is a great help to me. I would much rather focus on how to bring flirtation and play back into your relationship than sit around worrying about my situation. So let's get to work on you and we'll all forget about me. And actually, you'll be doing me a favor."

I smiled at them. They smiled back.

"Well, we are making some progress," started Bret hesitantly and then she blushed.

It seemed to work. My more personal disclosure: that I needed them for my own well-being appeared to help. But isn't that a contradiction with the earlier statement that therapy is supposed to allow the clients never to have to take care of the therapists? Yes. It is a contradiction, but first and foremost we are simply human beings. In this case, opening up about my need to be the therapist helped Bret and Elliot regain their comfort being the clients. It worked for them. It might not for the clients I see right after them.

Looking back

Clearly, I am an advocate for careful and creative self-disclosure for the client's sake. The value of self-disclosure has also proven itself in my 35 years of training therapists. We therapists practice an art, but feel the weight of expectation that we should be scientific and objective. No wonder many of us feel sometimes as if we are frauds or hypocrites. We look to experts to teach us and make us wise. We go to workshops and read books so we can feel that we know what we are doing, so we can feel competent. But where do the experts get answers? They find the answers through years of hard work, constant pondering, and their life experience. The same as we do. Many of my students have found it to be reassuring that despite my being a successful, well-known therapist I still have anxiety and confusion about my work. I still need to get help to untangle my unresolved issues from my clients and I still make mistakes that do harm. It's the nature of our calling. Therapists are frequently relieved to know that none of us are exempt from limitations no matter how much experience, training, and skill we might have.

We need to accept that after all the theories are spoken and all the therapeutic techniques applied, often the best we have to offer our clients is our own flawed humanity without shame or self-indulgence. We are not all-knowing guides, marching fearlessly ahead of our clients along harrowing mountain trails. Yes, we have pitons, ropes, and hammers. Yes, many of us have made the climb before. It is good to have experience and equipment. But, ultimately, our willingness to share the risk, to give gentle voice to the fear, and to hold the sweaty palms is the gift that heals.

What happens in therapy may be a mystery. But therapists aren't. We are people with a calling: people who risk opening our hearts to the suffering of others. We believe that being one caring person, in one session, even one moment, can be the difference that makes a difference. Learning how and when to share a personal part of ourselves that joins us with our clients in our shared humanity is often that difference.

Supervision, best practice guidelines

chapter twenty

Self-disclosure in clinical supervision

Eva L. Feindler and Jennifer J. Padrone

A brief history of clinical supervision

Clinical supervision may be one of the most influential yet understudied relationships in the development of professional practice and identity. These powerful relationships throughout training often shape more than the therapeutic work with clients; theoretical orientation, career development, and professional aspirations may be affected deeply. The supervisory process and the inherent asymmetrical power dynamics of this relationship therefore demand careful attention.

Initially, supervision was construed as didactic consultation directed toward the symptomatology, personality, behavioral patterns, and dynamics of the client. The supervisor's task was to teach the trainee about the practice of therapy with an adherence to a particular theory or model. Supervision was usually structured around the trainee's verbal report of the patient data, a discussion of clinical issues and treatment objectives, and recommendations for trainees in their plans for the next session. Then, attention shifted in both the content and process to the psychology of the supervisee/therapist. Supervision began to be considered an experiential rather than simply a didactic process in which resistances, anxieties, shame, vulnerability, and other interpersonal issues between supervisor and supervisee are brought into focus. Still the emphasis remained on the characterological and developmental issues of the trainee, while the supervisor assumed the role of objective observer who helped to identify these issues within the supervisee and consider how the treatment process might be impacted by them.

Currently, there is increased attention to the definition of clinical supervision as a shared interactional phenomenon wherein the dynamics and alliance of the supervisory relationship are paramount. In fact, a strong supervisory alliance as well as repair of ruptures and impasses within may have direct bearing upon the development of the working alliance in the therapeutic dyad. Clinical professionals agree that critical relational principles, such as mutuality, authenticity, shared meaning, collaboration, and trust, must be emphasized within the supervisory matrix. Structural as well as dynamic similarities of psychotherapy and supervision are thought to create a context wherein parallel processes can occur. However, Berman (2000) cautions that "Parallel processes should be understood as one potential aspect of the complex network of cross-identifications within the supervisor-therapist-patient triad. Some supervisory stalemates may develop irrespective of the identity of the supervised; these problem's require full attention despite being 'unparalleled'" (p. 280).

Becoming an effective supervisor initially depended upon the personal experience of having been in supervision. Novice supervisors learned and conducted supervision as they had been supervised. Yet, we all know that clinical supervision through the course of training can be a variable journey. Research has been conducted on effective and ineffective supervisory experiences, and much of the available post hoc data indicates that relationship variables stand out as key. In this chapter, we will begin with a brief review of the literature on effectiveness in supervision with a decided focus on a more relational model of supervision. The second half of the chapter will give clinical examples of supervisor self-disclosure from our own qualitative research and practice, followed by our suggested guidelines for good practice.

Models of supervision

In the scant literature on clinical supervision there have been several streams of influence on the practice of supervision. The developmental stream focuses on the movement from novice clinician to experienced clinician and from novice supervisor to experienced supervisor. Across time, a variety of developmental struggles are resolved as the clinician develops his or her professional identity. Both didactic and experiential components are crucial. In the psychotherapy stream, the theoretical orientation of the supervisor will dictate the focus, the objectives, and the techniques of the supervision experience. Some of these supervision approaches emphasize psychodynamic methods and others cognitive behavioral or behavioral analytic methods. Many supervisors blend in an emphasis on the supervisory relationship. This approach requires attention to interpersonal dynamics such as power, authority, evaluation, disclosure, conflict resolution, as well as to phases of the development of this assigned relationship.

Frawley-O'Dea and Sarnat (2001) provide a comprehensive and historical overview of various psychodynamic models of supervision. They compare and contrast the major dimensions of the supervisor's authority, focus, and mode of participation in the patient-centered model (classical), the therapist/supervisee-centered model (ego psychological, self-psychological, and object relations), and the supervisory matrix-centered model (relational). Although each supervisor will work in his or her own unique way and the models will overlap, these authors suggest that supervisors are informed by and influenced by their theoretical orientation as well as training and experience in supervision. As the psychodynamic field has expanded from a one-person to a two-person framework, it is accepted that both the supervisor and the supervisee contribute to the interpersonal dynamics, the misattunements, the impasses, and the quality of the relationship. This development has provided increased opportunities to examine unconscious phenomena, transference-countertransference dynamics, and parallel processes that occur in the supervisory dyad (Teitelbaum, 2001).

Early on, the tutorial or didactic model of supervision dominated and presented a context wherein the less experienced and less knowledgeable supervisee apprentices him- or herself to the more experienced teacher or mentor (Ricci, 1995). Most supervision is still structured as this didactic, mentoring relationship between a more experienced advisor and a less experienced colleague, where the supervisee's task is to learn and the supervisor's task is to guide in the achievement of the supervisee's clinical competence.

In early psychodynamic models, the role of the supervisor was to help the supervisee decipher the patient's clinical material presented through unconscious communications, enactments, and the transference dynamics. Personal difficulties that emerged in the supervisee's work, either with patients or in supervision, were located in the intrapsychic structure of the student, and psychotherapy for the supervisee was often suggested. Psychoanalytic training programs have clear requirements that each candidate participate in a training analysis in addition to supervision, as part of the preparation to conduct psychoanalysis.

Other psychodynamic models offer a supervision model which likens supervision to aspects of psychotherapy. Since treatment and supervision take place in a similarly structured intersubjective field, the same rules that regulate human interaction would logically direct the process (Ricci, 1995). Because the purpose of supervision is to facilitate the development of the supervisee, the supervisory relationship reflects opportunities to understand important elements of other relationships and issues related to autonomy, authority, and individuation. Riggs and Bretz (2006) suggest that critical and personal attachment processes are elicited in the supervisory context and that supervisors ideally function as a secure base from which supervisees explore and develop their clinical capacities. According to Coburn (2001), the value of supervision is not just the enhancement of the supervisee's clinical competence, but the opportunity for new object experiences vis-à-vis the supervisee's professional identity, self-experience, and self-organization.

Over the past decade, supervisors have been encouraged to be more attuned to the emotional needs of their supervisees and to consider that a psychoanalytic stance can inform the content related to the therapeutic dyad as well as process between the supervisor and supervisee. Sarnat (1992) emphasizes supervisor characteristics critical for effective psychoanalytic supervision. First, the supervisor must be able to keep the supervisory task differentiated from therapeutic tasks when engaging the supervisee. This guideline harkens back to the "teach-or-treat" controversy and the need to decipher what material is appropriate to the supervisory context. There certainly is a degree of overlap between the contents of psychoanalysis and supervision, and the centrality of the complex transference-countertransference dynamics in the supervisory relationship cannot be overlooked. In fact, the supervisory process is markedly enhanced when supervisors consciously study manifestations of transference within the supervisory relationship and respond to them correctively (Schamess, 2006). However, unlike in psychoanalysis, the supervisee's transference to the supervisor is not systematically analyzed or interpreted (Astor, 2000), unless of course there is a parallel process enactment.

A second critical supervisor characteristic is the capacity to acknowledge and tolerate his or her own anxieties and conflicts as they enter the supervisory relationship (Sarnat, 1992). Here the shift is on the experiences and contributions of the supervisor to the interpersonal dynamics. Supervisors who are attuned to the relational aspects of supervision recognize that transference-countertransference starts as soon as the supervisor and supervisee meet and each partner appears with positive or negative transference predispositions based upon prior teaching and general relational experiences (Schamess, 2006). A main task for the supervisor then becomes the monitoring of countertransference (Ricci, 1995) and the expression of those reactions becomes a decision related to supervisor self-disclosure. Sarnat (1992) suggests that a direct acknowledgment of countertransference is highly compatible with the supervisory frame in which the development of a regressive transference is certainly not an aim and supervisor anonymity is both unnecessary and inappropriate.

Many would agree that the essence of supervision is that it provides a space for thinking—a space that has a certain quality of attention, not dissimilar to psychoanalysis, in that communications are being thought about from multiple perspectives (Astor, 2000). It is assumed that both the supervisor and the supervisee can learn something from their work together and that the supervisory relationship contains rich and complex facets. Inevitably, intricate interpersonal dynamics will be triggered between the partners (Ringel, 2001), which can then inform the work with the patient as these intersubjective phenomena become diagnostic of the case.

Relational supervision

In a relational model, the supervisor and the supervisee participate in and observe their own emerging relationship in a way that is analogous to an interpersonally oriented treatment situation. Supervisor and supervisee coconstruct, mutually derive, and negotiate meaning about the content and process of both the therapeutic and supervisory work. If possible, they share power and authority but remain mindful of the asymmetry of the relationship and manage this power differential within the frame of the supervision. When a supervisor can model nondefensiveness and mutuality in constructing the supervisory relationship, the supervisee is given permission to be fallible and is given the skills to examine and negotiate a therapeutic relationship. It seems impossible to teach a psychotherapist to be open, nondefensive, and authentic without modeling it relationally. The willingness of the supervisor and supervisee to work through supervisory conflicts with mutual openness and honesty and to admit mistakes serves as a model for the supervisee in work with her own patients (Ringel, 2001).

Relational supervision is seen as a highly personal learning process for both partners, and its emotional climate is a crucially influential factor in its evolution into a space for reflection and generation of new meanings (Berman, 2000). The relational phenomena that arise out of continued contact and dialogue are determined by the natural and complex interpersonal interplay among the three participants (the relationship itself becoming the third), often called a matrix of triadic object relations. Coburn (2001) suggests that the exploration and examination of these relational experiences may be what is potentially most valuable to both the supervisee's growth and the patient's progress. Although both supervisor and supervisee contribute to the coconstruction of their relationship, the mutuality and vulnerabilities that emerge are experienced in the context of asymmetry and inequality, which should not be denied (Berman, 2000). A main function of the supervisory relationship is to help facilitate a reflective stance, an internal dialogue and a tolerance for *not* knowing or *not* understanding (Coburn, 2001). A supervisor may best accomplish this goal by modeling this analytic posture and also helping the supervisee to consider the supervisory relationship as a mutual interactive process to explore. Much has been written about the supervisory alliance as key to facilitating the supervisee's learning experience. According to Angus and Kagan (2007) a strong supervisory working alliance fosters an increased sense of self-efficacy and personal agency in supervisees. The supervisory alliance is influenced by many of the same variables involved in establishing the therapeutic alliance such as personality characteristics and relational style. Parallel to the psychotherapy situation, the bulk of responsibility for the quality of the supervisory alliance lies with the supervisor (Riggs & Bretz, 2006).

Effective relational supervision evolves into a transitional space within which the dyad generates new meanings not accessible by each partner in isolation (Berman, 2000). The supervisee's understanding of relational dynamics and his or her capacity to stay attuned to the nuances of the intersubjective field are enhanced. At its best, supervision will increase supervisees' understanding of latent content, improve their clinical skills, promote empathic listening, enhance functioning, and expand relational competencies for both partners (Schamess, 2006). This approach emphasizes the supervisor's participation in the development and maintenance of the relationship and challenges the supervisor to set the stage for the processing of interpersonal material. This type of participation, and certainly the analysis of the dynamics in the relationship, necessitate a certain level of comfort with self-disclosure. We will now turn our attention to issues related to self-disclosure in clinical supervision.

Qualitative research project

Throughout our consideration of issues related to self-disclosure in supervision, we frequently discussed our own experiences as supervisors primarily with predoctoral clinical psychology graduate students. It became apparent that little research had been conducted on the aspects of a relational model of supervision that influence the occurrence and/or use of self-disclosure in supervision. We therefore decided to begin a qualitative investigation of phenomenon of supervisor self-disclosure and allow some of these data to serve as case examples for our discussion.

We began our research process with an extensive review of the literature and our own experiences as supervisors and had an ongoing collaborative discussion of issues, concepts, dilemmas, and outcomes related to supervisor disclosure. A list of interview research questions was generated and was submitted to a qualitative research specialist for review. Table 20.1 lists the final questions we used in interviews with senior clinical psychologists.

Our initial sample consisted of six clinicians with a mean of 18 years conducting clinical supervision from a psychodynamic perspective. These three males and three females worked in various settings at the time of the interview: Three were faculty in a graduate academic program, one was in private practice and teaching as an adjunct in a postdoctoral training institution, one was director of psychology, and the other was director of inpatient psychology at different teaching hospitals. All completed a consent form for anonymous recording and transcribing of their interviews for use in this project.

Each of us conducted several practice interviews and wrote extensive field notes. We then reviewed the interview transcripts and finalized our research approach. To date we have completed six comprehensive qualitative interviews that have been transcribed. After considerable review and discussion of these interviews, we began to identify recurrent themes. We hope eventually to use structured qualitative methods to code these transcripts with a research team and to have these results available. However, for the purposes of this chapter we have culled a number of case examples

Table 20.1 Interview Question for Supervisors

1. What comes to mind when you think about self-disclosure in clinical supervision?
2. How do you understand supervisors' self-disclosure?
3. Can you tell me about your decision-making process relative to self-disclosure in clinical supervision?
    How do you decide to self-disclose?
    When do you self-disclose?
    What do you self-disclose?
4. Can you tell me about a time when you experienced self-disclosure in supervision?
    Taking that example, can you elaborate:
    How did you chose to self-disclose?
    What was the outcome?
    How did you reflect on that as a dynamic in supervision?
5. Can you tell me your thoughts about the role of the supervisee in your self-disclosure?
6. Can you think of a time when self-disclosure was helpful?
7. Can you think of a time when self-disclosure was *not* helpful?

in order to illustrate the many variables affecting self-disclosure by supervisors. What follows are case examples described by senior clinical supervisors as they answered our interview questions.

Self-disclosure in supervision

The notion that supervisors' thoughts and feelings about their supervisees deserve attention was proposed by Searles in his 1965 work, "The Informational Value of the Supervisor's Emotional Experiences." Searles suggested that consideration of the supervisor's "private, 'subjective' fantasy experiences and his personal feelings about the supervisee," could offer insight into the therapeutic relationship between supervisee and patient (p. 157). Searles viewed the feelings of the supervisor as "highly informative reflections of the relationship between therapist and patient," and was among the first to propose that supervisors not dismiss their own feelings an simply an aspect of countertransference (p. 158). He recommended that the supervisor "be alert to the possibility that the source of this emotion may lie chiefly in the therapist-patient relationship and, basically, chiefly in the patient himself," as in parallel process (p. 159).

Years later, Epstein (1997) turned our attention to the experience of the supervisee, and suggested that given the authoritarian nature of what he calls the "traditional tutorial model" of supervision, it would be very difficult for students to verbalize negative experiences of supervision during the supervision hour. Epstein asserted that the supervisory dyad may collude to avoid investigation of negative experiences and warned that these experiences can have adverse impact on the treatment relationship, especially if they remain unspoken. In order to create an atmosphere of safety and recognition of mutual influence on one another, Epstein suggested that the supervisor "be consistently alert to the impact of his personality style, his interventions, and of the entire supervisory process on the supervisee," in order to assist the student with disclosing such experiences should they arise (Epstein, p. 296). A supervisor whom we interviewed holds a similar view of this process and explained his approach:

> I say to them at the beginning, "If you're sensing
> something that's going on here, that's interfering
> with your learning, I . . . want to know about it." But
> I still feel, with interns and externs and even post-
> docs, that it's the responsibility of the supervisor to
> bring it up first, as a first step, rather than the other
> way around. Because I think no matter how we look
> at it, there's still an asymmetry, a power differential,
> especially when they're being evaluated.

Types of self-disclosure

Investigating supervisors' self-disclosure in clinical supervision can begin with categorizing types and patterns of disclosure. Ladany and Lehrman-Waterman's (1999) study generated the following categories of self-disclosure: personal issues, counseling struggles, counseling successes, neutral counseling experiences, professional experiences, reactions to trainees' clients, dynamics of the training site, supervisory relationship, and experiences as a supervisor. In terms of frequency of self-disclosure per category, disclosures related to "personal issues" were the most frequent type, followed by "neutral counseling experiences" (interventions or strategies employed), followed by "counseling struggles." The authors question the rationale for personal disclosures and ask us to consider whether these disclosures are being made in the service of the supervisor or for purposes of training. In addition to types of self-disclosure, our case examples consider issues related to spontaneity, timing, and impact of supervisor self-disclosure.

Personal issues

A supervisor whom we interviewed shared an experience of a personal disclosure that exemplifies the post-disclosure thought process:

> In supervision with a novice trainee, we were discuss-
> ing an adult case related to issues of loss. The patient,
> it seemed, never had opportunity or means to grieve

the loss of her father when she was a young woman, and the supervision was focused on the implications of that unprocessed loss. I responded with some self-disclosure about the profound impact of death of a parent regardless of the qualitative nature of the relationship. I shared a bit about the recent death of my own mother and the impact on my clinical work. This seemed to open up the trainee's disclosure about the death of her sibling while she was a teen, as well as disclosures about her then-entrance into therapy. We seemed then vaulted into a personal exchange about loss and I struggled with how to weave this back to the work with the patient. As I listened, I realized that the trainee had gone on to say that she subsequently became friends with her therapist and now will run into her at the gym. I noted some significant concern that this trainee had been exposed to professional boundary violations in her youth and that keeping the supervisory frame with her would be challenging but very necessary. I regretted having self-disclosed as I saw it as a spontaneous repetition for her in terms of relational confusion and I worried that this would also repeat in her work with her own patients. Because of her novice status and the early stage of our supervisory relationship, I chose to disclose neither my concerns nor my rationale for working more closely on boundary issues. Interestingly, the patient was about my age, while the trainee was my daughter's age. So I wondered much about the multiple relational configurations that may have contributed to my spontaneous self-disclosure.

[handwritten margin note: ✱ therapists are not friends]

This vignette is a valuable illustration of supervision as a cocreated experience. Additionally, it is clear from this example that given the interactive influence of participants, it is not possible to anticipate the precise impact or outcome of a self-disclosure until after the disclosure has been made and received. What is most important in this exchange in terms of our current objective is that the supervisor listened closely for reverberations that might follow her disclosure. She remained in the role of supervisor rather than allowing herself to get lost in the personal exchange and she was alert to the supervisee's process, which was communicated both directly and indirectly. Even after regretting the disclosure, the supervisor was able to make use of her experience by hypothesizing possible transference-countertransference enactments that might have been at play.

Counseling struggles

Ladany and Lehrman-Waterman (1999) caution that supervisors' disclosures of counseling struggles have the potential to increase anxiety in the
student, who may have previously regarded the supervisor as expert and
may be comforted by such a view. Our perspective differs from this position; we suggest that such a cautious approach serves to reinforce the "myth
of the supervisory situation," wherein the supervisor's abilities are idealized while the supervisee's capabilities are devalued (Berman, 1997, p. 168).

Given the anxiety typical of inexperienced psychotherapists in supervision, we have found that disclosure of the supervisor's professional
struggles, especially from a time when the supervisor was a novice in
the field, can be somewhat inoculating against the student's anxiety.
Reifer's (2001) description of the beginning psychotherapist reminds us of
the challenge of being supervised for the first time: "He worries that his
personality will be judged along with his work and, should he be unsuccessful, he is likely to suffer serious narcissistic injury" (p. 67). Given this
potential for shame, we have found that disclosures of the supervisor's
beginner anxiety, as well as struggles that continue to emerge even as an
established professional, can combat the apprehension that often interferes
with supervisees' ability to get the most out of supervision. Supervisors
we interviewed made reference to this issue:

> I think it's a necessary part . . . share what you've been
> through. Your own process . . . . The old ideas of ano-
> nymity *really* don't apply in supervision to me. It cre-
> ates a kind of discourse. I think supervisees remember
> those self-disclosures, especially ones where you're
> able to place yourself back during the moment, when
> you were a supervisee, and the kinds of developmental
> changes that occur over time as a therapist, and look at
> the cycles that you went through, one goes through, as
> a therapist and as a supervisor. I think it's very helpful
> to trainees so they also feel maybe disarmed by that
> and are able to talk about themselves more.

Another supervisor shared the following regarding disclosures she
has made about her own professional experiences:

> Sometimes I'll disclose things that happened to
> me as a beginning therapist so that I put myself in
> their position and I remember usually big mistakes
> that I made [*laughs*]. And part of that is modeling,
> part of that is to make them comfortable because

sometimes they feel very intimidated. Like they'll say, "Well, you always have the right answer," or "You always would know what to do." And so . . . I might pick from the repertoire of early experiences and sometimes not so early. Sometimes I'll tell them, "Look, I'm still struggling. Last week this situation happened and I wasn't sure what to do." So also to help them see that this is an ongoing, never-ending process of discovery and working on oneself. So I use it for that, too. It's to model what to do, but also to help them see that even a seasoned professional is constantly working and struggling and there are situations where you're not sure. Sometimes I'll . . . disclose mistakes I've made . . . even recent ones: "Look, you know, last week I did this . . . ."

Sometimes the disclosure has to do with, it's around the work, but my examples might be when a patient made me embarrassed or did something that put me on the spot, or that I felt ill-equipped in some way. . . . Of course I'm disclosing it from a position of authority and looking back, and "look what we can learn from this," but I'm still disclosing a weakness.

Hahn (2001) described the experience of shame in psychotherapy supervision and explained, "Supervisor self-disclosure and normalization of treatment hurdles can help supervisees feel competent relative to their level of training" (p. 280). "The goal is to create an atmosphere within which the experience of shame can be assuaged" (p. 281). As a supervisor whom we interviewed explained, disclosures may be

"about my own anxiety that I had in supervision, if I'm picking up on something. Or if felt like I'm contributing to shutting them down a bit, or I've criticized or shamed them in some way, I try to take a look at that."

Another supervisor shared a similar view: "I have self-disclosed to not only normalize what a supervisee had done, but also to indicate that we are more equal. We are not that dissimilar, different from each other."

In contrast, one supervisor remembered occasions of disclosing his history as a beginning psychotherapist that, in retrospect, he felt did not have such a positive impact:

I think that when I acted like a father who's saying, "I've been through this," "I went through the same process you did," "You'll see when you grow up." Sharing too much was just a burden to them. Because they felt like: "I feel like I should know this already. He's been through this, why don't I know this?" Rather than, they have to go through their process.

Developmental level of trainee

It reasons that supervisory self-disclosure would differ depending on the developmental stage of the trainee. One supervisor described his frequency of self-disclosure as linked with the developmental level of the trainee: "The more sophisticated the supervisee is, the more likely I am to self-disclose. That is because I think I probably experience that as a more egalitarian relationship. . . . I feel like I develop a more collaborative relationship with the more advanced students. . . ." Sophistication was defined by this supervisor as "the capacity of the supervisee to be open and honest and to have access to their own unconscious . . . and to be able to bring that into the supervision."

Another supervisor also addressed the impact of the developmental stage of the supervisee on his types of self-disclosures:

> Definitely with post-doc supervisees . . . I think I do it in a less structured way and I use my free associative flow a little bit more easily with post-docs, because that's where they're at. Usually, they're wanting to have a treatment that's a little less structured . . . . And then there are people that I've been supervising for five or six years, who are functioning at a staff level, where there's a lot more interchange. The relationship becomes maybe even mutual supervision after a while, so in that context, I'm even *less* planful [sic] about my self-disclosures because of the quality of the relationship.

Evaluative feedback

Granted, some disclosures are easier to make than others. Researchers have found that it is easier for supervisors to share feedback about clinical issues such as psychotherapy skills and the status of a case than to address matters related to the personality of the supervisee or the supervisory relationship (Hoffman, Hill, Holmes, & Freitas, 2005; Farber, 2006). In keeping with these findings, Ladany and Lehrman-Waterman (1999) found that only 12% of trainees reported that their supervisor made a disclosure about the supervisory relationship.

Regarding factors that facilitate imparting feedback, Hoffman, Hill, Holmes, and Freitas (2005) found that supervisees' level of defensiveness along with the quality of the supervisory relationship function as mediating factors in terms of the ease with which feedback is offered to supervisees. Providing feedback about a student's performance, however, is not considered self-disclosure in the spirit of "self-revealing" (Stricker, 1990). We will limit our discussion of supervisory evaluative feedback and focus instead on disclosure as revealing aspects of self (Farber, 2006).

Regarding frequency of supervisors' self-disclosure, Farber (2006) suggests that "most supervisors, like most therapists, will likely be more disclosing, personally giving, openly reassuring, and even humorous than the literature suggests or they have acknowledged to all but their closest friends or colleagues" (p. 180). Farber asserts that "clinical work, or at least the quality of the dyadic relationship, is likely to suffer in the absence of a reasonable degree of disclosure" (p. 180).

Disclosures during supervisory impasses

Several supervisors interviewed reported using self-disclosure during supervisory stalemates.

> I think that if we hit a jam . . . an impasse in the supervision, I'm more likely to self-disclose. . . . If I find that a supervisee is stuck in a particular repetition that they have with several patients, I'll probably be more likely to self-disclose. Sometimes it's just spontaneous, I'm not sure exactly why, but usually when I review it, you know as my own internal supervisor, it's usually when they've become stuck.

Another supervisor shared the following experience related to a supervisory relational impasse:

> I had a student many years ago, who, a supervisee, who I felt, we never hit it off. I repeatedly would, in session, give her advice, she would cry—it was painful to go through. And she thought I really hated her and disliked her, and frankly after a while, I was beginning to feel that way towards her. So I said to her something like, "You know, this is what has developed between the two of us." "Uh, I don't think you feel comfortable at all with me, and I see

you as being very defensive with me and frankly
that's beginning to wear on me because I don't
know what to do about it, I don't feel like we're getting anyplace, I don't feel like I'm helping you, or
anything like that." I don't remember it working
very well. My sense was I became this kind of per-
secutor and it wasn't, it wasn't remediable.

And the response was, she got sort of quiet, and
listened and tried to think about it, but she cried some
more. And her response was either temporary, shifting, or more defensiveness. And the result of that was
that my beliefs about her became even more concrete.
I mean, in the sense that, I began to think, "Well, here's
a student who is so frightened, and so defensive, and
this is such a challenge for her that I can't penetrate
her at all, I can't get her to look at, at this."

I regret not bringing it up earlier, and not disclosing my observation about the two of us, earlier. I think
I may have waited too long and there was just too
much there for me to overcome. I could be wrong—I
could have brought it up earlier and it wouldn't have
made a difference at all. I would, if I had that to do
over again and my regret is that I didn't do it sooner.

Supervisory alliance

The supervisory relationship or alliance has been studied as a basis
for determining frequency and type of supervisory self-disclosure.
Ladany and Lehrman-Waterman (1999) hypothesized that supervisor
self-disclosure would predict the effectiveness of the supervisory working alliance. Their results indicate that "the more frequently a supervisor
self-disclosed, the greater was the agreement between the supervisor and
the trainee on the goals and tasks of supervision and the stronger was
the emotional bond between the two" (p. 156). More specifically, sharing
counseling struggles seemed to have the greatest influence on strength
of the supervisory alliance. The authors suggest that the sharing of such
vulnerability on the part of the supervisor may serve to strengthen the
supervisory relationship.

Countertransference disclosures

We consider a major function of supervisory self-disclosure as seizing the
opportunity to make use of countertransference reactions that arise during the course of supervision. We view the investigation of supervisory

countertransference not only as essential in an exploration of potential parallel process, but also as useful in modeling acceptance of a wide range of thoughts and feelings that arise in response to patients. One of our supervisors shared the following, which serves as a broad overview of this type of disclosure:

> I'll disclose my emotions, I'll disclose what's happening with us . . . what position I feel I'm being put in. . . . Certainly if there are some projections or projective identifications that are very powerful and I'm starting to feel pulled in whatever way, I'll find a way to try to address that. And that brings me into the picture a lot more than them just reporting to me.

Strean (2000) contends that countertransference disclosures can strengthen the supervisory alliance:

> Just as I believe that the therapist's disclosures of countertransference reactions to the patient can at crucial times strengthen the therapeutic alliance, I also contend that the supervisor's disclosures of her countertransference responses can strengthen the supervisory alliance. In my judgment, when the supervisory alliance is strengthened the therapeutic alliance between the patient and therapist is strengthened, thereby moving the treatment relationship toward a resolution of a therapeutic impasse. (p. 270)

The view of supervision as "the crossroads of several relational paths," acknowledges the need to attend to the intersubjective components of supervision rather than simply focusing on teaching "correct" technique (Berman, 1997, p. 162, 164). Disclosing countertransference responses serves as one form of articulating reciprocal influence. As Strean explained: "When I observed that my supervisees did not respond positively to my teaching or my clarifications and interpretations of the parallel process, I decided to disclose some of my countertransference reactions to my supervisees" (2000, p. 276).

In terms of impact of supervisory disclosures of countertransference, Strean (2000) suggests the outcome is positive:

> As my supervisees observed that I was taking some initiative in disclosing my feelings of anger, hurt, rejection, and so forth, they felt a freedom to identify with me and do the same. And, when I did not

mirroring effect

reveal very much about myself, they also tended to be withholding. . . . And when the supervisee felt less anxiety about revealing himself, he invariably made it safer for his client to face herself. One of the positive effects of disclosing the supervisor's countertransference is that it tends to clarify the supervisee's transference toward her. (p. 277)

Case example of negative outcome of process disclosure

Most likely there are instances in which a supervisor's disclosure may complicate the supervision process. For example, one supervisor reported:

> I think the *worst* example of a process self-disclosure was when it was a displacement. Expressing and feeling frustrated, irritated, impatient with some process that was going on between the intern and patient and then I realized that it had to do with my anxiety about how the work would be viewed and how much progress was being made. In particular how a physician at the setting would view it. And I didn't realize that I was feeling that kind of pressure. As a result, my impatience showed. It was not productive. I know the intern felt more stressed. And it wasn't that I was inaccurate in my observations or conclusions regarding the work of the therapy, but it was the expression or the disclosure of my impatience or my irritation with the *approaches* that were being used, and what was being *said* to the patient and it *really* had to do with how I was going to look and that was displaced anxiety, converted into anger at her. So that was not useful based on what happened at the moment. It was a long time ago, so I forget if I shared my realization of what had happened on the spot, after it happened, or if it were a few days later after I thought about it. I know I did share it, and shared the reasoning for it, the anxiety about it, and that it was displaced inappropriately, and unfairly.

Ladany, Constantine, Miller, Erickson, and Muse-Burke (2000) described the following example of a supervisee's uncomfortable feelings following a supervisor's countertransference disclosure; the overall outcome, however, remained positive.

One supervisor said that talking about the supervisor countertransference reaction made the intern feel uncomfortable, anxious, angry, and hurt at times. However, this discussion influenced the supervisory relationship by letting the intern know that whatever happened, they could talk honestly about it, which was different than previous supervisory relationships for the intern. Another supervisor considered the discussion of issues pertaining to the supervisor countertransference as a turning point toward more openness with one another. (p. 109)

Case example of a decision not to self-disclose

Certainly, the reflective and self-aware supervisor has an ongoing repertoire of thoughts and reactions during each supervision session. Analyzing his or her internal process is invaluable in understanding the intersubjective triadic field, and the decisions concerning which material to verbalize are complicated. One clinician reported:

> The first thing that comes to mind is when I have feelings towards a supervisee that I shouldn't have. I will want to keep to myself. Those can include angry feelings, sexual feelings, and judgments about the supervisee, like I'm sitting here sometimes thinking, "Oh my God. This person shouldn't be a psychologist." You know, and "How am I gonna get this across?" "How can I say this in a way that doesn't seem like it's too personal on, on my part?" But I think mostly it's these sort of forbidden, negative, sexual feelings that come to mind. If I don't like a supervisee, uh, I won't want to say that. I might, will work hard to try to like the supervisee, if, if I can. Um, but with some supervisees, that's an uphill battle, to come to get to like them and respect them. . . . I usually have maybe one or two a year, maybe one a year, who I don't get along with, uh, it doesn't click . . . and I don't really want to share that.

Effectiveness of supervisory self-disclosure

So, how do we determine the effectiveness of supervisory self-disclosure? Ladany and Walker (2003) found that "in most cases supervisor self-disclosures have a small influence on supervision outcome" but "the outcomes most directly affected are the supervisory working alliance, trainee self-disclosure and trainee edification" (p. 613). Farber (2006) points out "the disclosures of supervisors seem to be of minor import" when measuring impact on the treatment outcome (p. 192). However, if the supervisory alliance is deepened and the supervisee learns from the inter-personal process, most likely the therapeutic work will be enhanced.

We contend that even if supervisory disclosures do not have signifi-cant impact on the patient's treatment, such disclosures are influential when measuring impact on the supervisory relationship, the supervisee's ease in the supervision, and the supervisee's comfort level with expe-riencing, tolerating, and making use of the wide range of feelings that emerge while conducting psychotherapy.

Additional case examples

Our interviews with senior supervisors provided many relevant and detailed examples of self-disclosure process occurring both spontane-ously and deliberately. The following two examples are included here to further illustrate the intersubjective aspects of this dyadic interaction unique to clinical training.

Case example of personal self-disclosure

> A [supervisee's] . . . wife had a crisis that made him cancel and abruptly leave in the middle of the [work] day. . . . He shared his anguish about how he would tell a very caretaking, elderly female patient what had happened (and she would ask) and what was he going to do. And inasmuch as I left it for him to decide, I said, "Think about not presuming you know what she's going to need from you and not feeding her ahead of time before she asks." I then said, "I made a major decision during a medical cri-sis for my son, to do what I usually never do, which is to tell every patient why I would not be available for a month." I said, "And much to my surprise, I made the call that if I was lost in space, that would be much more disruptive to them than not know-ing, than if they actually knew what happened and that I was taking care of that." And I said, "We look afterwards at the impact of our decision." I said, "As startling as it is, 50 people waited. No one chose to use my colleagues, no one had a crisis." So I said, "And I thought later that I had somebody keep them informed she's OK, her son's doing better, and that seemed to make them feel very complimented and

very included, but everybody kept their distance, in
the sense they did not demand me or my attention."
I said, "But that was a MAJOR decision I made." I
said, "You know, you've got to decide, but be that as
it may, once you do, it's on record. Once you share it,
it's part of your process with that person."

I thought it would be a dramatic example of disclosing something personal that actually helped the
patients. . . . Um, why did I choose, at that moment?
I guess I thought that it was a very close match-up to
the idea of suddenly being hit with something that's
going to disrupt their process. That's the other thing
about disclosure—if something's happening in your
personal life for which your patients need not know,
because it is really not interfering with their therapy, why should they know? But if in fact, I mean
all of a sudden that patient's session was cancelled,
(everybody's sessions were cancelled with me), then
I guess it's prompting a different kind of decision
making. Your inability to hold your private crisis is
your inability to hold your private crisis. And then
you wonder are you using your patients as audience
or as containers for your anguish. Um, it's much
like we say to them: "Your interventions—you don't
know until you see how it unfolds." . . . But I guess
I disclosed to my supervisee in order to model for
him an option for his work.

Case example: Disclosure of clinical and personal material

I can think of another supervision case in which I was
disclosing about my work with a suicidal patient. In
a case of a suicidal patient, the position that I'm taking with the supervisee is . . . you know the whole
notion of how you think about suicidal thinking, as
pain becoming intolerable, interminable, inescapable.
I've said, "And then at some point, you do whatever
you can to keep that person believing there's a reason to stay alive, including your own feelings about
that person." So I said, "So in the case of one man,
he's on a phone, I'm on a phone, he's saying there
is absolutely no more reason for me to live, I've told
you this," and I said, "At that point I'll use my own
feelings," which I did, which is, "The reason that I

need you to live is because of my feelings about you. And that this has to do with somebody caring about you. You're not someone whose disappearance is not gonna matter. It's gonna matter to me." What I *didn't* tell the supervisee at the time was that I made mention of the fact to the patient, and maybe it's because it was such an emotional moment that I told the patient at the time, "I have already lost a father who disappeared. I can't have you disappear." And [for] the patient who also had lost his father (abandoned him), that was a tie-in that made my care relevant. And years later he would point to that.

Now, I have to tell you honestly, I can't tell you if I told my supervisee the details of the paternal piece, but that I shared *my* personal side with that patient and it mattered, in terms of that suicidal intervention. I think what it did in terms of this particular female supervisee with a female patient, was her being able to share her own personal care and love and concern for the patient—she was very reticent to do that. She was reticent across the treatment in sharing her feelings. But given that we both feared her patient was suicidal, my invitation was to do that. So, those are the kinds of things I guess in some ways . . . it would take some personal disclosure and you could see the domino [effect] of personal disclosure. But over the course of all these years of supervision, that is the point at which I'll say to people, "As far as I'm concerned, I'll say whatever's real; I will break the frame at the point." That supervisee then seemed to become more comfortable in disclosing her authentic feelings to her patient.

Summary and recommendations

After a review of the clinical and theoretical literature, Hill and Knox (2001) proposed guidelines for effective and appropriate psychotherapist self-disclosure. Following our review of the supervision literature and our initial qualitative research, we would like to suggest similar guidelines as to content, aims, and process for supervisors to incorporate when considering self-disclosure to their supervisees.

1. Generally, supervisors using self-disclosure should consider the developmental training level of the supervisee as well as the emotional sophistication of the supervisee. New supervisees may be calmed by

supervisors' self-disclosures of early clinical experiences and their attempts to cope with anxiety and perhaps mistakes. Disclosures concerning countertransference reactions as well as issues related to process in the supervisory relationship would benefit more experienced supervisees, while still being potentially useful for novice clinicians. That is, most beginning students can benefit from the modeling of supervisory countertransference disclosures. Additionally, if the novice clinician possesses a moderate degree of emotional sophistication, relational process disclosures may also be appropriate and of great value. Again, it is key to be mindful of level of training and emotional sophistication when considering countertransference and process disclosures.

2. Supervisors can use self-disclosure to validate reality, normalize experiences, model therapeutic responses, strengthen the supervisory alliance, or offer alternative ways to think or act (Hill & Knox, 2001). Self-disclosures can serve many functions and may be spontaneous or intentional on the part of the supervisors as they mentor their supervisees into the profession.

3. Given the variety of forms and functions of supervisor self-disclosure, it is imperative that the supervisor carefully monitor his or her use of self-disclosure and understand the motivation behind it. Supervisors should avoid disclosing personal material if they find they are doing so as a result of being unable to contain their own experiences. We suggest that supervisors self-monitor such disclosures by asking themselves, "Am I using my trainee either as audience or container for my own struggles?" Such self-disclosures would be serving the supervisor's own needs rather than meeting the training needs of the supervisee. Supervisor self-disclosure that shifts the focus away from the therapeutic relationship, interferes with the flow of sessions, or burdens, confuses, or overstimulates the supervisee should be avoided.

4. Given the power differential inherent in the supervisory dyad, supervisors need to pay particular attention to the impact of their self-disclosures on the supervisee. Supervisors who ask supervisees about their reactions to supervisory self-disclosures may hear about anxiety reduction, greater understanding of the supervisor's instructions, new ways of thinking, or stimulation of therapeutic ideas. However, supervisees will be less likely to report negative reactions to self-disclosures such as discomfort, shame, or humiliation. Supervisors must remain sensitive to these issues as their evaluative responsibilities create a context wherein supervisees will easily experience shame as their clinical inexperience is exposed (Schamess, 2006). However, self-disclosure by supervisors seems to reduce supervisee shame and can create an environment where vulnerabilities can be discussed (Talbot, 1995).

5. We encourage the use of carefully considered and well-timed self-disclosure with supervisees who are struggling within their therapeutic relationship. Many have indicated that self-disclosure will enhance the working alliance whether in a supervision or treatment relationship. Supervisors can easily model and process this developing alliance within the supervisory context and discuss its extension to the therapeutic relationship.

6. Self-disclosures should also be congruent with the personality, style, and theoretical orientations of the two persons in the supervisory dyad. Supervisors with a more intersubjective focus will likely create a supervisory atmosphere of mutual engagement, openness, reflection, and transitional space for exploring new meanings. The specific focus and style of each supervisory dyad depends on unique personality variables of each of the partners (Berman, 2000). Even if the orientations of the dyad differ, attention to the intersubjective field will likely expand relational competencies and enhance the supervisory alliance. Supervisors must also remain mindful that supervision is *not* psychotherapy and characterological aspects of the supervisee are considered only as they pertain to the crossover into the therapist–patient dyad.

7. Whenever tension, impasses, or ruptures occur in the supervisory relationship, supervisors should carefully consider how self-disclosure might help the supervisee understand this process as a near experience in order to model this approach and further their understanding of intersubjective phenomena and parallel process. Further, a focus on the dilemmas occurring in the supervisory relationship may help both partners in the repair of the relational rupture and move the alliance into greater trust and safety.

8. If there is an evaluative component in the supervisory relationship (either as part of a grade, a benchmark achievement, or a letter of recommendation), we would urge supervisors to make these types of disclosures throughout the supervisory relationship. There should be no surprises vis-à-vis feedback upon termination of the supervisory relationship, and the termination process should be openly and fully discussed. There often are continued interactions between supervisors and the supervisees, so a "good enough" closure is strongly encouraged.

References

Anderson, H., & Swim, S. (1995). Supervision as collaborative conversation: Connecting the voices of supervisor and supervisee. *Journal of Systemic Therapies, 14*(2), 1–13.

Angus, L., & Kagan, F. (2007). Empathic relational bonds and personal agency in psychotherapy: Implications for psychotherapy supervision, practice, and research. *Psychotherapy: Theory, Research, Practice, Training, 44*, 371–377.

Astor, J. (2000). Some reflections on empathy and reciprocity in the use of countertransference between supervisor and supervisee. *Journal of Analytical Psychology, 45*, 367–383.

Berman, E. (1997). Psychoanalytic supervision as the crossroads of a relational matrix. In M. Rock (Ed.), *Psychodynamic supervision: Perspectives of the supervisor and the supervisee* (pp. 161–186). Northvale, NJ: Jason Aronson.

Berman, E. (2000). Psychoanalytic supervision: The intersubjective development. *International Journal of Psychoanalysis, 81*, 273–290.

Bernstein, A. E., & Katz, S. C. (1987). When supervisor and therapist dream: The use of an unusual countertransference phenomenon. *Journal of the American Academy of Psychoanalysis, 15*(2), 261–271.

Coburn, W. (2001). Transference-countertransference dynamics and disclosure in supervision. In S. Gill (Ed)., *The supervisory alliance* (pp. 215–232). Northvale, NJ: Jason Aronson.

Downs, M. (2006). Between us: Growing relational possibilities in clinical supervision. *Work in Progress*, No. 105, Wellesley, MA: Stone Center.

Ellis, M. V. (2006). Critical incidents in clinical supervision: Assessing supervisory issues. *Training and Education in Professional Psychology, 2*, 122–132.

Epstein, L. (1997). Collusive selective inattention to the negative impact of the supervisory interaction. In M. Rock (Ed.), *Psychodynamic supervision: Perspectives of the supervisor and the supervisee* (pp. 285–311). Northvale, NJ: Jason Aronson.

Farber, B. A. (2006). Supervisee and supervisor disclosure. In *Self-disclosure in psychotherapy* (pp. 180–197). New York: The Guilford Press.

Fleming, J., & Benedek, T. (1966). *Psychoanalytic supervision: A method of clinical teaching*. New York: Grune & Stratton.

Frawley-O'Dea, M. G., & Sarnat, E. (2001). *The supervisory relationship: A contemporary psychodynamic approach*. New York: Guilford Press.

Gill, S. (Ed.) (2001). *The supervisory alliance: Facilitating the psychotherapist's learning experience*. Northvale, NJ: Jason Aronson.

Glickauf-Hughes, C. (1994). Characterological resistances in psychotherapy supervision. *Psychotherapy: Theory, Research, Practice, Training, 31*(1), 58–66.

Gray, L. A., Ladany, N., Walker, J. A., & Ancis, J. R. (2001). Psychotherapy trainees' experience of counterproductive events in supervision. *Journal of Counseling Psychology, 48*(4), 371–383.

Hahn, W. K. (2001). The experience of shame in psychotherapy supervision. *Psychotherapy: Theory, Research, Practice, Training, 38*(3), 272–282.

Heru, A. M., Strong, D., Price, M., & Recupero, P. R. (2006). Self-disclosure in psychotherapy supervisors. *American Journal of Psychotherapy, 60*, 323–334.

Hetzel, R. D., & Kroll, A. S. (in press). Relational psychotherapy supervision: A shared supervision story. *Texas Psychologist*.

Hill, C. E., & Knox, S. (2001). Self-disclosure. *Psychotherapy, Theory, Research, Practice, Training, 38*, 413–417.

Hoffman, M. A., Hill, C. E., Holmes, S. E, & Freitas, G. F. (2005). Supervisor perspective on the process and outcome of giving easy, difficult, or no feedback to supervisees. *Journal of Counseling Psychology, 52*(1), 3–13.

Hunt, W. (2001). The use of the countertransference in supervision. In S. Gill (Ed.), *The supervisory alliance: Facilitating the psychotherapist's learning experience* (pp. 165–179). Northvale, NJ: Jason Aronson.

Jordan, J. V. (2004). Relational learning in psychotherapy consultation and supervision. In M. Walker & W. Rosen (Eds.), *How connections heal* (pp. 22–30). New York: Guilford Press.

Ladany, N. (2002). Psychotherapy supervision: How dressed is the emperor? *Psychotherapy Bulletin, 37*(4), 14–18.

Ladany, N., Constantine, M. G., Miller, K, Erickson, C. D., & Muse-Burke, J. L. (2000). Supervisor countertransference: A qualitative investigation into its identification and description. *Journal of Counseling Psychology, 47*(1), 102–115.

Ladany, N., & Lehrman-Waterman, D. E. (1999). The content and frequency of supervisor self-disclosures and their relationship to supervisor style and the supervisory working alliance. *Counselor Education and Supervision, 38,* 143–160.

Ladany, N., & Walker, J. A. (2003). Supervisor self-disclosure: Balancing the uncontrollable narcissist with the indomitable altruist. *Journal of Clinical Psychology, 59*(5), 611–621.

Reifer, S. (2001). Dealing with the anxiety of beginning therapists in supervision. In S. Gill (Ed.), *The supervisory alliance: Facilitating the psychotherapist's learning experience* (pp. 67–74). Northvale, NJ: Jason Aronson.

Ricci, W. (1995). Self and intersubjectivity in the supervisory process. *Bulletin of the Menninger Clinic, 59,* 53–68.

Riggs, S. A., & Bretz, K. M. (2006). Attachment processes in the supervisory relationship: An exploratory investigation. *Professional Psychology: Research and Practice, 37,* 558–566.

Ringel, S. (2001). In the shadow of death: Relational paradigms in clinical supervision. *Clinical Social Work Journal, 29,* 171–179.

Rock, M. H. (Ed.). (1997). *Psychodynamic supervision.* Northvale, NJ: Jason Aronson.

Safran, J. D., & Muran, J. C. (2001). A relational approach to training and supervision in cognitive psychotherapy. *Journal of Cognitive Psychotherapy: An International Quarterly, 15,* 3–15.

Safran, J. D., & Muran, J. C. (2000). *Negotiating the therapeutic alliance: A relational treatment guide.* New York: Guilford Press.

Sarnat, J. (1992). Supervision in relationship: Resolving the teach-treat controversy in psychoanalytic supervision. *Psychoanalytic Psychology, 9*(3), 387–403.

Schamess, G. (2006). Transference enactments in clinical supervision. *Clinical Social Work Journal, 34,* 407–425.

Searles, H. F. (1965). The informational value of the supervisor's emotional experiences. In *Collected papers on schizophrenia and related subjects* (pp. 157–176). New York: International Universities Press.

Strean, H. S. (2000). Resolving therapeutic impasses by using the supervisor's countertransference. *Clinical Social Work Journal, 28*(3), 263–279.

Stricker, G. (2003). The many faces of self-disclosure. *Journal of Clinical Psychology, 59*(5), 623–630.

Stricker, G. (1990). Self-disclosure and psychotherapy. In G. Stricker & M. Fisher (Eds.), *Self-disclosure in the therapeutic relationship* (pp. 277–289). New York: Plenum Press.

Talbot, N. L. (1995). Unearthing shame in the supervisory experience. *American Journal of Psychotherapy, 49*(3), 338–349.

Teitelbaum, S. (2001). The changing scene in supervision. In S. Gill (Ed.), *The supervisory alliance: Facilitating the psychotherapist's learning experience* (pp. 3–18). Northvale, NJ: Jason Aronson.

Worthen, V., & McNeil, B. W. (1996). A phenomenological investigation of "good" supervision events. *Journal of Counseling Psychology, 43*(1), 25–34.

chapter twenty-one

Collective wisdom for good practice
Themes for consideration

Andrea Bloomgarden and Rosemary B. Mennuti

Judicious self-disclosure as good practice

Our authors shared their stories honing in on different aspects of what each believed to be judicious self-disclosure meant to be instrumental in the formation of a healing relationship. Therapists considered the whole of what was known about them, recognizing that what is disclosed goes far beyond what is said in words within a therapy office. Being aware of possible errors of too much, too little, or unattuned self-disclosure, therapists were willing to attend to and repair ruptures, evolving to become more flexible and skillful at using themselves, the instrument of their work.

Viewing the therapy relationship as the medium through which all good therapy is accomplished, empirically supported techniques and models are best served by a psychotherapy relationship that works for the client. In trying to create good quality relationships, our authors shared stories to illuminate different aspects of what each believed to be judicious, therapeutic self-disclosure. Mindful of too much, too little, or unattuned self-disclosure, they discussed their own evolving perspectives as they reflected back on cases that taught them something. In the process, they had to at times repair ruptures and become more skillfull at using themselves as the instrument of their work. False dichotomies pitting neutrality against self-disclosure as automatically leading to egregious boundary violations will hopefully soon be a thing of the past. In this book, our authors tried to model open, nuanced discussion about this complex aspect of therapy. A healing relationship, in our view, includes the personhood of the therapist, but thoughtful choices need to be made for it to be used wisely and therapeutically. Perhaps we are moving from the "blank screen" to a "judicious self-disclosure" ideal.

As we reflected upon the stories we read, we found that five themes emerged that may help the reader integrate the lessons learned in this book.

Therapist as well-tuned instrument

All therapists have past histories and current life challenges, ethnic/ racial/gender/sexual identities, wisdom from life experiences, as well as blind spots from lack of experience and understanding. In some way, all of who we are comes with us into the therapy relationship whether any of it is ever discussed with clients or not. With degrees of kinesthetic empathy, the assistance of the Internet, and all that is readily seen about us, our clients may well know more about us than we may think. It is our job to be responsible for teaching clients how to navigate that part of our relationship with them, and for choosing carefully to cocreate a relationship with our clients that will most facilitate their growth. They may not know if they are allowed to ask questions, to disagree, to need something from us, to write e-mails to us, to call us between appointments for additional support, to ask for a hug, to give us a gift.

We can begin by educating clients about therapist self-disclosure, modeling our own boundaries, and also respecting theirs, by giving them information to empower them in the therapy process. We model flexibility and ego strength when we respond positively to a request for something different from what we have offered, to change course in better attunement to their needs: Perhaps they want us to be less self-disclosing to give them more space; perhaps they need us to bring ourselves more into relationship and be more present. Sometimes they ask in words—sometimes we may observe that our way of relating seems ineffective, and we might seek feedback about how they experience their relationship with us. When we think of ourselves as instrumental in the therapy process, we take full responsibility for who we are and what we are bringing to our therapy appointments each day, and we are willing to question what we are doing to better attune with our clients' needs.

Expressing affect appropriately

As we listen to our clients, we often have feeling reactions to their words. We do not sit blankly, feeling nothing. We may have many tender, positive, and heartfelt caring feelings; by contrast, we may feel frustrated, annoyed, discouraged, or angry. When should we say something about what we feel, and how should we do it? When is it therapeutic to share, when is it therapeutic to keep it to ourselves? Although clients may sense what we feel even without our saying so, we may choose at times to specifically say what we feel about them, to them. Sometimes we sense that they need to know their value to us—at those times, telling them the positive ways we think and feel about them may be helpful. It could be crucial, even a lifeline, for a very isolated, depressed client to know that we care about them, that they matter to us. It could be helpful to let clients who abusively express their anger at us to let them know something about how that makes us feel, to teach them about the effects they may have on others. When we make these decisions, we are very careful, testing the waters, saying a little bit, and observing the effect of our choice on them. We can watch carefully and see what seems to happen next—do they open up more? Do they look at the clock? Change the subject? We can ask them directly for feedback, "How do you feel about my saying that?" "What was it like to hear that?" "Do you know why I told you that?" Based on their answer as well as their nonverbal cues, we can attune to them, to learn which clients find our interventions helpful and which ones feel uncomfortable in some way.

In sum, when we choose to purposely and explicitly share our affect, we do it because we have reason to believe it might help the client; we can find out whether it helped, and decide whether or not to do it again in the future. We also believe, as numerous authors in this book mentioned, that there are some absolute limits—we don't believe there is ever a benefit to expressing a therapist's own sexual feelings about a client to a client, even if a client asks. We also hesitate to express anger at a client—we believe that if a client is provoking anger in us, then in part we are responsible for our own reaction, and need to translate to the client about their behaviors, for example, if they are crossing our boundaries and mistreating us. In sum, we delicately and thoughtfully consider our clients' needs to know our feelings, our thoughts, and our reactions about them, and with feedback from them, we learn what will be most helpful with each client regarding affective expression.

Perils of too much or too little: Striking a balance

We are bound to make errors, sharing too much or too little about ourselves, in affect, facts revealed, bringing too much (or too little) of our personality into the relationship, or being too rigid or loose with our boundaries. Whether we are extroverted, introverted, or somewhere in the middle, we each bring our inherent personality to the therapy setting and must start with awareness of our personal style and preferences. Sometimes that preference is a hindrance and has to be overcome to be a better therapist—for example, if we are extroverted and prone to talking, we may have trouble holding back a story that seems relevant, but in fact is unnecessary to share. Perhaps we feel bored, lonely, and want to talk just for the sake of it. Conversely, if we are introverted, we may have something relevant to share, but purposely hold back due to our own shy-ness and tendency to be reticent. In these cases we are responding to our own preferences rather than client need. Thus, the "perils of too much and too little" include the peril of staying within our comfort zone, at the client's expense. The goal is to be ourselves, but as therapists, to be able to move beyond our preferred style and perhaps expand our repertoire when client need calls for something different from us.

Identity factors: Age, culture, ethnicity, racial, spiritual, gender, sexual

Clients' needs for disclosure and boundary flexibility vary not only by their personality, but age, cultural and ethnic factors, and identity issues all may need to be considered. For example, if therapist and client share a particular identity, they may have some common understandings and clients may find that they want to know something about the therapist's relevant life experience. Some clients seek out a therapist who has a simi-lar identity, particularly when part of a marginalized group. Similarities and differences in life experience, with the therapist being willing to share some of his or her understandings, may be appropriate and help-ful. Younger clients too have different expectations of and needs from therapy, and there, some more disclosure about everyday things may be called for to help the client feel comfortable; being too nondisclosing may be off-putting and seem abnormal. Thus, as therapists consider what con-stitutes too much or too little, client age and identity factors should be considered in making self-disclosure and boundary crossings even more or less appropriate. Ultimately, the client need drives the therapist's deci-sion, and therapists consider these factors about their clients, using the same methods of testing the waters, getting feedback, and being willing to change if whatever they are doing is not serving the relationship.

Legitimate therapist needs and boundaries

Therapists too have some legitimate needs and the right to honor their own boundary or self-disclosure preferences, and this should be con-sidered along with client need. Perhaps they have a useful story to tell that would demonstrate something and help a client, but they may not want to share it because it breaches their own privacy. Therapists, simply because sharing something or doing something might be helpful, need also to honor their own limits, and when relevant, make a judgment that balances both their own needs and the best interest of the client. This is equally true of clients' desire for minor boundary crossings—perhaps a client wants to e-mail a therapist some of their journaling or an agenda for the next appointment. While some therapists might feel perfectly comfortable with this, others may not. Some clients may want a therapist to attend their special event (e.g., their wedding, a performance they are in, a funeral of someone significant in their life)—some therapists may be comfortable doing so, others may not. Or, therapists may need to decide on a case-by-case basis, considering the particular client, the circumstances, the therapeutic value, and the therapist's own comfort with going. Although these clients are not wrong or inappropriate for asking, therapists don't have to meet their needs either—therapists know how they work best. Knowing who we are, what we are comfortable with, we can express our limits with our clients without shaming them for having those needs. Thus, while the major emphasis has been on thinking first about what clients need, we are not selfless beings, and we have limits too. By honoring them, we model for our clients a way of setting our boundaries without making the other feel ashamed for having wanted something different.

Moreover, it is necessary to prevent burnout from giving too much. As many of the therapists in this book have shown, we may care deeply about our clients and give to them regularly, and there will be times when we, too, must rest and know that we do not want to do more.

As we bring this volume to a close, we hope that you've found these stories thought-provoking and that you've reflected, in turn, about your own self-disclosure and boundary decision-making processes. In this chapter we highlighted the themes that emerged, putting the collective wisdom of the various authors into a form that we hoped would be helpful to you in consideration of your own self-disclosure perspective and boundary challenges. We hope, too, that you will participate in the ongoing shift in the psychotherapy community, by being willing to write, research, and openly discuss your own ideas about how therapeutic and judicious self-disclosure affects the healing relationship. We need to come together as a community to learn more about this important and powerful factor in effecting change, healing, and mutual growth, and move beyond unproductive and divisive discourse.

If you are so inclined, to make this process of dialoguing within the psychotherapeutic community about self-disclosure a broadly collaborative exchange, we welcome you to send your thoughts, ideas, or reactions to us at http://www.psychotherapistrevealed.com. We welcome your thoughts and look forward to hearing from you.

Index